SIMON &
SCHUSTER

Also by James P. Womack and Daniel T. Jones

Lean Thinking

The Machine That Changed the World
(with Daniel Roos)

The Future of the Automobile
(with Alan Altshuler, Martin Anderson, and Daniel Roos)

Seeing the Whole: Mapping the Extended Value Stream

LEAN
SOLUTIONS

*How Companies and Customers
Can Create Value and Wealth Together*

James P. Womack
and Daniel T. Jones

SIMON &
SCHUSTER

London · New York · Sydney · Toronto

A VIACOM COMPANY

SIMON &
SCHUSTER

First published in Great Britain by Simon & Schuster UK Ltd, 2005
A Viacom Company

1   3   5   7   9   10   8   6   4   2

Simon & Schuster UK Ltd
Africa House
64–78 Kingsway
London WC2B 6AH

www.simonsays.co.uk

Simon & Schuster Australia
Sydney

A CIP catalogue record for this book is available from the British Library

ISBN 0-7432-7595-0
EAN 9780743275958

Printed and bound in Great Britain by Mackays of Chatham plc

For Carrie and Katherine,
Two thoughtful consumers of the future,
who often got me what I wanted when I wanted
where I wanted while writing this book.

JPW

For Michael, Kate, and Simon,
Three thoughtful participant-observers of
provision, who often told me whether I was
getting it right.

DTJ

For Pat and Anne,
For bearing with us while we wandered off
on consumption-stream walks—sometimes
only in our minds—and then huddled in
our garrets to write up our findings.

DTJ and JPW

Contents

LEAN
SOLUTIONS

From Lean Production to Lean Solutions

In the summer of 1982 we had a revelation. We were visiting a series of companies in Japan, trying to understand why they were winning in global competition. Then we encountered Toyota.

We quickly realized that this company was quite different from the others we had seen. Toyota's success lay in brilliant management of its core processes: the series of actions conducted properly in the correct sequence at the right time to create value for customers. Its management of product development and production and its collaboration with suppliers and customers in Japan were far better than anything we had ever encountered.

At the moment of revelation we turned to each other and said, "It's not brilliant product innovations or culture or a weak currency or strong government support that makes this company stand out in global competition. It's the brilliant focus on core processes." This was an exceedingly useful insight, because quirky product brilliance or culture-specific advantages can't be copied. But superior process management can.

It took us a while, but by 1990 we were able to describe

these processes in *The Machine That Changed the World*.[1] We presented exhaustive evidence that Toyota's key value-creating activities were better on every significant dimension, not only in comparison with foreign auto companies but with other Japanese companies. Toyota's product development, supplier management, customer support, and manufacturing processes were collectively the "machine" that was changing the world. This conclusion naturally raised the question of how companies in any industry in any country could also achieve process brilliance, a question we tried to answer in our next book, *Lean Thinking*.[2]

We proposed five simple principles to guide any firm:

Provide the *value* actually desired by customers. Resist the urge to work forward from existing organization, assets, and knowledge to convince customers that they want what the firm finds easiest to provide.

Identify the *value stream* for each product. This is the sequence of actions (the process) needed to bring a good or service from concept to launch (through the development process) and from an order into the hands of the customer (through the fulfillment process). Challenge every step in these processes to see if they really create value for the customer. Eliminate the steps that don't.

Line up the remaining steps in a continuous *flow*. Eliminate waiting and inventories between steps to slash development and response times.

Let the customer *pull* value from the firm. Reverse the push methods used by firms with long response times, which try to convince customers that they want what the firm has already designed or produced.

Finally, once value, the value stream, flow, and pull are established, start over from the beginning in an endless search for *perfection*, the happy situation of perfect value provided with zero waste.

The Triumph of Lean Production

As the years have passed, we have been cheered that the internal processes in many organizations are improving. The simplest indicator is that most manufactured goods work a lot better today and cost less to buy than when we started our collaboration. For example, defects per car have fallen steadily in the auto industry, even as the real price of a motor vehicle of a given specification continues to decline.[3] And we have been equally gratified to discover that lean production works in every company, industry, and country where it is seriously tried.

Meanwhile, Toyota marches from victory to victory in global competition as it closes in on General Motors for the leadership of the world car industry. By contrast, most of the other Japanese firms we encountered on our 1982 visit have failed or fallen by the wayside. (Honda is still independent and healthy, but Nissan is controlled by Renault; Mazda is part of Ford; Subaru, Suzuki, and Isuzu are tightly tied to GM; and Mitsubishi has suffered a dramatic loss of market share.)

But curiously, despite a growing variety of better products with fewer defects at lower cost available from a growing range of sales channels, the experiences of consumers seem to be deteriorating. In recent years, we've frequently found ourselves discussing this phenomenon with managers. They report that when they are wearing their producer hats in the office or the factory, things seem to be getting better. But when they go home and put on their consumer hats, things seem to be getting worse.

And we have felt this acutely in our own lives. It seems that every conversation the two of us have, working as busy authors separated by an ocean, starts with an account of a consumer frustration that has gotten in the way of getting our work done:

- The custom-built, delivered-in-three-days computer that refuses to work with the printer, the other computers in our home offices, and the software from different providers.
- The car repair requiring many loops of mis-communication, waiting, and complaints about work done wrong.
- The long drive to the "big box" retailer, stocking tens of thousands of different items—most of them better and cheaper than those available 25 years ago, only to return home without the one item we actually wanted.
- The medical procedure that was deeply impressive from a technical standpoint yet unpleasant and time-consuming from a personal standpoint.
- The business trip with endless queues, handoffs, and delays.
- The exasperation of "help desks" and "support centers" that neither help nor support.

Consumption should be easier and more satisfying due to better, cheaper products. Instead it requires growing time and hassle to get all of our goods and services to work properly and work together. Stated another way, today's consumers are often drowning in a sea of brilliant objects. And this seems very strange when we stop to consider that satisfying consumption—not just making brilliant products—is the whole point of lean production.

The Emerging Challenges of Consumption

In the late 1990s, we passed off these observations as short-term phenomena, the consequence of the bubble economy when consumers were offered many new capabilities supported by immature technologies. Surely things would get better in the future.

By the end of the bubble, however, we could see that these consumer problems weren't anomalies; they were normal. We then asked a very simple question: What's going on in the world that we should come to feel this way, gradually shifting our view of the next big challenge for business from producing better products to making consumption more satisfying?

As we reflected on consumption problems, we began to see five key trends that collectively create the challenge now facing consumers:

First, producers are relentlessly adding choices as they "mass customize" their product offerings[4] and steadily increase the number of channels through which products can be obtained. Choice is wonderful but it requires more and more decision time from the consumer.

Second, the regulated economy of the mass production age is steadily contracting. This gives all of us more freedom—which is good.[5] But it also gives us many more activities to manage and decisions to make: How do we invest our pension funds? Which telecommunications providers do we sign up with? What airline/rental car/hotel combination do we pick? The cost associated with making the right choice from this busy menu can easily exceed the time and energy required to make it.

Third, we are shifting from a service to a self-service economy in which we obtain more and more personal capital goods to manufacture our own value—like the computers, printers, scanners, personal digital assistants, and software that surround us as we write this book. (Our fathers and mothers had secretaries with typewriters; we have PDAs and PCs.) And we don't just obtain these personal capital goods. We must also install, maintain, upgrade, and recycle them, often integrating goods and services from many vendors, using our own time and energy.

Fourth, households are changing in every advanced economy in ways that create time and energy pressure for consumers. Workforce participation has risen dramatically, meaning that in two-adult households the member of the household (typically female) who previously managed consumption is now working. And in a growing fraction of households there is only one adult present to earn the living and to manage the consumption. This may mean more money per capita to buy more goods and services, but there is less time to manage them.

Fifth, and finally, the advance of the Internet and information technology are steadily blurring the distinction between consumption and production, often pulling the customer into the provision process. For example, one of our wives recently ordered office equipment online from a well-known manufacturer. Due to confusion about a taxpayer identification number, the order was rejected, but no e-mail with this information was sent. When the equipment failed to arrive on the promised day several weeks later, a trip to the web showed that the order had been canceled. When a human was finally reached at the manufacturer's help desk to discuss how this could have happened, the "customer relationship manager" explained that it is now the customer's responsibility to check the web frequently to make sure the production and shipment process is proceeding to plan. As the wife noted, "I had been appointed operations manager at this company at zero pay, but they forgot to tell me."

This widespread trend toward transparency and direct participation by the consumer in the production process is touted by providers as an unalloyed boon. But to busy consumers with other priorities, it often feels like the gift of unpaid work.

Today's situation of more choices and more knowledge for the consumer, gained at the expense of more responsibility and more decision and management time, can be summed up very simply:

(1) There are more and more consumption decisions for consumers to make—more categories of products from more suppliers available through more channels to be obtained, installed, integrated, maintained, repaired, upgraded, and recycled.

Plus,
(2) The evolution of the production process, facilitated by information technology and the steady introduction of more personal capital goods, claims more of the consumer's (unpaid) time and energy while blurring the boundary between consumption and production.

But,
(3) Consumers will never have more time in their day (the one real constant and constraint in life) and most consumers will actually have less useful time and energy in the years ahead because of changing households and aging populations in all advanced economies.

Collectively, these forces constitute the consumer's dilemma in the 21st century.

Rethinking Value

As we grasped this situation, we realized that we needed to heed our principles of lean production by returning to the starting point, the question of value. We needed to ask what consumers really want in the era ahead. Then we needed to rethink consumption from first principles as a process—like production, but from the opposite direction—in order to discover a better way for consumers to obtain the goods and services they now want. We call this improved process *lean consumption*.

Lean consumption must have a companion process. Firms must provide the goods and services consumers actually want, when and where they are wanted without burdening the consumer. We've used the term "lean production" in the past, but too many managers act as if production stops at the office door or the factory gate. So we now use the term *lean provision*, which comprises all of the steps required to deliver the desired value from producer to customer, often running through a number of organizations.

Most of us find it easy to think about consumption when we are consumers and easy to think about provision when we are at work. But all of us find it difficult to see these interlocking processes together as a unified value stream. As we have walked through a range of industries in recent years, from airlines to healthcare to insurance to automotive repair services, we have repeatedly observed consumers and employees struggling valiantly with misaligned consumption and provision processes that alienate customers, drain away profits, and burden staff with feelings of rage and despair. Yet they soldier on in a fog of mutual incomprehension.

As we continued our investigations—visiting many companies in many industries in many countries—we began to see that if truly lean provision can be married to truly lean consumption, life can be better for consumers, more satisfying for employees, and more profitable for providers. A win-win-win is possible in which providers, employees, and consumers create lean solutions together. This fundamental insight led directly to this book.

Lean Consumption Meets Lean Provision

Consumption. It sounds so easy. Indeed, in advanced market economies, it's often portrayed as effortless. Consumers can get just what they want easily, even instantly. And yet, the problem is that consumption often isn't easy and consumers can't get what they desire. And this is true in every category of consumption, for all types of goods and services. In this book we will see why consumption is often hard work for the consumer and is unpaid work to boot.

Consumption Is a Problem-Solving Process

Let's start with a very simple observation. Consumption is a continuing process—a set of actions taken over an extended period—to solve a problem. It involves searching for, obtaining, installing, maintaining, repairing, upgrading, and, eventually, disposing of many goods and services. All of this obtaining, installing, maintaining, and disposing involves time, effort, and—far too often—hassle for the consumer. To make this clear, let's look at the process followed in one simple act of consumption.

As we set out to write this book, Dan needed a new computer and went to the web to do a bit of research on competing products. He gave the matter some thought, then went back to the web, reached the preferred manufacturer's web site, and typed in all the information necessary to make the purchase and arrange a shipment date within his acceptable wait time. The manufacturer shipped the product as promised, and it arrived on the promised date. So far, so good.

But the software installed was not all of the software needed, and when additional software was installed for additional applications, the computer didn't work. This led to a visit to the manufacturer's web site and then a call to the manufacturer's help line. After a considerable wait, Dan was told that the problem was with the new software. This triggered a call to the help line of the new software provider—who blamed the hardware maker. This caused a search for a computer expert with experience with this problem and a service call to fix it. Unfortunately the expert, after much time, some money, and many false leads, was stumped. This caused a search for a second expert who finally solved the problem.

Dan's computer finally worked, but his consumption was hard work, time-consuming, and exasperating. On the next page, a list of the steps, time, and experience involved shows the complete consumption process.

Note that this simple act of consumption was actually an extended process involving 11 steps over seven days. Of these steps, four actually created value in some way, but seven were pure waste. One was fun, two were tolerable, and the rest produced anxiety and exasperation in varying degrees. (The two "help" lines were particularly exasperating.) What should have consumed no more than three hours and 30 minutes of Dan's time—still a surprisingly large amount for "effortless"

Steps	Dan's time	Dan's experience
Day 1		
1. Web search for information	1 hr.	Fun. "Lot's of interesting new stuff out there, and I never left home!"
2. Product selection, option selection, and order entry	30 min.	OK—"But I do begin to feel a bit like a file clerk as the novelty of web ordering wears off. Why do I need this tracking number to check on my order? Aren't they responsible for getting it to me on time?"
Day 4		
3. Receipt of product and unpack	1 hr.	OK—"Bit of tension as I try to follow all the instructions, but the computer does turn on and boots up."
4. Load additional software	1 hr.	Some frustration—"Seems like this should be easier at this point in the computer age."
5. Test complete, but hardware/ software "product" quits working	1 hr.	Extreme frustration—"It was working, but now it boots up and suddenly shuts down."
6. Visit to manufacturer web site and call to help line	1 hr.	Exasperation—"How can I spend an hour, mostly on hold, to learn that the problem is someone else's fault?"
7. Call to help line of software vendor	1 hr.	Extreme exasperation—"How can this industry survive when nothing works and no one takes responsibility?"
Day 5		
8. Search for an expert	1 hr.	Mild frustration—"How come you can't figure out in advance what anyone wanting to work on your computer systems really knows?"
9. Expert visit	2 hr.	Extreme exasperation—"I love the way my time and money become this guy's learning curve."
Day 6		
10. Search for a new expert	1 hr.	Extreme exasperation—"The web sure isn't helping me now; I'm reduced to desperate calls and e-mails to friends."
Day 7		
11. Expert visit	1 hr.	Anxiety followed by relief—"Will this 'expert' be any better?" followed by "I can finally get some work done!"

web-based consumption—actually burned up 11 hours and 30 minutes, nearly one and a half standard working days.

But this is not the end. Dan's real objective is not to own a computer. It is to solve the problem of processing words and images, transferring them to others as necessary. The computer, its software, and the technical support required are only a means, not an end, and are only a first step.

The complete consumption process to solve Dan's problem over several years will involve not just one "buy and install loop," but also a number of repair and upgrade loops, followed by a replacement and disposal loop. The steps involved in each of these loops will be very similar: many actions (a few of them value creating) and lots of personal time (much of it exasperating). All to solve the simple problem of processing words and fashioning images for books and articles.

On one level, personal computing is a miracle. We know because we started writing books together years ago on IBM Selectric typewriters, exchanging drafts by mail and then by fax. But on a different level it's highly exasperating. The individual products involved are often very impressive—once you get them to work right and to cooperate with each other. But the overall experience is full of frustration.

If this typical experience is the current negative, let's think about the future positive. What would we really like to experience as consumers? What are the objectives of what we term lean consumption?

What Do Consumers Really Want?

First, we need to remember that most of us consume in order to solve problems. These may be little problems, such as finding, buying, and using the apparatus needed to enjoy music as we go through the day; or they may be big problems, like finding, buying, and maintaining a comfortable home in which to live and work. Often we aren't as interested in the goods and services themselves—the iPod or even the house— as we are in what they can do for our lives. Therefore, it follows that our acts of consumption must actually solve the problem, from our simple music problem to our complicated shelter problem. A partial solution—a new computer that won't talk to the printer, or a health maintenance organization (HMO) that can't find an appropriate specialist in a timely manner—is no solution. We want our problems solved completely.

Second, we would like our problem solved cost-effectively, with minimum expenditure of our time and effort. As society develops and standards of living rise, the one item we never have more of is time. (To the best of our knowledge there is no research underway in any laboratory anywhere on increasing the numbers of hours in the day or days in the week.[1]) Thus the conservation of personal time and effort for more valued uses becomes an ever more important objective.[2]

Third, we would like to obtain exactly what we need to solve our problem, including all the necessary goods and services in the exact specification required. We don't want to make substitutions or go away empty-handed.

Fourth, we want to solve our problems where we need them solved. In a bygone age of personal services, items were often brought to the customer: the cleaner, the grocer, the butcher, the vegetable gardener, and the doctor all made house calls. In the more recent age of self-service, the customer has either gone to the store or ordered directly from the producer. We believe that in the emerging age of lean consumption many products will be available at multiple locations for comparable prices. That is to say, you will be able to solve your food problem by going to the "big box" warehouse, the traditional grocery store, or the small convenience store, or get home delivery with web-based ordering. You will diagnose your health problem by going to the HMO or the stand-alone medical lab, or perform tests at home with personal capital goods. You will have the choice of buying life insurance from the agent at your dining room table or by filing the application yourself over the web.

Fifth, we want to solve our problem when we need it solved. As we will see, current provision systems typically involve strangers ordering goods and services from strangers. It's not surprising, therefore, that most consumers give the provider no warning that an order is coming. Unfortunately, typical production systems—including even the touted build-to-order systems of companies like Dell—can't provide a high level of service in this environment. And, as we will see, consumer desires are actually much more complex. It turns out that in the world of lean consumption, the notion of when means very different things to different consumers.

Finally, many of us would like to reduce the total number of problems we must solve. The obvious means is to bundle them. For example, many of us might appreciate a "solution provider" to put the vehicles we need in our driveway for a simple usage fee in order to solve our mobility problem without our ever having to think about it. Or a shelter provider to cost-effectively maintain our homes without any of our mindshare or emotion-share. How about a shopping solution so the items needed arrive at our homes when we need them, without fetching them ourselves nights and weekends? Or a single computing and communication provider so we deal only with a single party and expend no time on the solution? Moving the fundamental unit of consumption from many individual items to a few aggregated solutions is a major leap. But it is a leap that we believe is the end destination of lean consumption.

The Principles of Lean Consumption

These six simple principles of lean consumption provide a new definition of value for today's consumer, which we'll express in the voice of the customer:

- Solve my problem completely.
- Don't waste my time (minimize my total cost of consumption, which is the price I pay plus my time and hassle).
- Provide exactly what I want.
- Deliver value where I want it.
- Supply value when I want it.
- Reduce the number of decisions I must make to solve my problems.

Note that none of these principles focuses on the specific attributes or performance of products themselves: the car, the software, the insurance policy. Today the product is often not the problem. Unfortunately, many firms making goods and providing services cling to a product-centric focus. Because they oversee only one element of the total consumption process, they often overlook the consumer's total experience in finding, obtaining, installing, maintaining, upgrading, and disposing of the products needed to solve the problem. And they are seemingly oblivious to the total cost of a solution, including the consumer's time and hassle.

The Challenge for Lean Provision

Provision. Like consumption, it also sounds so easy. Surely with modern technology—especially information technology—providers can supply the value desired by consumers easily, even effortlessly. The problem is that provision is actually very hard and few firms today do it well. Indeed, as consumers struggle with broken consumption processes, providers struggle with defective provision processes. The evidence is everywhere:

- Growing spending on product features and options that fail to attract new customers.
- Unrealistic delivery promises, which providers feel they must make to be competitive.
- High levels of out-of-stocks (due to too few goods) and remaindering (due to too many).
- Increasing spending to retain customer loyalty, even as customers become less loyal.
- Larger investments in bigger assets (big stores, big distribution centers, big computer systems), which have shrinking ability to create competitive advantage.
- Spiraling spending on help desks and other forms of customer support, now outsourced so that direct customer contact is lost.
- Chronic employee dissatisfaction in almost every activity with intensive customer interface, causing high turnover and training costs and low customer satisfaction.

No provider wants any of these outcomes, but with current provision processes most of them are unavoidable. And most providers seem to think that actually solving customer problems while providing value when and where the customer wants would cost much more. As a result they have pushed harder down the traditional path of mass consumption. They offer ever more brilliant products in splendid isolation at steadily lower prices, even as consumers signal they really want something else.

Fortunately, as we will see in the pages ahead, a few firms have learned a new way to think about consumers and providers and how they can create lean solutions together. They have discovered that just as high quality costs less, not more, we now know how to provide the value that consumers really want and at lower total cost. The simple objective of this book is to demonstrate this new approach—marrying lean provision to lean consumption—so we can all progress from mass to lean.

Chapter 1

Learning to See Consumption

"Let's take a walk." This has been our standard response for many years when an organization asks us to talk about lean thinking. The firm's managers usually want to meet in the conference room or the CEO's office. But we know from long experience that value is only created on the gemba—the Japanese word for the place in the office or factory where the real work is done. So that's always the place we insist on starting, to learn what the true situation is.

Consumers have a gemba, too. It's the path they follow to solve their problems. And most managers seem to have a very hard time seeing it, even when they follow the path themselves, once they take off their provider hats and put on their consumer hats. So, in recent years, we've spent a lot of time walking the consumer gemba, dragging along managers whenever we can.

Our objective is simple: We aim to teach managers to see all of the steps a consumer must perform to research, obtain, install, integrate, maintain, repair, upgrade, and recycle the goods and services needed to solve their problem. We then challenge each step, asking why it's necessary at all and why it often can't be performed properly. Once worthless steps are eliminated, we can talk about flow and pull, heading toward perfection.

To make this method clear, let's take a walk right now, putting ourselves in the position of a consumer. Let's experience a simple car repair, following the path of Bob Scott, a prototypical consumer whom we first encountered in *Lean Thinking* when he bent the rear bumper of his pickup.

Walking the Consumer Gemba

This time the process started when the mysterious "check engine" light began glowing on the instrument panel, and Bob needed to search for a repair outlet. The choices were the new car dealer he felt victimized by the last time he needed service, other dealers within driving range who sell and service the same type of vehicle, and several local garages, which may or may not have the latest equipment and knowledge about the specific vehicle.

After several phone calls describing the problem and inquiring about the likely cost, Bob decided to go to a new car dealer he had not visited previously.

The next step was to schedule an appointment—the equivalent action to placing an order in the case of a product, for example, Dan's computer. Bob then took the car to the dealer at the appointed time.

At the dealer, the problem needed describing. Because Bob was a stranger, the dealer knew nothing about the history of the vehicle and no information had been collected prior to his arrival. This circumstance required a wait in a queue at the service desk to fill out and sign the appropriate forms.

The vehicle couldn't be fixed immediately, and Bob needed to get to work, so a "loaner" car was provided. This caused another wait while the replacement vehicle was transferred from its storage area. Fortunately, the actual commuting time was no longer than Bob's normal commute, although in many cases it would be.

During the day, the dealer's service department made the dreaded call to Bob to describe the problems found and to reveal the cost of the repair. Later, Bob received a second call sharing the bad news that the vehicle would not be ready until the next day because of a lack of parts. As we will see, this is a typical experience when the consumer and the provider are strangers who fail to discuss the nature of the problem up front or share any data on the product's "as is" condition. As a result, parts have to be ordered and shop time can't be scheduled accurately.

The next evening, Bob returned to the dealer to pick up the vehicle. This required a short wait in line to fill out the paperwork—reviewing the statement, providing the credit card, collecting the keys. After paying, he encountered a second wait, while the vehicle was brought around from the remote parking area used to store vehicles once repaired.

With the addition of the trip home—counting only the travel time in addition to the daily commute time necessitated by the need to get the car serviced—the consumption process was seemingly complete. However, on the drive home the problem recurred. The mysterious "check engine" light that instigated the initial service went on again.

This is actually a common outcome, as documented by the International Car Distribution Programme (ICDP).[1] The chances in North America and Europe of getting a vehicle fixed right the first time are only about 80 percent. And the chances of getting it fixed right the first time and on time are only about 60 percent.

Because the dealer had failed to fix the problem but the repair had already been paid for, the search process moving forward was very simple. Bob made another appointment at the same dealer, the vehicle was returned to go through the check-in and checkout steps, and—two times lucky—the car actually worked properly.

On the next page we have listed the steps that Bob needed to take to complete what appeared to him to be a simple act of consumption. None of the 16 steps was by their nature complex, and each took only a small amount of time. However, when they are added up, the magnitude of effort and time required is striking. Bob expended three hours and 30 minutes of his own time to solve his problem.

Drawing a Consumption Map[2]

Step lists of the type we have just created can be constructed for any consumption process. They are designed to help managers learn to see the process and its implications. However, we find that many managers and employees are more visual than verbal, so we also draw simple consumption maps to show a process at a glance.

In the consumption time map (*The Long and Winding Repair Path*) depicted on page 24, we've arranged the steps involved from upper left to lower right to illustrate the flow of the process from start to finish, with a back-flow loop of Step 10 through Step 16. We have also drawn the boxes for each step in proportion to the time taken.

Consumption Step List

Steps	Consumer time
1. Search for the best repair facility	25 min.
2. Make appointment with selected facility	5 min.
3. Drive vehicle to facility	20 min.
4. Wait in queue, describe problems, and do paperwork	15 min.
5. Wait for loaner car and sign form	10 min.
6. Discuss problem with service staff and authorize repairs	5 min.
7. Second call to say the car will not be ready until the next day	5 min.
8. Fill out paperwork and wait for delivery of the car	15 min.
9. Drive vehicle home (and discover problem was not corrected)	20 min.
10. Make appointment with same facility	5 min.
11. Drive vehicle to facility	20 min.
12. Wait in queue, describe problems, and do paperwork	15 min.
13. Wait for loaner car and sign form	10 min.
14. Discuss problem with service staff and authorize repairs	5 min.
15. Fill out paperwork and wait for delivery of the car	15 min.
16. Drive vehicle home	20 min.
Total consumer time (16 steps)	**210 min. (3 hr. 30 min.)**

The Long and Winding Repair Path

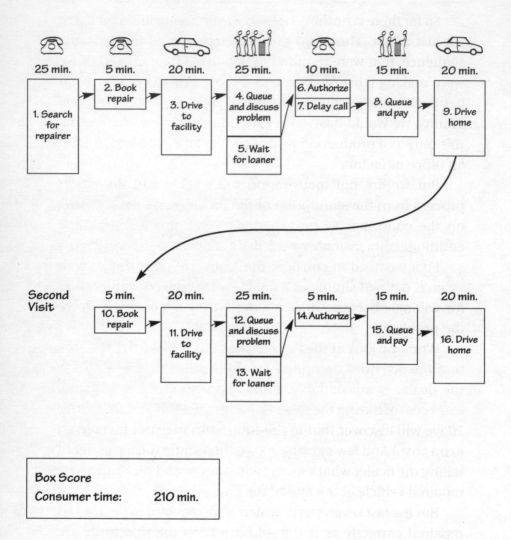

25 min. — 1. Search for repairer

5 min. — 2. Book repair

20 min. — 3. Drive to facility

25 min. — 4. Queue and discuss problem / 5. Wait for loaner

10 min. — 6. Authorize / 7. Delay call

15 min. — 8. Queue and pay

20 min. — 9. Drive home

Second Visit

5 min. — 10. Book repair

20 min. — 11. Drive to facility

25 min. — 12. Queue and discuss problem / 13. Wait for loaner

5 min. — 14. Authorize

15 min. — 15. Queue and pay

20 min. — 16. Drive home

Box Score
Consumer time: 210 min.

24

From Consumption Process to Consumer Experience

So far there is nothing right or wrong about all this activity. It's just a fact. These are the steps, conducted in a specific sequence, that were required of Bob to get his car fixed. If we were making a list of steps and a process map only for what happens to the car during the repair cycle, we would be done. That is, we would have a very useful map if we were treating this only as a production process of the type we might find in an office or factory.

But we are not focusing on the vehicle and the repair process from the standpoint of the provider. We are focusing on the consumer as he experiences this process. So some additional dimensions are needed for our step list and map.

First we need to consider the "value" of each step, where value is defined simply as an activity that the consumer pays for willingly because it seems to be truly necessary to solve the problem.

When we look at the list and the map in this light, we note that the activities described are quite different. The drive to the dealer is unavoidable, unless Bob is willing to bear the extra cost of having the dealer pick up the vehicle. (In Chapter 10 we will discover that in the future this may not involve an extra cost.) And few consumers would dispute the necessity of telling the dealer what's wrong with the car and picking up the repaired vehicle at the end of the day.

But the last seven steps, which were required to get the car repaired correctly as it should have been the first time, are unlikely to be considered valuable by any consumer anywhere. Indeed, why isn't the dealer compensating Bob for these steps by refunding some of the cost of the repair to offset the value of his wasted time?

And even for the first nine steps that seem on their face to create value, what about all the waiting involved: The "please hold for the next available service representative" message when calling the dealer to inquire about the cost and to make an appointment? The wait at the service desk to describe the problem? The time needed to fill out the forms with information the dealer could have obtained beforehand? The wait for the loaner car? And the wait at pickup time, both at the service desk and for the repaired car to be fetched?

When we restate the step list to break out the steps and expenditure of time as "wasted" vs. "value-creating," we see something very interesting. More than 70 percent of the total time expended by the consumer in this case was "wasted" rather than "value-creating."

Anyone observing the queues at the dealership could easily see the waste of time in waiting. And any dealer even casually analyzing this process could challenge the repairs that aren't really repairs by installing a more robust, first-time-quality process. So why do these waits and wastes persist? The simplest answer—which we believe is almost universally true in consumption processes—is that providers ignore the customer's value of time. They either don't see it, or they choose to ignore it because they think that doing so saves them money. And as long as all providers think this way, and consumers fail to demand a better process, this logic goes unchallenged.

To help raise managers' consciousness, we find it useful to enhance the consumption map by shading the fraction of value-creating time in each step. This consumption-time waste map (*Many Steps, Mostly Waste*) reveals activities that create value and those that do not.

The clear and simple message of the completed map—with only a small portion of the available space shaded to indicate value-creating activities—is that even simple consumption activities involve many steps and significant consumer time. And most of this time is wasted.

Consumption Steps: Value-Creating vs. Wasted Time

Steps	Value-creating time	Wasted time
1. Search for the best repair facility	5 min.	20 min.
2. Make appointment with selected facility	1 min.	4 min.
3. Drive vehicle to facility	20 min.	
4. Wait in queue, describe problems, and do paperwork	5 min.	10 min.
5. Wait for loaner car and sign form	1 min.	9 min.
6. Discuss problem with service staff and authorize repairs	5 min.	
7. Second call to say the car will not be ready until the next day		5 min.
8. Fill out paperwork and wait for delivery of the car	1 min.	14 min.
9. Drive vehicle home (and discover problem was not corrected)	20 min.	
10. Make appointment with same facility		5 min.
11. Drive vehicle to facility		20 min.
12. Wait in queue, describe problems, and do paperwork		15 min.
13. Wait for loaner car and sign form		10 min.
14. Discuss problem with service staff and authorize repairs		5 min.
15. Fill out paperwork and wait for delivery of the car		15 min.
16. Drive vehicle home		20 min.
Total consumer time	**58 min. (28%)**	**152 min. (72%)**

Many Steps, Mostly Waste

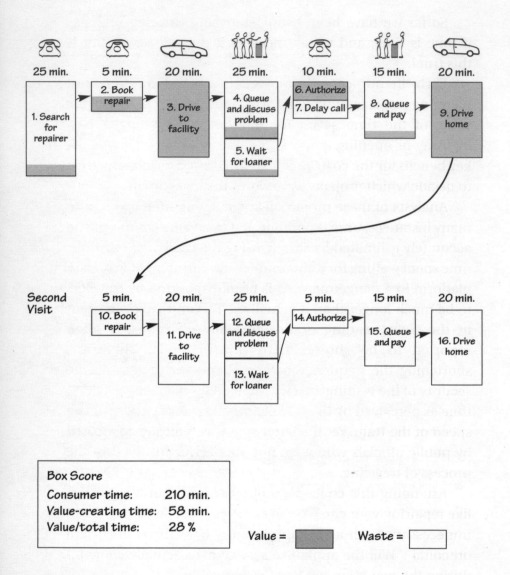

25 min.

5 min.

20 min.

25 min.

10 min.

15 min.

20 min.

1. Search for repairer

2. Book repair

3. Drive to facility

4. Queue and discuss problem

5. Wait for loaner

6. Authorize

7. Delay call

8. Queue and pay

9. Drive home

Second Visit

5 min.

20 min.

25 min.

5 min.

15 min.

20 min.

10. Book repair

11. Drive to facility

12. Queue and discuss problem

13. Wait for loaner

14. Authorize

15. Queue and pay

16. Drive home

Box Score

Consumer time: 210 min.
Value-creating time: 58 min.
Value/total time: 28 %

Value =   Waste =

Perceptual Time vs. Clock Time

So far we have been listing steps and drawing maps as if time is time, and we all measure it the same way. But is this true?

Early in our careers, one of us worked on transport planning projects in which it was important to measure the value of the time saved for travelers by building a new highway or opening a new commuter rail line. This was the key benefit for the cost/benefit analysis used by governments to decide which projects were worth the investment.

Analysts of these projects learned a long time ago that in many instances, time is not time and that value cannot not be accurately estimated by simply using the clock. For example, time spent waiting for a commuter train late at night on a dark platform in a dangerous area is usually reported by travelers to be much longer than it actually is. By contrast, time spent in the train, reading or dozing while en route, is often reported to be shorter than it actually is. Therefore, shortening the frequency between trains or increasing the security of the waiting area was actually a better way to "save" time as perceived by the traveler than increasing the cruising speed of the train. Yet the latter step was typically advocated by public officials who were not themselves involved in the process of traveling.

Extending this concept to other consumption activities, like repairing your car, we can easily see that steps that seem unnecessary, such as waiting in lines, or with an uncertain outcome ("Will the appliance service man actually show up during the two hour window I've agreed to wait at home for him?"), seem to take longer and be more onerous than steps requiring the same amount of "clock" time that do seem to actually create value and where a successful result is assured. We call the former "hassle time," or time that seems longer than it is. The successful consumption process always seeks to minimize this form of waste.

This insight gives us one final way to enhance our map, this time with the steps adjusted to take account of perceptual time as shown on the consumer's face. The consumption experience map (*Was My Experience Really that Bad?*) on the next page illustrates the hassle level for the consumer.

What the consumer really wants and what providers should be offering is a much shorter map with all areas shaded and every face smiling. That's the signature of lean consumption.

A World of Unpaid Work

You may think that fixing your car or successfully buying and installing a computer are irritating tasks, but that problems of this sort don't happen very frequently. After all, products like cars actually are getting better, as we noted in the Preface, and surely computers will work better some day as soon as the industry matures.

Then, once you've had these latest problems solved, along with a few others on your list at the moment, everything should be fine and you can get on with what you really want to do. But this is rarely the case. New problems just keep popping up as quickly as you slay the old ones, like the plastic monsters in the arcade game that our kids smacked down with a mallet.

As it happens, this reality has been documented by a little-noticed cottage industry within the academic world that studies the use human beings make of their time.[3] To categorize time use, studies conducted across the world have divided the 24 hours in our days into four categories: personal

Was My Experience Really that Bad?

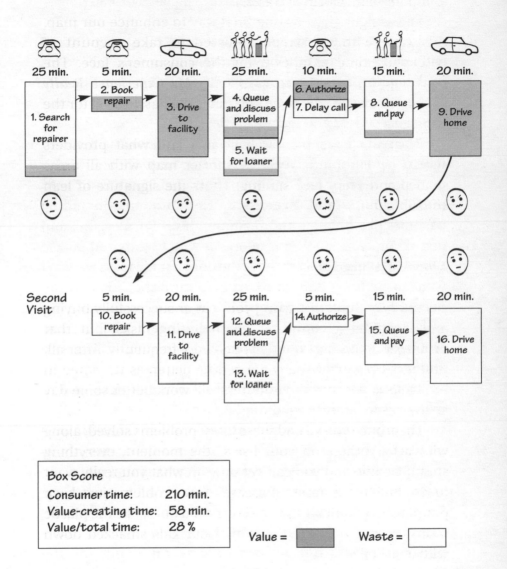

Box Score

Consumer time:	210 min.
Value-creating time:	58 min.
Value/total time:	28 %

Value =   �   Waste = □

time (sleeping, dressing, personal hygiene, and eating), paid work, leisure, and—a wonderfully suggestive category—unpaid work.

Personal time is known to have been constant at about 540 minutes a day (or nine hours) for more than 200 years. And time expended on paid work has fallen steadily over many decades in the advanced economies, except for some senior executives and technical specialists.

The real contest for our time, as it turns out, is between leisure and unpaid work. Leisure is easy to define. It's activities we enjoy and that we perform paid work in order to afford: sports and exercise, entertainment (including pastimes like hobbies and reading), travel for pleasure, and just sitting around relaxing, alone or with friends and family. But what is "unpaid work"? It is the bothersome tasks we don't want to perform and aren't paid to perform, but that are necessary to solve our daily problems and conduct our lives. This includes cleaning up, doing routine chores, and obtaining, installing, maintaining, and disposing of the goods and services we need.

Despite the introduction of labor-saving devices, and in many cases because of these labor-saving personal capital goods, unpaid work has been rising in advanced economies in recent years at the expense of leisure. The growth in unpaid work mostly involves the management of consumption—shopping trips, medical visits, bill paying and financial management, home repairs, motor vehicle maintenance. This is not only by the consumer for his or her personal needs, but in many cases on behalf of the consumer's parents and children.

If the amount of unpaid work needed to operate our households and conduct our lives is rising and if this work is often stressful, what can managers in a wide range of organizations do to make it less time consuming and more satisfying? Even better, what can they do to make this a business opportunity that reduces their costs while increasing their customers' satisfaction? To begin the escape from the world of unpaid work, we now need to go to the other side of the equation and look at the value-provision process.

Chapter 2

Learning to See Provision

At the end of a consumption walk, managers invariably want to sit down and think about the many questions that have been raised. But there is really no point without also looking at the matching provision process consisting of the steps the business takes to deal with the consumer. We need to see why consumption is so challenging for the consumer even as the provider expends large amounts of energy, frequently without much economic reward.

So after catching our breath, we need to take a second walk, now through the provision gemba for the same product to see what a firm is actually doing to serve its customers. We need to record all the steps taken and the amount of human effort expended by employees. As we do this we need to remember that this also is a provision *experience* for the managers and employees operating the process. How they feel about the process will have a major bearing on how well they do their jobs and how well they satisfy the customer.

As we walk, we will also want to identify the points of interconnection between the consumption and provision streams, where the consumer and the provider directly engage each other. These are often the points of greatest dissatisfaction for both consumers and employees.

Walking the Provider Gemba

In the case of Bob Scott's car repair, the process started when the Service Desk received the call from Bob, heard about the problem, described the nature of the repair, and provided an estimated price. Next, Bob called back to schedule an appointment.

Then Bob brought the car to the dealer on the agreed day and time, which was a pleasant surprise to the dealer, since many customers booking service appointments in North America do not actually show up with their vehicle at the agreed time. This permitted the dealer's Service Desk to take down all of the necessary information—remembering that this dealer had never seen this vehicle before and had no prior record to work from. The desk then wrote up the nature of the problem for the technicians in the Service Department.

Now it was time to get to work, except that the schedule of work for the day called for doing other vehicles first, the cars whose owners had brought their vehicles in earlier. So the next step was for the service assistant to drive the vehicle to the remote parking area and return with the keys.

When the repair sequence got to Bob's vehicle, the service assistant retrieved it from storage and drove it to the designated service bay.

In the service bay, a service technician finally looked at the vehicle to fully diagnose the problem and order the necessary parts from the Parts Department. Note that this is the first activity that actually creates any value from the standpoint of the customer. It occurred after the vehicle had already been at the dealer for more than three hours.

The service technician recognized immediately that this was another of the dreaded "check engine" problems, and he also knew that simply changing out electronic parts, as recommended in the manufacturer's latest service bulletin, might not solve it. However, replacing certain parts was the currently recommended first step, so the service technician estimated the cost of the job and went to the Service Desk. There he asked the staff to call Bob and get permission to make the repairs.

The Service Desk reached Bob—after several calls and a bit of a wait for him to return the last call—and listened to his complaints about the cost before reluctantly authorizing the repair.

From long experience the service technician knew that Bob would complain about the cost but that he lacked a realistic alternative and would approve the repair. Therefore, the technician took advantage of the wait time to go to the dealer's Parts Department and wait at the window for the parts assistant to find the parts in the parts storage area.

After 10 minutes, the parts assistant reported that one of the needed parts was not in inventory and that it would be necessary to "call around town" to see if it could be located at another dealer. The manufacturer had a regional parts distribution center with this part in stock, but the center was 150 miles away and only delivered parts overnight. Therefore, in order to get the car back to the customer that day, the only alternative was to check the inventory of other service shops in reasonable driving distance.

After several calls to independent repair shops and a look at a computerized inventory of parts at local dealers for this brand of vehicle, the parts assistant delivered the bad news. The vehicle could not be repaired until the next day when the missing part arrived from the manufacturer's regional distribution center.

The delay in obtaining parts necessitated taking the vehicle back to storage. It also triggered the next step, which was the hardest for the Service Desk: Call the customer and explain the delay. This was a frequent occurrence but was never easy because most customers challenged the need for the delay and were often harsh with employees at the Service Desk, even though the need for more time was obvious from their standpoint.

The next morning, with parts in hand, the repair could proceed. Once the vehicle was moved to the bay, the service technician was ready to make the repairs, the second activity thus far to actually create value from the standpoint of the customer. Given the modular nature of the vehicle and the lack of any need to adjust or tune these electronic items, the actual repair required only a few minutes.

From this point, only three more steps were required to get the vehicle returned and have the customer on his way: Take the car back to storage to await pickup. Do the paperwork at the time of pickup. Fetch the car from storage and wave goodbye to Bob.

However, as you remember from Chapter 1, the car—like 40 percent of those cars serviced every day in America—hadn't been repaired properly or on the same day. The "check engine" light came on again after only a few miles, and the repair cycle had to be restarted.

The key difference in the second repair cycle was that a special factory-operated, technical-assistance line was consulted, and a wider range of parts was replaced. Also, the vehicle was test driven to make sure that problem was completely solved. Fortunately, the vehicle ran properly and the repair cycle was completed.

This process was indeed cumbersome. In the last chapter, we listed the sequence of steps in the process. Now we have combined all of the steps and employee time required in the two repair cycles and shown on the next page. Note that 29 distinct steps were required, consuming three hours and 40 minutes of employee time:

Drawing the Provision Map

Just as we visualized the consumption process in Chapter 1 by drawing a map, we can do the same by creating a provision map with the steps, proceeding from left to right (*Should the Repair Shop Be Repaired?*). However, note that we have grouped the steps into blocks of actions whenever they occur in a rapid sequence, such as the steps related to booking an appointment, making the actual repair, and delivering the vehicle to the customer.

We have done this in order to make the map easily readable. The critical challenge for any map is to include all the significant activities at a scale that can be understood in a glance. The following provision time waste map reveals how many—or few—of these activities deliver value.

For greater insight about the provision process, we can also shade those steps that actually create value as defined by the customer. And here we make an important finding: Almost none of the 29 actions performed actually created any value from the perspective of the customer. In fact, there were only two: the second diagnosis and the second repair, together requiring 35 minutes of employee effort.

For all the rest, although they were unavoidable in the current configuration of the process, the customer would have been equally happy with the result if the steps could somehow have been left out and certainly did not wish to pay for them.

Provision Step List

Steps	Provider time
1. Answer customer inquiry about repair	5 min.
2. Record appointment and schedule work	5 min.
3. Take down info and prepare work order	15 min.
4. Ferry vehicle to storage	5 min.
5. Ferry vehicle from storage to service bay	5 min.
6. Diagnose vehicle problem	10 min.
7. Draw up cost estimate and parts list	5 min.
8. Contact customer and obtain permission to repair	5 min.
9. Seek parts in parts department	10 min.
10. Determine when parts can be delivered	15 min.
11. Ferry car to storage	5 min.
12. Call customer to explain delay	5 min.
13. Ferry vehicle from storage	5 min.
14. Repair vehicle	15 min.
15. Ferry vehicle to storage	5 min.
16. Prepare invoice, run credit card, etc.	5 min.
17. Ferry car from storage and hand over to customer	5 min.
18. Record appointment and schedule work	5 min.
19. Greet customer and prepare work order	10 min.
20. Ferry vehicle to storage	5 min.
21. Ferry vehicle from storage to service bay	5 min.
22. Diagnose vehicle problem with factory help	20 min.
23. Draw up parts list	5 min.
24. Contact customer and obtain permission for repair	5 min.
25. Repair vehicle	15 min.
26. Road test	10 min.
27. Ferry vehicle to storage	5 min.
28. Prepare invoice, run credit card, etc.	5 min.
29. Ferry car from storage and hand over to customer	5 min.
Total provider time (29 steps)	**220 min.** **(3 hr. 40 min.)**

Should the Repair Shop Be Repaired?

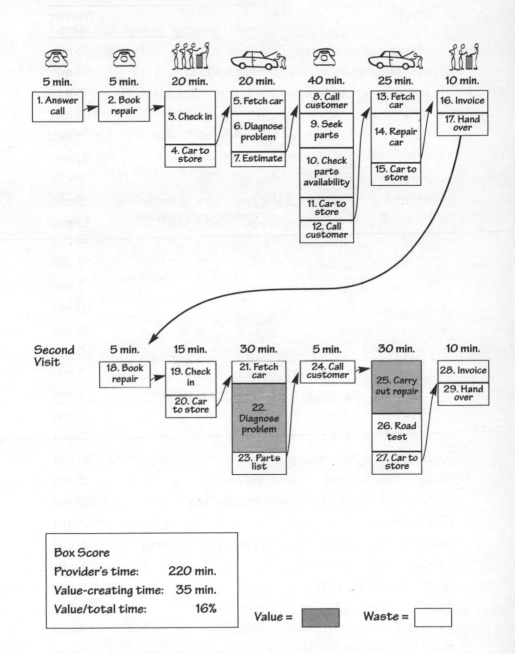

5 min.	5 min.	20 min.	20 min.	40 min.	25 min.	10 min.
1. Answer call	2. Book repair	3. Check in 4. Car to store	5. Fetch car 6. Diagnose problem 7. Estimate	8. Call customer 9. Seek parts 10. Check parts availability 11. Car to store 12. Call customer	13. Fetch car 14. Repair car 15. Car to store	16. Invoice 17. Hand over

Second Visit

5 min.	15 min.	30 min.	5 min.	30 min.	10 min.
18. Book repair	19. Check in 20. Car to store	21. Fetch car 22. Diagnose problem 23. Parts list	24. Call customer	25. Carry out repair 26. Road test 27. Car to store	28. Invoice 29. Hand over

Box Score

Provider's time: 220 min.

Value-creating time: 35 min.

Value/total time: 16%

Value = ▨   Waste = ☐

What Do Workers Really Want?

We can also use the map to show the experience of the employees operating the process. We do this by assigning a satisfied face to steps which are fulfilling as work experiences and attaching a frowning face to those steps which are full of frustration and hassle. The provision experience map (*Why Isn't Work More Satisfying?*) illustrates how workers who experience the wasted steps respond.

For example, diagnosing the problem and making the repair are satisfying to the Service Technician. Solving technical problems with complex equipment was the original attraction for the technician of getting into this line of work. Similarly, shuffling the vehicles from one point to another, while of no value at all to the consumer, was at least satisfying to the young staff members who sought work at the car dealer because of their love of cars. But explaining to the customer why the car was not ready and furiously filling out forms for impatient customers standing in a long line are stressful activities, as indicated by the frowning faces and by the high turnover levels in these types of jobs in all service businesses.

Connecting the Two Maps

We can complete our mapping process by arraying the consumption map from Chapter 1 in parallel with the provision map we have just drawn. This portrays a complete *value stream* consisting of the consumption stream plus the provision stream for the simple activity of getting a car repaired. The combined consumption and provision map (*Seeing the Entire Value Stream*) tracks the entire process for the first time from both perspectives.

Why Isn't Work More Satisfying?

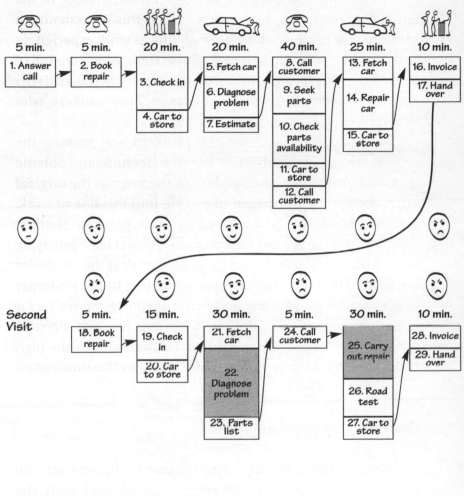

5 min.	5 min.	20 min.	20 min.	40 min.	25 min.	10 min.
1. Answer call	2. Book repair	3. Check in 4. Car to store	5. Fetch car 6. Diagnose problem 7. Estimate	8. Call customer 9. Seek parts 10. Check parts availability 11. Car to store 12. Call customer	13. Fetch car 14. Repair car 15. Car to store	16. Invoice 17. Hand over

Second Visit

5 min.	15 min.	30 min.	5 min.	30 min.	10 min.
18. Book repair	19. Check in 20. Car to store	21. Fetch car 22. Diagnose problem 23. Parts list	24. Call customer	25. Carry out repair 26. Road test 27. Car to store	28. Invoice 29. Hand over

Box Score

Provider's time:	220 min.
Value-creating time:	35 min.
Value/total time:	16%

Value = ▓▓▓   Waste = ☐

Seeing the Entire Value Stream—First Visit

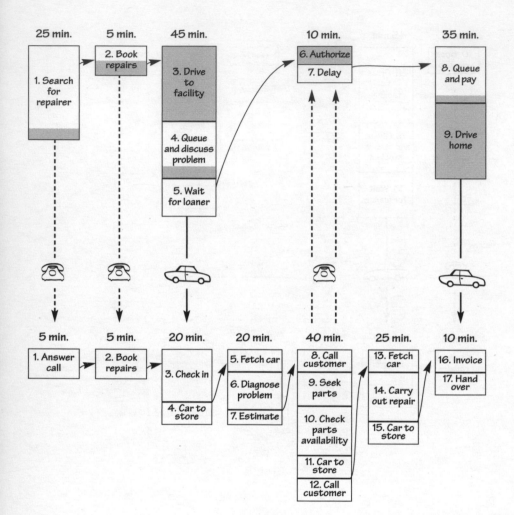

Seeing the Entire Value Stream—Second Visit

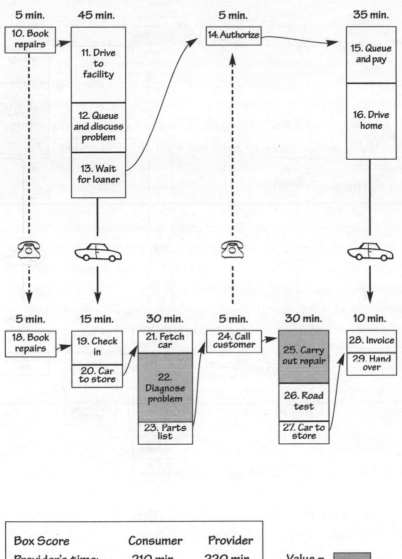

Nobody Wins in a World of Broken Processes

Learning to see the entire value stream can be a revelation. What's striking when we look at the completed step lists and value-stream map is how much of everyone's effort is wasted and how frustrating everyone finds the process. What's more, the points of maximum frustration are precisely where the consumer and provider deal directly with each other, as one stands in line or waits on the phone while the other tries to explain problems and justify delays. What might be the points of greatest satisfaction, as the customer and the provider work jointly to solve a problem, are often the times of greatest discomfort.

The net result is that the customer is actually paying too much for all those wasted activities, which cost the provider real money and which must be passed along. In addition, the customer is suffering stress from not knowing when the car will be fixed, how much it will cost in the end, and whether it will work. Meanwhile, the dealer's employees are also feeling stress as they wrestle with faulty processes that thwart their work and require them to explain unpleasant facts to the customer. And the dealer is not making the economic return he desires. In short, it's a lose-lose-lose situation.

Good People in a World of Bad Processes

How do we typically deal with this (far too typical) situation as humans? Mostly we default to "bad people" analysis. The customer concludes that the provider is either an idiot or a crook while the dealer decides that the customer is an overbearing incompetent, and the employees conclude that both the owner and the customers are a bad lot.

And yet the problem is not bad people, although, of course, a few providers and consumers are idiots or crooks or both. The root cause of the problem is a bad process that no one can clearly see or manage. And the one thing we can conclude for certain, based on our years of observing faulty processes, is that if you drop good people into a bad process you quickly end up with a lot "bad" people assigning blame to each other. Even worse, there's usually no trend toward a better process because assigning blame to the people rather than the process is just another form of waste.

Because our lives as consumers and as producers are critically dependent on a large collection of shared but poorly specified processes, surely we need to do better. And surely we can do better if we can learn to see and think together about improvements. The prize is very large if costly waste can be removed along with the unpaid work of consumers, the unfulfilling work of employees, and the high-cost activities of businesses. In the next chapter we will begin to see how this prize can be attained by applying the principles of lean consumption and lean provision.

Chapter 3

Solve My Problem Completely

We've now examined the auto repair value stream, combining consumption and provision, because it is typical and pervasive. Once you learn to see value streams, you will discover them everywhere because no value can be created without them. Equally important, the methods used to analyze the flow of value can be applied to any type of consumption and provision process. These techniques also can link all of the steps in a complete value stream, beginning with the search for the right goods and services and ending with recycling.

It is now time for a creative act that lean thinkers perform every day. This is to look carefully at the current value stream, from the standpoint of the consumer and the provider, to envision a better "future state." This is the beginning step in the search for the perfect process, one that feels right and is best for all three parties—consumer, employee, and business owner.

Where do we start?

We need to remember that consumers obtain goods and services in order to solve problems. And the first principle of lean consumption is to solve the consumer's problem completely. So let's begin there. Any consumption process that can't totally solve the problem is unacceptable. Period.

But note that failures can and do occur at many points between searching and recycling:

At the outset, for example, the customer may not be able to find the right goods and services to solve his or her problem during the search process—despite the extraordinary increase in publicly available information and low-cost, web-based search tools. And even if the consumer manages to track down the precise item he or she set out to find, the consumer cannot obtain meaningful feedback from the search process to confirm that he or she will actually solve the problem. That is, the customer may finally locate what he or she thought was needed, but will have done so without any input from assistants who in other settings might be able to steer the consumer to a better actual solution to the problem.

Yet even when the consumer successfully searches for and identifies the desired product, he or she must resort to extreme time-consuming measures to successfully complete the buying process. For example, his or her order is lost, like the computer order cited in the Preface. As we will see in a moment, help lines have proliferated to deal with these consumption failures, but they have been directed to solving problems the wrong way.

The next failure point often involves delivery and installation, which is when problems with individual items and with items in combination may first be discovered. Consider your own experience with "ready to assemble" furniture for an example of an individual item that often fails at the installation point. And think of Dan's computer as an example of a failure in combining solution elements, when the goods purchased wouldn't work together, and the service provider couldn't convince them to.

Then, once the products required to solve the problem are installed and working, they may soon prove faulty in service. Even worse, the repair process also may be faulty. Think of Bob Scott's car and, very likely, your own vehicles.

Next, products may need upgrading, initiating yet another process that may run over budget, finish late, and still not get the upgrade done properly. This describes practically everyone's experience in rehabilitating or upgrading their home. It's often true in upgrading software as well.

Finally, the products used to solve the problem eventually will need disposal and recycling at the end of their useful lives. But the process often is so complex and its outcome so uncertain that we take environmentally harmful shortcuts. In fact, this describes our experience recycling old computers and printer cartridges while writing this book. The packaging and shipping requirements to do the right thing by sending the products to a recycling center were so onerous that we did the wrong thing by putting these items in the trash. The real victim in this failure was the environment.

Note that a failure in any one step disrupts the entire consumption process—a dangerous situation considering that consumers may encounter failures in many or even most of the steps as they set out to solve their problems. But note also that the design of the individual goods and services involved often isn't the problem. Dan's new computer performed well once properly installed, easily solving his word-processing problem. And current-day cars usually are satisfying to drive, as long as there is no need to go near the dealer. So the challenge is to place and keep these isolated goods and services—whose specification is often excellent—in a context where they can get their jobs done.

Solving Problems Completely by Understanding and Eliminating Them

Looking over the list of consumption failures, it's apparent that the best approach is to prevent them from ever happening.

The best search process is the one that always works, not the one with the best help line.

The best maintenance interval—servicing cars, for example—is "no maintenance required" during the (long) life of the product.

And the best repair process is the one that is never required because the goods and services always work. Remember, that the entire car repair process described in Chapter 1, which consumed three hours and 30 minutes of the customer's time, was pure waste from Bob Scott's standpoint. No matter how well the task was performed, he would have been much happier if the need for the repair had been entirely avoided.

So what can providers do to avoid these "consumption failures"?

Manufacturers of physical goods, such as toasters, lawn mowers, and cars, have come to accept the idea that their products ought to work perfectly, both "out of the box" and over an extended period. They also expect to incorporate the out-of-pocket costs of repair in their selling price. This attitude is not borne out of benevolence: Producers have had little choice in the past 20 years. Japanese producers, led by Toyota, made a low level of defects in new products, along with a low level of problems in the first years of use, their key competitive weapon, forcing everyone else to respond.

These remarkable improvements have occurred even as real, inflation-adjusted prices for most manufactured goods have fallen. Phil Crosby's famous claim in 1979 that "quality is free"[1] has actually turned out to be true. Companies that create provider processes that are designed to ensure quality at the source with instantaneous feedback loops (both human and automatic) are able to detect every problem as it occurs.

As a result, product quality, measured as delivered defects and defects occurring during an extended period of use, has steadily improved in most industries. Quality measures that are publicly available for a large range of products bear this out. Service intervals are increasing, many products work much longer before they wear and need repairs, and warranties are getting longer in practically every product category, now reaching 10 years and 100,000 miles for some car makes.

Even better for the consumer, in a few product categories regulation has forced manufacturers to eliminate the need for maintenance entirely. Emissions regulations for cars around the world now require that vehicles produce less than a given amount of pollutants per mile driven up to 100,000 miles or more without the need for any maintenance of the emissions controls.

We highlight this achievement with emissions because we believe that with the right incentives, producers of many products would take advantage of the existing technologies to create designs that are far less maintenance- and repair-intensive. Just ask yourself how often your car or your appliances or your computers would need service and repairs if manufacturers internalized the whole cost, rather than making high margins on service calls and service parts instead.

By contrast, the software world, with its allied hardware makers, has long embraced the notion that consumers will accept products that frequently fail to work, in return for a steady stream of new capabilities and cutting-edge performance when they do. In addition, warranties are much more difficult to fashion for software, which is easy to copy and hard to "return" to the manufacturer. And warranties are more difficult still for software and hardware in combination, whose problems often defy simple analysis and which seem to have a remarkable ability to absorb consumers' time.

Fortunately, the maturation of products in the software/hardware industry—have you noticed that the capabilities of PCs and the office software driving them haven't actually changed in years?—and the growing integration of sophisticated software/hardware into more mature mechanical products like cars is rapidly changing the willingness of consumers to accept product defects.

So help is on the way. But note that the number of items and elements we possess to solve our problems is growing steadily. So even if the number of failures per item or relationship is falling, the total claim on our time goes up and no warranty currently reimburses the customer for the time and hassle of a faulty search process, a faulty order process, a faulty installation process, or a faulty repair process. Yet time is often the largest "cost" to the consumer.

It's our expectation that a great leap lies ahead in which providers of all types will embrace the idea that products actually ought to work every time and that some providers will make history by taking responsibility for the total cost—out-of-pocket *plus* consumer time and hassle—of fixing defective products through the entire consumption cycle. This will have profound implications for the design of goods and services. To put it simply, if providers must pay the full costs of faulty consumption—internalizing the cost of the consumer's currently free labor as they do this—solution elements will be much less likely to fail.

The tipping point for this transition is likely to be a switch by manufacturers and service providers from selling or leasing products to subscription services and life-cycle management arrangements. As this happens, the solution provider's expensive labor, rather than the consumer's free work, will be used to solve problems; and the goods necessary to solve the problem never leave the control of the provider. In Chapter 10, we will show how this solution economy can work.

Using Intelligent Feedback to Solve Problems That Do Occur[2]

We are optimists by nature. But it will be a long time before every product works every time, in combination with many other products, through long lives after a fault-free, search-obtain-install process. Today's challenge for consumers and providers is to find a better way to rectify the failures that do occur as imperfect products—often developed in isolation by different organizations—break or fail to cooperate in actual use. Fortunately, lean methods can move us steadily toward consumption processes that are much less likely to fail. The key innovation is gathering intelligent feedback about each "consumption failure." This will permit the current problem to be rectified quickly and completely while future occurrences of the same type of failure are eliminated.

To understand how this might work, let's look at the most visible device companies use to deal with consumption failures—the help desk. Car companies use these to deal with customer complaints about dealers and with on-the-road failures in their products. (OnStar is the best-known service in the latter category.) Computer and software companies, like Dell and Microsoft, use help desks to deal with failures in searching for, ordering, installing, maintaining, repairing, and upgrading their products (accounting, by the way, for a substantial fraction of their total operating costs). And most firms providing goods and services to other firms—ERP (enterprise resource planning) systems, airline reservation software, garden-variety IT systems for small offices, complex process machinery—help their customers to keep their products working through extensive use of service desks.

Typically these firms have automated the answers to as many problems as they can, using a web site or phone lines to lead consumers down different decision paths using voice recognition or touch tones. But, as you have no doubt noticed, your problems are often those that the automated systems can't address. Thus by the time you get to human help at a service center, usually after a wait on hold, your experience is already frustrating.

What do we see if we take a walk through a typical "help" operation? Physically, it's simple. A big room with a lot of people wearing headsets, looking at screens, and interacting with customers, perhaps on the other side of the world. But what are they actually doing, and how are they doing it?

In most instances, the people communicating with the consumer by phone or e-mail are the least informed and the lowest paid in the organization. And their job—upon which management measures them—is to dispose of as many callers as possible per hour using standard answers to standard questions. They rectify failures as best they can at the lowest possible cost per reported failure. Meanwhile, the managers are looking at large screens on the walls that show the average queue time for those on hold or the average wait time to get a response by e-mail, and they are continually redeploying resources to keep the waits within the targets accepted in the industry.

Many of the problems being reported are new or unusual and the organizational units to which the help desk must refer all but the most standard problems are often poorly connected and unresponsive. Indeed, they are often in another company or another country because a substantial fraction of help lines are now outsourced to contractors, many in foreign locations. As a result, the consumer's helper often finds it as hard to get help from the organization where the failure originated as the consumer finds it to deal with the help line. Not surprisingly, employee morale in the help desk and call-center industry today is very low, with turnover typically 40 to 50 percent per year.

But there is actually a much bigger problem lying under the surface in this big room. The help desk is designed to solve the problems that the service center and its client firm (the provider) know how to solve. It is not designed to ask each customer what his or her real problem is. In addition, there is no mechanism in place to rapidly trace the real problem to its root cause back in the client firm and to devise a fix that quickly eliminates future calls about the same problem. Finally, there is no mechanism to actually enhance the consumption experience by providing the customer with new knowledge or ideas that are well known within the client organization but never passed on to the user of existing products. A lean help desk operates in a completely different way.

For starters, the lean call center takes a fundamentally different approach to the issue of staffing, training, and motivation. The first step is to deploy more highly trained help-desk staff and to stop grading them on the number of calls answered per hour. Instead the lean organization encourages its help staff to ask the customer to say more about the nature of the problem, even though this may take considerably more time. The problem, for example, might not be a software feature that is hard to configure, but the lack of another capability in the software, and repairing or providing this would solve the user's problem more directly.

Next the lean provider creates linkages across its departments and functions (and those in the client firm) to quickly trace the causes of problems reported to the help desk, in order to quickly devise permanent fixes. These are both for products already in use and in similar products still to be built and shipped. (The provision stream maps introduced in Chapter 2 are an excellent way to help everyone in the organization see this process of tracing root cause and to identify and improve the process for taking out the wasted time and steps.) The central idea is to stop the help requests at the source by finding and fixing the ultimate cause of the failure.

Then, while the customer is already in communication, a properly configured help desk can turn a frustrating failure into a positive experience. For example, the skilled help-desk expert can far exceed the expectations of the customer by offering new information on the use of the product, such as features in the software that the user has never learned about or forgotten. The help desk can also offer ideas about new and better products to solve emerging problems reported by the consumer during the interaction.

Any contractor or internal help desk pursuing this approach will look terrible on the basis of conventional efficiency metrics used in the call center industry because the amount of time spent with each customer is much greater. When the process is constructed properly, however, the number of callers with a given problem rapidly decreases to a negligible level and these can be helped with a more structured or even automated response system. This means that costs rise at the point of information capture, but that total system costs fall, including the cost of customers' time. And revenues are likely to rise as well, as superior customer support causes happy customers to obtain additional products.

Intelligent Feedback in Action

This all sounds fine as described. But can real firms with real customers actually implement such intelligent feedback? We were delighted in our research to discover that Fujitsu

Services, one of the largest providers of IT support services in Europe, has convincingly demonstrated that these ideas work.

For many years, Fujitsu was mainly a computer hardware company that provided technical support only for its own products. Seeking to grow, the company decided in the late 1990s that it should take advantage of the trend toward outsourcing of IT support. It created a subsidiary, Fujitsu Services, to help the wide range of companies seeking outside contractors for customer service and technical support.

To succeed in this new endeavor Fujitsu soon discovered that it would need to play a very difficult role. It would need to mediate between customers calling with problems and a range of independent hardware and software vendors contributing goods and services as part of the customer's complete solution. Often these parties were complete strangers to each other.

In addition, it would need to deal with an industry model in which help-desk operators bid for contracts from provider firms to respond to their customers' complaints on the basis of the lowest cost per complaint handled. This revenue model gave help-desk contractors no reason to reduce the number of calls handled. Instead it created a disincentive because contractor revenues fell if call volume fell. As a result, traditional firms in the industry worked hard to figure out how to answer calls faster and cheaper by use of poorly paid employees reading scripts addressing routine queries. From the help-desk operator's perspective, the fact that calls kept coming about the same type of problem was a virtue rather than a vice.

As a new player in the industry, Fujitsu decided to approach the problem with the completely different mindset of intelligent feedback. For example, when Fujitsu took over the help-desk contract in 2001 for BMI (the European airline formerly known as British Midland), it immediately analyzed the different types of calls coming from BMI employees.[3] Then it set to work to understand the nature of the problems that gave rise to the calls. This meant identifying what Fujitsu terms "customer purpose." At the same time, it tracked the time and effort required to actually fix the problems the customers were calling about. Most importantly, it measured the impact on BMI's business of the different types of failures being reported by IT system users and the delays in fixing them.

Fujitsu soon found that more than half of the calls to the BMI help desk were complaints about recurring problems. For example, one of the most common reasons for calls, accounting for 26 percent of the total, was malfunctioning printers at check-in desks. Ticket agents kept finding that they couldn't print boarding passes and baggage tags for passengers. It was immediately apparent that this was an important business problem for the airline. Given tight airport security, the inability to print boarding passes and baggage tags that could be scanned at a number of points caused passengers to miss their flights, with major revenue consequences for the airline. Or it caused delayed flights to miss their takeoff slots at crowded European airports—with even more costly consequences.

The previous help-desk contractor had taken the common-sense approach of trying to get service technicians from vendors to respond more quickly to broken printers so that check-in staff wouldn't keep calling about the same complaints. (The normal practice in this industry has been that only the first call about a specific problem is counted toward the help-desk operator's call total for billing purposes.) They had done this mostly by complaining loudly to a contractor servicing the printers, but with limited results.

Fujitsu's conclusion, after its quick analysis, was that the most cost-effective way to proceed was to eliminate the root cause of the calls, which was that the printers were poorly designed for their actual use. BMI senior management was persuaded to spend money to install new printers optimized for their service environment.

As the new printers arrived over the next 18 months, the number of calls about malfunctioning printers fell by more than 80 percent. Much more important to BMI, gains in passenger revenues and reductions in the cost of flight operations vastly exceeded the cost of the new printers. However, because check-in staff still called occasionally with printer problems, Fujitsu also worked diligently with the vendor of the new printers to design a new service process. As a result, the average technician-response time to fix a printer fell from 10 hours under the old system to three hours.

Fujitsu then coupled this problem-solving approach with a different business proposition for BMI. Instead of being paid for each call handled, Fujitsu asked in the future to be paid a set annual fee based on the number of potential callers to the help desk. (In this case, this was the number of check-in staff using the system.) This arrangement allowed Fujitsu to profitably offer BMI a lower bid than alternative vendors, as long as Fujitsu could continue to solve problems in order to reduce call volume. Everyone involved now had the right incentives.

By addressing root causes, Fujitsu was able to reduce total calls to the BMI help desk by 40 percent within 18 months. It also greatly improved customer satisfaction and drastically reduced help-desk staff turnover from 50 percent under the previous vendor to 8 percent. Turnover fell because the staff members now saw their jobs in a totally different light. They were converted from rote responders to recurring problems into active problem solvers.

In applying these concepts across practically all of its help-desk contracts between 1999 and 2002, Fujitsu was always able to dramatically reduce the number of calls for help, in some cases by as much as 90 percent. More highly skilled and better-paid employees were often needed for this new approach, which cost Fujitsu Services money. But the dramatic reduction in the total amount of employee effort needed meant that the cost of a help desk serving a pool of potential callers of a given size fell by 30 percent while doubling reported customer satisfaction with the calls that were still required. At the same time, Fujitsu's annual staff turnover fell from 42 percent to 8 percent, providing another major savings in the form of reduced training costs.

In addition, as Fujitsu applied its approach in different business situations, it began to generate new product ideas for its clients as help-desk staff took the time to ask callers what problems in their lives the callers were actually trying to solve. Conventional help lines steer callers toward conventional answers in order to make call resolution more efficient. By contrast, Fujitsu employees took time to probe, often discovering that the caller's real purpose—once discovered—opened up new opportunities for providers of hardware and software.

For example, in supporting the personal financial software offered by a leading software firm, Fujitsu help-desk staff quickly discovered that the whole mission of the help desk was misunderstood. The software company, dominated by engineers, thought the help desk was there to solve technical problems with the software. But by querying callers about their real problem, it turned out that most were simply trying to figure out how to configure the software to solve their specific problem. There was actually nothing wrong with the software from a technical standpoint. This insight quickly led to a suggestion to the software company that it create a separate help desk, which charged a small fee to take a few minutes with customers to help them get the full use of the software.

As an incentive to keep its staff doing the right things and as a way to sell its services to additional clients, Fujitsu also transitioned in this period from charging other client firms by the number of calls handled to charging them for the total number of customers using the products who might call if there were failures. The new system, which rewarded the elimination of calls by eliminating failures at the source, became a win-win-win for Fujitsu, the customer calling with a problem, and the firm paying Fujitsu for its efforts. Not surprisingly, Fujitsu's market share also surged during this period along with its profitability. For example, BMI soon concluded that Fujitsu should be handling all of its IT support tasks, not just employee help lines.

Outsourcing and Offshoring:
The Wrong Answer to the Wrong Problem

We believe that the implications of this lean approach are quite broad. Instead of measuring results in terms of efficiency in rectifying the same failure over and over, lean thinkers with a new approach concentrate relentlessly on eliminating the failures altogether and reducing the total human effort required to solve customer problems. (To use a term now familiar in the manufacturing world, every failure is an excellent opportunity for kaizen.) This suggests that the current debate in the developed countries about outsourcing call centers and help lines along with "offshoring" them to low-wage countries largely misses the point.

Rather than seeking ever-lower wages for evermore remote workers performing mass production jobs, the lean thinker asks why they need to be done *at all*. In the lean consumption approach, fewer employees are needed to solve an ever-declining number of customer problems in a better way. To do this the employees must be more highly skilled and intimately familiar with the products in question and their uses. Ideally, they also should be able to talk directly with the engineers and managers at the root cause of the problem in order to devise permanent fixes. Therefore, their best location may be near the corporate technical centers that developed the products or near the operations center of client firms like BMI. And it may be inside the company rather than through a contractor.

If firms continue to keep mass production office jobs in high-cost areas without finding ways to truly solve problems, it is very hard to see how wages for these jobs won't decline in the future. And it is hard to see why the distance between firms and their customers won't grow. In any business, employee compensation in the long term must be based on how much value is being created. And revenues from customers will be based on how satisfied customers are.

One of the greatest problems we see with traditional business practices—and it is a problem for society as well—is that jobs directly touching customers are being continually decontented, contracted out, and remotely located. (The widespread resort to part time and temporary workers is another manifestation of this trend.) These expedients reduce the value employees can create and the degree to which consumer problems can be truly solved.

Every Consumption Failure Is a Rich Opportunity

So far, we've been talking about call centers and help desks and these are certainly prominent players in the "failure industry." But don't we all seek help in many ways in our consumption activities only to encounter similar failures?

The clerk at the car dealer, for example, has very little

product knowledge and races to stay ahead of the growing queue. So questions about the full nature of the consumer's problem are never asked. And even if they are asked, there is frequently no way to convey this information to the service technician who will actually solve the problem or to the parts department that will obtain the necessary parts and tools.

Similarly, the clerk in the store who discovers consumer frustration with the features of a DVD player or cell phone/PDA/camera often has no channel for passing the information along. Thus the features continue to be produced, even though the sales staff collectively has a clear understanding of what should be done.

And moving one step backward up the provision stream, the sales director of the complex machinery company actually knows in depth the problems his customers are experiencing with the new model. But the manufacturer's engineering change process is slow and inaccurate in hearing the voice of the customer. It's easier for the sales director to develop a patch kit in collaboration with the service-parts organization than it is for the sales director and the engineering group working together to eliminate the root cause of the problems in the design.

The key point is that every consumption failure provides invaluable information for the provider about the real needs of the consumer and a valuable opportunity to turn frustration into satisfaction. The challenge is to install an intelligent feedback loop that progressively reduces failure while providing new customer insights. The alternative is to perpetuate current systems that become ever more efficient at dealing with repetitive failure but that never solve problems completely and alienate customers in the process.

Solving Problems Without Wasting Customer Time

Let's make the heroic assumption that in the future most goods and services will be much more likely to work as they are supposed to and that consumption failures will steadily decline. Does this mean consumption will be approaching perfection? Unfortunately, no. There will still be a major problem with the use of consumer time, specifically the time that consumption activities consume in the form of unpaid work even when everything goes properly. Fortunately, lean thinkers know how to remove wasted time and hassle from practically any consumption and provision process. We will turn to this challenge in Chapter 4.

Chapter 4

Don't Waste My Time

"Your time is free." This is one of the most curious convictions providers seem to have about their customers. No provider actually says this of course. And some may not think it consciously. But the evidence of this conviction is everywhere.

Just look at queues. Any time you find consumers waiting in a line—at the airport, at any service desk, on any help line, at any healthcare organization, and, of course, at the post office, which is truly the global benchmark—ask two simple questions:

Is the amount of work to be done by the provider reduced by having customers wait? The answer of course is "no," unless some customers give up and go away, taking their revenue with them. Indeed, as we will see, managing the queue actually requires the provider to deploy extra assets and to do more work.

Would there be a queue if the providers had to pay customers for waiting time? This one is harder to answer, since no provider currently pays for waiting time. But intuitively we believe that this answer surely would be "no," unless customers value their time as worthless. Try this exercise: Ask how long it would take to process the traveler from the curb on to the airplane at the airport—being careful, of course, to employ the highest level of security screening—if the airline had to subtract an amount from the ticket price for every minute of elapsed time. Would flyers still need to show up an hour or two in advance and sit (or stand) in several waiting rooms in addition to standing in several queues? Note that all of the waiting areas—which account for much of the space in a modern airport—cost money and must be incorporated in the ticket price.

Looking beyond the highly visible queue, where consumers actually stand in line, there are many additional instances when customers must wait for the value they desire. Examples include the wait for an appointment with their own doctor at their healthcare provider, and for the service technician to fix their personal capital goods. And there are many other instances where customer time is wasted on repairs that shouldn't be necessary (because the product should never have broken), and on visits to doctors, lawyers, financial advisors, and other service workers that wouldn't be required if providers thought carefully about their process or had to pay for customer time.

While a complete list of the ways customer time is wasted would be quite lengthy, this is only part of the time waste in the economy. There are consumers at many intermediate points along each provision stream (employees) whose time is also treated as if it is not highly valued. These consumers include the technician fixing cars, the service man fixing the furnace, the help-desk operator trying to solve customer problems, and the medical technician in the lab. They all "consume" goods and services from other parts of their organization as they try to solve the end-user problems.

Their time is clearly not free to their employer, but, when we observe a business, we typically see many employees in customer service standing around. The reason is not that they are lazy, but rather that they are waiting to obtain the parts, tools, and information from other parts of the organization that they need in order to serve the end customer. How can these wastes of time persist? Because, from the provider's standpoint, the customer's money used to pay for unnecessary time is also free, as long as competitors adopt the same attitude and leave customers with no choice.

Think about the last time you signed the invoice for any type of service. It very likely consisted of two lists—hours of work and parts consumed. The provider then presented this list to you as proof that the job had been done and that the requested fee was justified. Whenever we encounter this type of invoice our first instinct as consumers is to ask how much of the time was truly value-creating time—the technician turning screws on the parts to be installed—and how much was wasted wait time while the technician looked (or waited) for work space, parts, tools, information, and technical help. We're happy to pay for the former, but opposed in principle to paying for the latter. And we usually have no choice in the matter.

By contrast, we note that our friends—many of whom run businesses—generally challenge the cost per hour when the bill seems too high. Like offshoring help lines to a low-wage area, this focus largely misses the point because it concentrates on the cost per hour of labor rather than the number of hours actually needed.

The Process Determines the Time Expended

To make any progress in ending the waste of consumer and employee time, a provider must do more than try harder. Indeed, just getting employees at the help desk in the computer company or in the laboratory at the healthcare provider to work faster may cause mistakes. These may actually increase the total time commitment of a consumer, in addition to introducing risks, because they cause work to be repeated. The key, as always, is to clearly understand the consumption and provision processes and why they require so much time from both the consumer and from the provider's employees.

Let's return to our auto repair example from Chapter 1 and Chapter 2 to understand how the consumption process determines the time expended. We'll then rethink the whole process to see how the lean provider can save both the consumer's and the employee's time.

If you will remember, Bob Scott's first step in repairing his car was to search for a repair shop as shown in the consumption maps on the following pages (*Car Repair before Lean—First Visit* and *Second Visit*).

This involved a wait in several queues for telephone responses. Why? We've already noted that the existence of queues doesn't change the amount of work to be done. The dealer still answers the same number of calls requiring the same number of staff hours of effort. So longer queues don't reduce the dealer's cost of doing the actual work, and they do cost the customer time, increasing the total cost (time plus money) of the repair.

So why do they persist? Partly because of old-fashioned thinking that a queue makes the staff work faster. And it's partly that there is no flexibility in work assignments at the dealer, even though the rate of incoming calls is highly variable. The consequence is that the staff hurries in order to keep the queue as short as possible and often makes mistakes in the process. And the worst mistake, as we saw in the last chapter, is failing to ask in detail about the nature of the real problem. Then, in periods of peak demand when the amount of staff is held constant, some calls are simply not answered.

After enduring the telephone queues to get an appointment, Bob took the vehicle to the dealer and waited in a queue at the Service Desk. Why? The problem is partly the failure to prediagnose the problems with the vehicle and to gather necessary information in the initial contact. This makes the queue longer because it takes more time to deal with each customer. It is also due to the highly variable demand because the number of people bringing in their vehicles peaks in the early morning as dealers schedule arrivals to coincide with the rush hour as people drive to work.

Next, Bob waited to pick up his loaner vehicle to use during the repair. Why? Because the dealer was unable to predict exactly who would need a loaned vehicle and how many of those who did would actually show up. In addition, the crunch at the service entrance to the dealership, where many customer vehicles piled up during the peak, made it seem obvious that the loaner fleet should be kept in a remote storage area until needed.

When Bob's vehicle was not ready for pick up on time—due to a lack of parts—a new type of time issue emerged. This is the hassle of Bob not having his own vehicle for an extra day, just when he had planned to take a trip. We'll talk more in the next chapter about why the parts weren't there and what can be done about it. For the moment, let's just note this hassle factor.

Finally, when Bob went in to pick up his vehicle, he experienced all the waiting and confusion again, and for the same reasons. The fact that the repair also was done incorrectly, requiring a return visit, simply doubled the amount of hassle.

But this is not the full story of lost time due to waiting. Once Bob left his faulty car at the dealership, new types of waiting emerged for the dealership employees trying to fix the vehicle.

Car Repair before Lean—First Visit

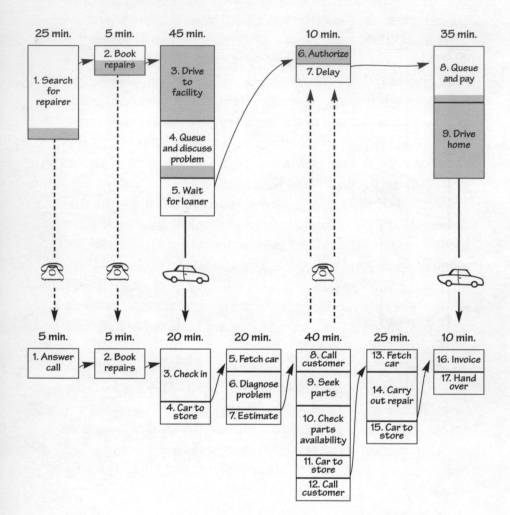

Car Repair before Lean—Second Visit

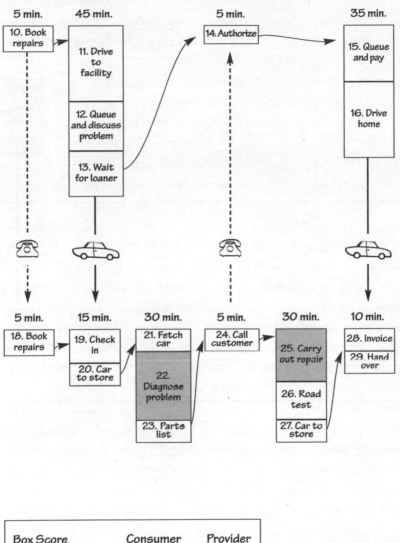

Box Score	Consumer	Provider
Provider's time:	210 min.	220 min.
Value-creating time:	58 min.	35 min.
Value/total time:	28%	16%

Value =

Waste =

These time losses were frustrating for the dealership personnel and costly (although Bob paid), so let's take a closer look.

The heart of any service activity is the technician who does the actual value-creating work. Think of this person as the brain surgeon in the hospital or the lawyer actually writing the contract in the law firm. They are conducting the primary, value-creating process of the organization and need to be supported by many individuals in support processes.

In the case of the car dealer's service department—which we can think about in the same way as an operating room in a hospital—the technician needs four items to succeed at his task: a service bay with the vehicle where he can begin working, the necessary tools to do the job, the necessary parts to do the job, and the necessary information to know what to do with the tools and parts. Some of the tools are always in the bay along with a few of the most common parts, and a lot of knowledge is in the technician's head. However, a few extra tools, a lot of parts, and some additional knowledge in the form of manuals, service bulletins, or advice from a more senior technician are almost always needed as well.

So what do you see in a typical dealership when you follow a service technician through his or her day? Despite the best efforts of the shop scheduler, there is often a wait for a bay to work on the car. And there may also be a wait for the vehicle to arrive from storage once the bay is open. This is because demand is unpredictable and the actual repair time for each vehicle is often unknown.

Once the vehicle is available, and the technician diagnoses the problem, he goes to the tool crib and to the parts window to pick up the necessary tools and parts. Since he is not expected at any particular time and there may be several technicians there already, there is generally a wait— and sometimes a long wait—while the employees in the tool crib and the parts warehouse look for the necessary items.

Finally, as the job proceeds and things don't go to plan, the technician often leaves the work area to look for help from other technicians or the shop manager.

The result is that the technician usually incurs lots of expensive waiting time (charged to the customer) when no value is being created. And this reverberates through the system as other jobs fall behind schedule. In the case of Bob's car, the rush to get the assigned number of jobs done by the end of the day, after a number of delays, meant that the vehicle was not road-tested. It then failed when Bob performed his own road test on the way home.

Surely there is a better way.

How to Create a Lean Process Saving Everyone's Time (and Money)

The lean thinker who looks at this typical situation sees opportunities for improvement at every turn.

Let's start with the search process. The first question, of course, is why any search was necessary. In Bob's case the answer was clear: There was a consumption failure during the previous repair in which the performance of the dealer was so deficient that Bob felt compelled to search for an alternative. We'll not provide an answer to this common circumstance just yet—we'll wait for Chapter 10—but it's important to realize just how much cost, in time and money, results from typical consumption failures.

What we can do here is tackle the queue-time problem. The root cause was that the staff at the dealership all had fixed jobs, but the demands from customers were variable through the day. The staff were frozen to their specific tasks, such as taking orders by phone, taking orders at the counter, and doing walk-arounds of arriving vehicles. They couldn't move around as the volume of the work changed. A better approach would be to train every worker to use a variety of skills, and let them shift tasks as necessary—dealing with the customers waiting in line during the morning rush, for example.

Once Bob had decided which repair outlet to use and contacted the dealer to schedule the repair, a second problem arose. (This is in addition, of course, to a second trip through the telephone queue.) As in the case of the help desks examined in the last chapter, the service agent was the least knowledgeable person in the organization and was being measured by the dealer on the "efficiency" metric of how many calls per hour were handled.

Because the service agent's technical knowledge of the product was roughly the same as Bob's, or approximately zero, the discussion of the problem was unavoidably superficial, along the lines of, "There's this light on the instrument panel and the owner's manual says that if it comes on I should call you." This was a huge missed opportunity for the service representative to ask questions such as: "What's the mileage on the car? ... Does the light only come on in specific conditions? ... How long has it been coming on? ... Has this ever happened in the past and when? ... Is there a funny noise or roughness in the motor?" And equally important, "Are there any other problems with the vehicle that should be dealt when you bring your car in?"

But these additional questions weren't asked. Not only that, but the information gathered couldn't have been passed along to the service technician if it had been. Nor was it possible to make an informed guess about the nature of the problem and make sure the parts were available by the time the car was brought in. This is because there was no link between the two tasks of talking with the customer and fixing the product.

And there was a second problem. The service agent faced a peak of activity at the dealership early in the morning because the dealer was offering only one option. This was to bring the vehicle in between 7 a.m. and 8 a.m., and leave it in order to get it fixed that day. For some customers, this might have been the only feasible option because of their work schedule. But the work world has changed and many people are actually much more flexible today.

The service agent instead could have created a precise profile of the customer, the vehicle, and the job. Then he could have sorted problems by type, into simple repairs that could be done while the customer waited, repairs that truly required the whole day, and repairs that could be started later in the day but still finished that day if the customer brought the car in later. With a bit of probing of customer preferences and flexibility, in combination with more knowledge of the problem, the peak could easily be reduced. Perhaps off-peak pricing for some repairs could have been offered as a way to smooth demand further by letting price-conscious consumers trade convenience for money.

Note that the failure to take a bit of extra time at the outset to ask probing questions and to smooth demand then led to a chain reaction of wasted time for both Bob and the dealer's staff as the process proceeded.

The lean alternative is to make time to talk with the customer at some length when the appointment is made, starting the process of converting a stranger into a partner. Then the service representative can call back the night before the appointment to make sure the car will be brought in at a precise time and that there are no new problems requiring attention. This can have a startling effect on the likelihood that the customer will show up at all or at the precise time agreed.

Then, when Bob arrives, because there is no crush in the service area—remember that demand has been leveled—and because the service representative has already taken the important information about the vehicle and its problems, the walk around can be very brief. The loan vehicle can be in the adjacent parking space ready to go. A 25-minute wait in two queues can be reduced to a two-minute swap of the vehicles.

The benefits are equally visible for the employees in the service bay. There the jobs have been presorted into categories. For example, one bay is devoted only to the recent recall on a certain type of vehicle, and another handles only routine service intervals (24,000 mile, 48,000 mile, etc.) requiring a known set of parts and tools. The jobs can flow much more smoothly with standard work for each task. (And, obviously, the less skilled technicians are given the simple tasks while the most skilled tackle the complex problems.)

Even better, the tools, parts, and information needed can be delivered by the support staff to the service bay in time for the scheduled start of the job so that the technician—the expensive brain surgeon—does nothing but create value through the day. Because jobs tend to be completed on time when using this approach and can be sequenced for pickup at different times during the day, the end-of-the-day jam-up and the tendency to cut corners on testing and checkout can be reduced as well. This means that fewer jobs are likely to return because they weren't done correctly. This is a major savings of everyone's time and money because, as we have seen, these major process failures are both the biggest single time waste for the customer and largest revenue loss for the dealer in the entire repair process.

Finally, back at the pickup point at the end of the repair process, the benefits of taking time up front, getting acquainted with the customer and the problem, and leveling the schedule are apparent once again. Because the jam-up at the service area to pick up all jobs at once has been eliminated, the repaired vehicle can be waiting next to an empty space for the loaner and the service rep can be waiting in the lot just the way service reps wait with electronic point-of-sale devices at rental car returns. Two additional waits by the customer totaling 15 minutes can be reduced to a painless two-minute handoff even as the cost to the dealer is lowered.

In summary, the drawn-out process shown in our "current state" consumption map can be shrunk to the tight lean process shown in the "future state" map on the next page (*Lean Car Repair*). And, as noted in the *Car Repair Box Score*, the time expended by the consumer can be reduced from 210 minutes to 75 minutes, with the fraction of total time spent actually creating value rising from 28 percent to 71 percent. In addition, the hassle factor can largely disappear because there are no needless queues, no rushing to take down customer information, no phone calls hours later with bad news about the cost of the repair, and a near certainty that the job would be done right and be ready at the time promised.

Car Repair Box Score

	Before lean	After lean
Consumer		
Total time	210 min.	75 min.
Value-creating time	58 min.	53 min.
Value/total time	28%	71%
Provider		
Total time	220 min.	80 min.
Value-creating time	35 min.	35 min.
Value/total time	16%	44%
Technician		
Total time	85 min.	45 min.
Value-creating time	35 min.	35 min.
Value/total time	41%	78%

Lean Car Repair

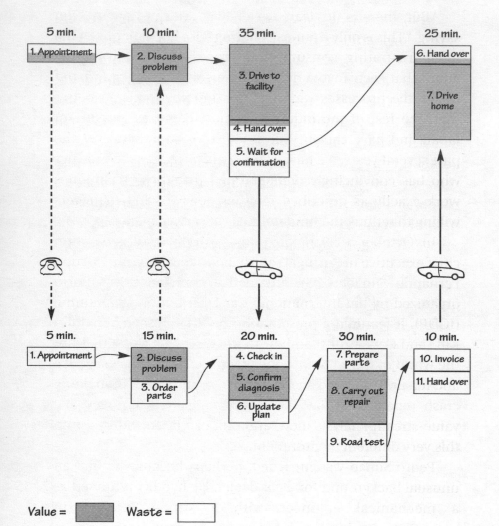

Value = [shaded]   Waste = [ ]

Simao: A Case Study of Lean Service in Action

"But, there is no 'lean' car dealer," we can imagine you saying. "This is only a fantasy offering false hope for one of the most frustrating consumption processes." And we must admit that even Toyota dealers, who should understand and utilize the processes we have just described, are no better than the rest of the industry in most countries outside of Japan and have shown little interest.[1] Fortunately, over the past several years, we have carefully investigated a car dealer who has convincingly demonstrated that these techniques work exactly as described for those owners and managers willing to rethink the fundamentals of service businesses.

In October 1999, Pedro Simao, the second-generation chief executive of Portugal's third largest dealer group, Grupo Fernando Simao (GFS), attended a conference in Oporto organized by the International Car Distribution Programme (ICDP). It featured a presentation by ICDP researchers John Kiff[2] and Dave Brunt[3] on how to translate lean thinking from the world of the factory to the realities of automotive service and repair. They used an example of an auto body shop doing crash repairs to show that standard lean techniques like value-stream analysis, flow, and pull can be introduced into this very different environment.

Pedro Simao was intrigued, perhaps because he had an unusual background for a car dealer. He had been trained as a mechanical engineer with a strong interest in manufacturing and would probably have gone into a manufacturing company for a career except for the relative lack of major manufacturers in Portugal. Instead he wound up taking over the family car business, and wondered why standard dealer practices were so chaotic and inefficient.

At the end of the conference Pedro proposed coming to the UK to learn more about what John and Dave were proposing. At a meeting in London, John walked him through the complete concept of a lean dealer that he had summarized in an ICDP paper, "From Hunting to Farming."[4] He explained that dealers need to move beyond their current "hunting" of customers for one-time transactions based on price. Instead, in order to grow their business and their margins, they need to develop continuing relationships ("farming") based on continually solving customer problems through the life-cycle of multiple vehicles. He argued that the place to begin was in vehicle service, where most dealers currently lose their customers as soon as vehicles are out of warranty.

Early in 2000, Pedro called back to ask Dave Brunt to provide specific advice on a lean conversion of his business, asking him to take a look at the body shop for crash repairs in one of his 17 dealerships. Upon arriving in Oporto, Dave followed standard lean practice and suggested that they simply take a walk together through the repair process from beginning to end. This involved separate areas for stripping off damaged parts, straightening the body, welding on new panels, preparing the vehicle to paint, painting, refitting good parts removed at the start of the process, and polish up.

As they walked, Dave began picking up rolls of masking tape on the floor and left in cars as they were prepared for painting—10 in all—a simple gesture to show that the process was completely out of control. There was no standard place to store things, and tools, parts, and materials were lying everywhere. As Dave remembers, "It was just a typical body shop. There were 'dead' cars everywhere, just sitting there waiting for parts or technicians. Every activity was taking place as an isolated island with no flow and no sense of whether jobs were ahead or behind schedule. Meanwhile, managers were scurrying through the shop resequencing jobs in response to customer, planning, or parts issues."

Dave showed the Simao team how to draw a map of the current provision process as well as a future-state map of how the process would work if lean principles could be applied. To get to the future state he made a number of suggestions: "Look at the whole process from beginning to end rather than trying to optimize the individual steps. Try to flow every vehicle smoothly through the entire process. Don't launch cars into the repair process unless you have fully diagnosed them and have all the necessary tools and parts. Separate types of jobs—from simple to complex—and run them down separate paths. Create a process control board so every employee can see at a glance the status of every job. Let each work area go to the previous work area to pull the next job ahead."

He placed special emphasis on carefully measuring "customer fulfillment." This meant precisely tracking if vehicles were being delivered to customers on time with everything done right the first time. Then, whenever there was a "failure to fulfill," it was critical to find the root cause and permanently remove it so the provision stream could be shortened and smoothed further.

As he went away, Dave didn't expect to come back. "Almost all dealers I had met at that point were hunters. I wondered if Pedro could really learn to be a farmer."

To Dave and John's surprise, after about a year, Pedro and his improvement team began to report substantial progress. Dave received an e-mail with a large batch of photos documenting remarkable changes at all 17 sites (not just in the body shops). This convinced him that he needed to return. He was amazed with the new practices. "What I found was a terrific 5S process[5] to create a precise place for every tool and kit of parts. There was a progress control board clearly visible showing the exact status of every job. Parts were now being delivered in kits—containing every item needed for each job—from a centralized warehouse serving the body shops in all of his dealerships. And each work area was going to the previous work area to get its next job. Meanwhile, no new jobs could be started unless the next downstream area signaled it was time. As a result, jobs were being completed faster and customers had a shorter wait for their vehicles."

Simao had also started to transfer lean provision concepts to the service shops of all of his dealerships, which were separate from the crash repair operations. These are the types of activities we described for Bob Scott's "check engine" problem. Soon Simao had lean provision practices in place all the way across every service area in his $400 million business with 900 employees.

Today, GFS diagnoses every car prior to the start of repairs. Because this is done over the phone prior to arrival, parts can be ordered in advance. However, not all problems can be identified over the phone and the practice of many customers in Portugal is to simply show up for service rather than calling ahead.

To deal with these problems, Simao has created a diagnosis bay at the front of each repair shop. Upon arrival at the dealer, the customer drives the vehicle directly to the bay and onto a lift. Where the customers are prepared to wait, the customer and the service technician inspect the vehicle using a standard check sheet designed to identify all needed work including items the customer may have been unaware of. The technician and the customer agree at this point on all the work to be done, the cost, and the completion time. This eliminates the need for callbacks to the customer during the day and any unwelcome surprises about the cost of the repairs.

A key advantage of diagnosing the vehicle the instant it is brought in is that in many cases the repair can be done within the time the customer is willing to wait, typically an hour or less. This saves the customer time for the total repair process because the trip back to the dealer to pick up the vehicle is eliminated. And it saves the dealer money because the multiple movements of the vehicle and storage at the dealership are eliminated along with the need for a loaner vehicle. To save more time, Simao is now introducing a "pit stop" method in which several technicians work on the vehicle at the same time as soon as it is diagnosed in order to get it back to the customer faster.

Once the nature of a repair is specified, the technician places an order for all the parts needed. These arrive before the repair is scheduled to start, in a kit from the central parts department delivered on periodic "milk runs" to many dealerships. (Standard parts for the simple jobs that can be done while the customer waits are kept in the service bay and replenished frequently by a simple pull signal to the parts department.)

The application of lean principles has also permitted Simao to create a profitable new business in the preparation of used vehicles for placement with new customers. By lining up all the steps in the preparation process in a tight sequence, standardizing the work, ordering parts in a kit, and maintaining a steady work pace, the cost of vehicle preparation has been reduced by 50 percent and the time needed has been reduced by 70 percent. As a result, Simao is now performing this task for many leasing firms not part of GFS.

Simao is hardly finished with his lean journey, but already the company has cut the time expended by the average customer almost in half while reducing the total cost of the average service to GFS by 30 percent. The dramatic decline in vehicles coming back to do the job right the second time has been a big contributor to cost savings along with the 75 percent reduction in the number of loaner cars needed and a near doubling of the service technicians' time actually creating value. Other savings resulted from the central parts department, which reclaimed all of the parts previously lying around the dealerships, reduced the total stocks held by GFS, and raised the parts availability by ordering more frequently in small amounts from suppliers. (We'll see further evidence of the power of this simple idea in the next chapter.)

At the same time, the likelihood of being able to fix vehicles correctly on the first visit and to deliver them to the customer at exactly the time guaranteed has increased from about 60 percent (the service industry average) to more than 80 percent. Simao recognizes that there is still a long way to go. But as a result of progress to date, GFS has climbed to the top of the car manufacturer's customer-service rankings for many of its brands and has dramatically increased the share of the service business that it retains during the life cycles of the vehicles it sells. By saving everyone's time, GFS is achieving a lean success for customers, employees, and the owner.

Simple Rules for Saving Everyone's Time

What we've just seen in the case of car service can easily be generalized to any consumption experience where scheduling and knowledge of the customer are needed. Here are four simple rules to follow.

First, *create a knowledge dialogue with the customer* from the outset to gain a full understanding of the problem, including dimensions the customer may not even be aware of. Remember that customers can't ask for goods and services they don't know about, but can easily be steered into suboptimal paths convenient to the provider that wastes both parties' time.

Creating this smart conversation requires the use of highly trained employees who can ask insightful questions, rather than unskilled employees who are not prepared either to ask the right questions or to pass along interesting information.

Companies must also create a knowledge base th.
the information, and create paths that convey this w.
those in the organization who can act on it.

Second, whenever possible, *prediagnose the problem*
taking extra time to learn exactly what tools, parts,
knowledge, and time are likely to be required to fix it. This
permits kitting of all the needed items ahead of the time of
use and avoids the need to make repeat trips to get the job
done. To verify this need, consult your memory as to how
often a service technician has arrived to work on your
computer, your air conditioning system, or your gutters only
to inform you after a few minutes that he or she will have to
come back later with the right tools, parts, and knowledge.

Fortunately, the trajectory of information and diagnostics
technology is such that most of our personal capital goods
will soon have their own diagnostic systems and an ability to
explain what ails them directly to the provider. And the
miniaturization of medical diagnostic devices increasingly
means that the patient can report useful information on their
condition to their healthcare provider.

This is good news, but progress is not nearly as fast as it
could be. This is largely because interfaces between
manufacturers of products and service organizations are
unstandardized and weak. Remember that adding
diagnostics to the product costs the manufacturer money and
costs the service organization money for equipment to
receive the diagnostic information remotely. Unless these
parties can work together to develop ways to use the
information creatively to better serve customers while
reducing costs and increasing provider revenues, results will
be suboptimal. We'll return to this issue in Chapter 10.

Third, *level demand* wherever possible. If all customers
show up at the same time, the first question should be,
"Why?" Often the cause is not the customer's own desires but

the operating practices of the provider. For example, we visited the central laboratory of a world famous healthcare organization that took all blood samples and other specimens at 7 a.m. in order to analyze them in large batches during the course of the day. (The leaders of this organization were classic mass production thinkers and believed that doing analysis in batches—for example, with large centrifuges able to hold hundreds of blood samples—would minimize the cost per analysis.) This meant building a large auditorium to hold a batch of a thousand or more patients as they queued for the early morning tests. Then the facility was empty during the remainder of the day.

Similarly, motorists queue to get their cars inspected for emissions and safety as their stickers expire on the last day of the month. Why not have the same number of stickers expire every day of the year? (Of course, one can also make the argument that Christmas should come every day in order to level demand on toy stores, so there are some limits to applicability of this concept.)

Going further, if a stable relationship can be built between customer and provider, the provider can approach the customer in advance to suggest convenient times for activities that aren't urgent in order to level demand further. Routine auto service, tied to mileage and unrelated to breakdowns, is an obvious possibility. The dealer can roughly estimate the amount the customer drives the car and maintain a knowledge-sharing relationship with the customer to suggest when service is needed. Similarly, medical providers can proactively schedule routine checkups at times when health centers aren't flooded with flu patients, an option made even more attractive by the health benefit of keeping healthy patients away from health centers when they are most likely to be exposed to contagious illnesses.

The fourth and final rule for saving everyone's time is to also *save the time of the employees* serving the customer, who consume inputs from other parts of their organization. This requires creating predictable work flows through the organization by separating types of activities into what lean thinkers call product families. For example, put simple activities with stable cycle times down one path, activities that require complex analysis with unknown cycle times down another, and activities involving complex but stable tasks down a third.

Doing this also requires the development of standard work for every task and prekitting of the tools, parts, and knowledge that will be needed. These sound like activities that can only work in industrial applications, but they are actually even more valuable outside the factory. They can be achieved in almost any environment where employees can see the benefits and give the methods a fair test.

Then as activities proceed much more smoothly, the chances are much greater that the work will be done within the time promised and that the customer will regain the use of his or her home or car or computer (or even his or her body) precisely when promised, and with a lower risk of failures that require rework loops.

Attacking Time Waste in Healthcare: The Triumph of 'Open Access'

Many consumers would say that their most painful instances of wasted time occur while obtaining primary healthcare. And there are three different ways in which they feel this pain. The first is the wait on hold when calling their doctor, followed by further waits for calls back in order to fully explain the problem and make an appointment. The second is the wait of many days or weeks to get an appointment with their personal physician (the alternative being a trip to urgent care to be treated by someone unfamiliar with their circumstances). The third is the wait at the doctor's office when they arrive for their appointment.

In 1994, Dr. Mark Murray, a family practice physician at Kaiser Permanente, the large West Coast HMO, had a revelation: All of this waiting was unnecessary.[6]

Murray had been placed in a new job to rethink operations and improve patient service while spending no money on additional staff or facilities. After analyzing the situation, he realized that all of the telephone queues and callbacks to get an appointment were caused by a lack of knowledge by low-level employees answering the phone. They needed to "triage" patients—to separate acute cases from those that could wait— but they couldn't do this well partly because they couldn't communicate quickly with busy nurses and doctors to reach these decisions. (The introduction of a complex, computerized scheduling system seemingly only made matters worse.) If only patients could talk directly to their doctor or at least make an appointment on their first call, this hassle would go away.

He then noted that the waiting interval in his practice before patients could see their own doctor was constant at about two months. Murray reasoned that if the length of the queue was constant, the cause couldn't be a capacity problem. "The amount of work to be done was the same," he said. "We were just pushing it out two months."

Finally, he noted that the waits in the office were caused by the scheduling practices demanded by health insurance companies that were only willing to reimburse the doctor's time for a 15-minute appointment as a way to contain costs. Because the amount of time needed with some patients went longer than 15 minutes, delays tended to stack up during the day and physicians had to stay late to do paperwork that couldn't be handled during the tight schedule.

With these simple observations in hand, Murray devised a strikingly simple solution. He called it "open access."

Rather than asking patients to call in and wait for a callback from a higher-level decision maker, Murray proposed that any patient expressing the need to see his or her doctor should come in at the first available time that day. One quick phone call and it was done. Murray had looked carefully at the actual pattern of patient demand and believed there was a very high chance that every patient could see his or her own doctor that day, once the doctors put in some overtime to work off the backlog. Murray said, "The queue wasn't actually serving any purpose except to provide doctors and administrators a security blanket. Their big concern was that the most expensive asset in the practice—the doctor—would not be fully utilized, and a queue meant no doctor would ever be idle."

Murray also proposed to lengthen the intervals scheduled for patient visits with the doctor so doctors could catch up on their paperwork between patients rather than at the end of the day. To make this work from a financial perspective, the number of hours each day during which appointments were booked was extended. But doctors would now be going home immediately after the last visit rather than staying for hours to catch up on record-keeping details that were often hard to remember many patients later.

Of more interest to the patient, Murray believed that appointments would actually start on time, eliminating the third significant source of wasted time in traditional systems. This was because appointments would be scheduled to be longer than the amount of time needed by the average patient. The doctor would then do paperwork or respond directly to patient calls when patients required less time than the scheduled appointment. This in turn was how the doctor could go home immediately after the last appointment.

When Murray first proposed his new system, it was greeted with skepticism. He decided to try a simple experiment in a six-doctor practice in Roseville, CA, that was isolated from the rest of the vast Kaiser system. Because these doctors suspected that management's true intent was to increase their work load and billable hours while paying the same wage, it was important to get agreement at the outset that their patient load would not be increased.

After the backlog was worked down and the doctors got used to the new approach, they discovered they liked it—and so did their patients. As Murray notes, "They were doing today's work today and discovering that there was a lot less work." The doctors found that their lives were easier because they weren't always behind, apologizing to patients for being behind, and staying late to do paperwork at the end of the day.

Even more important to Murray as a physician, patient outcomes were better. Practically every patient was now dealing only with a doctor who knew the patient's personal history, rather than with a highly trained stranger in urgent care or during an appointment scheduled quickly to avoid a long wait for their personal physician. Misunderstandings were reduced, and patients were more compliant with treatment plans. Diabetics had lower blood sugar, those at risk for heart disease had lower cholesterol, and patients at risk for strokes had lower blood pressure. Clearly the move to open access would provide better care while saving the entire healthcare system money in the long term.

Given the deep traditions in medicine and the fact that many doctors seem to be process-challenged,[7] it was not surprising that it took three years to spread open access across the complete Kaiser Permanente system and had taken many years more to become a common practice in American medicine. In fact, when we first met Murray in 1999, he was still not sure that open access would be more than a noble experiment. Fortunately, the adoption rate is now in a steep upswing portion of the familiar "s" curve. Nearly 50 percent of primary care practices in the U.S. report that they are experimenting with open access, and perhaps 25 percent have fully implemented the system.[8]

Beyond Open Access: Do You Need to See the Doctor at All?

A final leap in saving the patient's time may be to eliminate the need to spend it at all. Dr. Charles Kilo, a primary care physician in Portland, OR, reflected on the future of primary care, recently concluded that open access is a wonderful innovation for those who must really see a doctor. But he wondered how often this was really the case. He noted that traditional medical practice and the rules of the health insurance industry result in 90 percent to 95 percent of patient care taking the form of office visits. (Currently, most insurers won't pay unless the doctor actually sees the patient.)

He further noted the rising fraction of care focused on patient maintenance. This is the oversight by primary care organizations of patients with chronic conditions such as blood pressure, diabetes, and excessive cholesterol. These activities are likely to increase steadily as a fraction of total health needs as the baby boom cohort ages. Finally, he noted the rapid growth in personal healthcare technology available at modest prices: blood-pressure recorders, blood-sugar testers, and even blood-analysis devices.

He therefore set out on a new approach to practice in an organization appropriately named Greenfield Health, which has sought to reduce the need of the patient to go to the doctor, even as the standard of care is increased. He adopted all of the techniques of open access so any patient needing to see his or her doctor could get an appointment the same day. But by carefully building an accurate, computerized history of each patient, arranging for the appropriate personal technology at home, and making direct access to the primary care physician easy by e-mail and phone, Kilo found that the number of annual office visits per patient could be cut in half. This was even as patients reported higher satisfaction with their primary care relationship and had better outcomes on chronic care measures. This was partly due to the technology, but, more importantly, it came from the physician's knowledge of the history of each patient and the resulting ability to communicate by phone or e-mail to assess the situation and, often, to provide both care instructions and reassurance in place of a time-consuming office visit.

Just how the insurance industry will adapt to these innovations remains to be seen. But with studies indicating a 20 percent to 30 percent reduction in total cost (not counting patient time) from implementing the entire set of lean measures in primary care and with better outcomes as a result, it is now clear that we know how to save the patient's time, the employees' time at the healthcare provider, and everyone's money. Surely it is only a matter of time before everyone's time is being saved

For the Want of a Nail (or a 50-Count Box of #2 Galvanized Nails)

We have now shown, in a range of activities, how to create lean processes that save the customer's unpaid time along with the provider's paid time and that make the customer and the employees doing the work happier. But note that providers can only save customer and employee time if they have all the materials on hand to perform the needed tasks. For example, in our car repair example, much time was wasted when the dealer could not get the right parts to do the job the same day. This is a pervasive problem in many types of consumption, including healthcare, and one we will try to solve in the next chapter. In simplest terms, it's the difficulty customers have getting exactly what they want on their first try.

Chapter 5

Get Me Exactly *What* I Want

Let us assume that providers learn how to remedy the product failures described in Chapter 3 and the time wastes examined in Chapter 4. What if consumers still can't solve their problems simply because the specific items they need aren't available when needed? Most of us experience this annoyance routinely in our lives as consumers, but it is easiest to see when we are searching for just one item. Let's take the example of shoes.

Human feet come in a wide distribution of lengths and widths. And the owners of these feet seem to want a wide variety of styles for each width and length. Therefore it's not surprising that when customers go to the shoe store, the clerk takes their measurements and disappears for an extended period to a mysterious back room to look among a large stock for the right size in the right style. Unfortunately, the right item often isn't there.

Most people would wonder why the retailer doesn't carry more stock and do a better job of forecasting. These methods have, in fact, been the traditional approach of retailers for decades in a continuing struggle to improve their "level of service," which they define as the fraction of time they have exactly the item the customer wants on hand. But when we look at how the provision stream actually works and how unpredictable demand is, it is easy to see why progress toward this goal has been limited.

The Provision Logic of the Shoe Industry

The shoe market in almost every country is largely focused on fashion. The basic problem of putting something comfortable between our feet and the street has largely been solved for almost all consumers, so the important issue is style. It's not surprising, therefore, that the industry has four selling seasons per year and that about half of all shoes currently on sale have a product life of one selling season. (That's roughly three months.)

Despite advances in technology, shoe manufacturing is still quite labor intensive, and labor rates for the types of tasks required vary remarkably around the world. Given these realities and the additional fact that trade in shoes is now largely free of tariffs and quotas, it's not surprising that many shoe companies in the "action wear" category, like Nike, Reebok, and Adidas, have decided to outsource shoe manufacturing to a few contract manufacturers operating at low-labor-cost sites in East Asia. Indeed, 90 percent of the action-wear shoes sold in North America and Western Europe are now made in China, Vietnam, Indonesia, and Thailand.

Let's look at what this means for the retailer trying to serve the customer. The process starts with the visit from the shoe company's representative to the retailer, bearing samples of the new models being offered. (In the curious custom of the shoe trade, they are all size nine—and the number of samples needed is so large that Nike produces more sample shoes each year than the total sales of the fourth largest company in the action wear category.) But these are not models for the next selling season—let's say the fall "back to school" season in the Northern hemisphere. They are models for two selling seasons out. This is because the lead time required from placing the order until delivery to the store is more than 150 days. The retailer knows with great precision what is selling at the moment, but has only a limited idea of what will be popular in the next selling season. Thus the order for two seasons out can't be much more than a guess. This is particularly the case since half of the models offered by the shoe company's representative are new, with unknown consumer acceptance.

The retailer therefore does the best job possible, by placing an order for what seems to be the likely sales for a given model. And this initial order must do: Because of the long lead time, once shoes go on sale at the beginning of a three-month season there is no time to place reorders for runaway successes or to stop a continuing flow of models rejected by the market.

Given this reality, a large number of "out-of-stocks" ("OOS" in the language of retail) are unavoidable, and a safety valve is necessary somewhere to deal with the equally unavoidable overstocks. The current-day safety valve is for shoe companies and retailers to dispose of excess goods through price markdowns in retail stores, sales in company-branded outlet stores, or transfers of goods to bargain-basement secondary channels.

These safety valves are well managed, in the sense that the entire order-taking and sales process utilizes the latest forecasting models. Electronic point-of-sale (POS) data are available in real time to the retailer, the shoe company, and the contract manufacturer. Everyone can see what is happening. Yet at the end of a selling season, shoe stores find on average that they only have the right style in the right size 80 percent of the time (meaning large numbers of lost sales), and that up to 40 percent of the total shoes manufactured are sold at reduced prices or sent to outlet stores and secondary channels (meaning more lost revenue and additional costs). It's a classic case of having too much of the wrong thing and not enough of the right thing, with the consumer[1], the retailer, and the shoe company suffering as a result.

To make this as clear as possible, we've drawn a map (*Shoe Current State*) of the current-day provision stream for shoes.

The boats and trucks in the diagram represent the physical movement of shoes, while the arrows represent the flow of information (in the form of orders) used to regulate the system. (This is what Toyota calls an information and material flow map and what lean thinkers more generally call a value-stream map.[2]) Note that at any time there are significant inventories of shoes at the shoe assembler, on the boat, at the shoe company's distribution warehouse, at the shoe retailer's distribution warehouse, and at the shoe store. There are also inventories of information in the form of orders waiting to be processed. These are at the retailer, the shoe company, and the contract manufacturer, as shown in the "in boxes." It's the long time lags for the system to respond to customer orders that require the inventories.

'Did You Find Everything You Were Looking For?'

We've started with shoes because these are a stand-alone item solving the customer's problem. Customers may also want to buy a hat or warmup jacket at the same time they buy their shoes, but usually there is little or no linkage between the different items as they visit the shoe store. The same can generally be said for shopping for clothes, books, or DVDs.

Shoe Current State

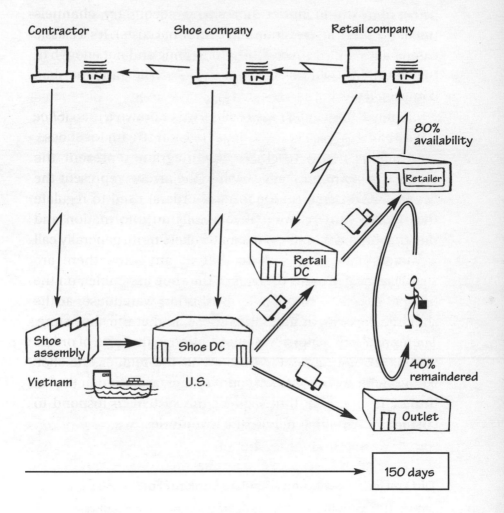

Consumers may end up obtaining several items on one trip or one visit to a web site, but their use and usefulness are not linked.

This is not true in many other situations. For example, most of us would like to obtain on one trip all the items we need for a home repair and all the drugs and personal care items we require to doctor our current health problem. In these circumstances, consumers grade the provider on a combined level of service; that is, on the ability to put in their shopping basket all of the needed items to solve the problem. (We'll call this "basket fulfillment.") We can see how this works with a quick trip to the grocery store.

In North America and Western Europe, about 40 items are purchased on a typical trip to a large grocery store to shop for the family. And in the typical store the level of service in keeping individual items on the shelves in the right place is about 92 percent.[3]

This level of service sounds acceptable until you do some simple math. To successfully complete a shopping trip, the consumer needs to find all 40 items, many of which will be combined into recipes and all of which are likely to be needed before the next shopping trip. Because each item is likely to be available 92 times out of 100, it follows that the chances are only 4 percent that all 40 of the items will be available. (This is the result of multiplying .92 by .92 40 times.) Twenty-four trips out of 25 will produce frustration.

One of the virtues of shopping in a large store is that consumers can often find substitutes for the items they really want. (Indeed, in our reluctant role as weekly grocery shoppers in big stores we have perfected a method for performing the necessary substitutions. We always take our cell phones and call our wives for specific instructions on what to substitute.) And one of the reasons grocers carry so many alternative versions of similar products is to help consumers substitute.

But even with many substitutes, grocers have long found

from survey data that the single largest complaint about their stores—and a major reason for switching stores—is OOS in items the shopper expects to find. This awareness has been greatly heightened in recent years by the introduction of home delivery from orders placed on the web. The grocer's employees now become shoppers on behalf of the customer and report to management the substitutions for missing products that customers were making all along without the grocer being fully aware. So grocers are now much more focused on raising the level of service.

Fortunately, there is a solution to the OOS problem, and we will reveal it in just a moment. But to complete the description of the problem, we need to note that the inability to get exactly what consumers need is manifest in just about every consumption activity, including services.

Bob Scott couldn't get his car repaired the same day because the car dealer discovered that one of the needed parts wasn't in stock and couldn't be replenished in time. And how many times have you had your plumber or your electrician or your computer service representative show up to solve your problem only to report that the parts were out of stock and that they will have to come back later, quite possibly many days later? In these situations, substitutions are rarely possible and the level of service falls to zero if even one of the needed parts is missing. In short, the inability to get exactly what they want is a pervasive problem for consumers.

What's more, this is a problem for consumers at all levels of a provision stream, not just end consumers. Service organizations, such as retailers and repair operations, and wholesalers, manufacturers, and their suppliers are also shoppers for items from the next organization up the provision stream. They can't solve their customer's problem if they can't first solve their own problem by obtaining exactly the right items exactly as needed.

How the Traditional Retailer Tries to Get You What You Want

The common-sense approach to raising the level of service is to position large inventories at every level of the distribution network and the supporting production system. These start with the store shelf in the back room at the retail store. (In many warehouse formats, like Home Depot and Costco, inventories are held vertically, in storage racks above the consumer touch point.) Stocks are also held in the retailer's distribution warehouse, in the wholesaler's warehouse (particularly for low-volume items), in the manufacturer's finished-goods warehouse, at the point of manufacture, and (in the form of parts) at many points all the way back to raw materials.[4] The retailer and every level in the system then try to reorder in time to avoid out-of-stocks on the basis of sophisticated forecasts of future demand. But they also tend to reorder infrequently in large quantities because they believe that this reduces freight and handling costs.

Information technology has come increasingly to the aid of common sense by means of barcode scanning systems (soon using radio frequency identification—RFID). As a result, everyone associated with provision streams can know how sales are proceeding and where all inventories are located. Yet these methods are still not providing a high level of service because the dynamics of the total system chronically tend toward too much of some items and too little of others.

To see why, we need to create a current-day provision map for the goods you might obtain from a retail outlet like a grocery store and follow their journey through each "shopping loop" backward, through manufacturing to raw materials.

The first step is for the grocer to form a rough estimate of the rate of sales of each item (easy to do from POS data) and to reorder this amount perhaps once a week, making adjustments for known spikes or troughs in sales just ahead. (For example, the first summer holiday weekend is sure to produce a big burst in sales of soft drinks.)

So far so good.

But then the problems begin. The grocer is not receiving the needed items directly from the supplier's factory but from the grocery company's distribution warehouse serving a number of stores. And the grocery distribution warehouse is not receiving goods directly from the supplier factory either, but instead from the supplier's distribution warehouse. There are inventories of finished products on hand at four points (at the least): in the grocery store, the grocer's distribution warehouse, the supplier's distribution warehouse, and the shipping area of the supplier's factory.

So who is going to place the order? The store manager, on the basis of point-of-sale data plus an educated guess about future needs? The grocery company distribution center manager, on the basis of an additional set of calculations about the rate of consumption across a number of stores? Or the grocery company's buyer at headquarters, who aggregates orders from many stores and several distribution centers?

And where is this order going to be received at the supplier? At the distribution warehouse? At the factory? Or at the supplier's headquarters where schedulers are trying to plan production and shipments for the whole company?

And what about promotions? Suppose the grocery company buyer discovers a great opportunity to order an extra amount of a given product because the supplier has made too much? Or suppose the supplier is trying to "make its numbers" at the end of its fiscal year and offers customers an incentive to take more product now rather than later? Who decides whether this deal makes sense, where the extra stocks should be stored, and who will keep track of them to know when to reorder?

Many questions indeed. When we put all this together in a diagram showing what is happening in this provision stream (*How Provision Systems Amplify Demand*) we always find the same thing. There are multiple order points, often in conflict. Orders are placed infrequently and often irregularly. Deliveries are infrequent and often unpredictable, to suit the needs of the logistics companies rather than the customer. And there are numerous promotions and other perturbations in the order cycle. All this means that true customer demand gets lost in the shuffle. And, the further we move up the system from the customer, the more tenuous the link between actual demand and what the operation at that step is hearing.

In this map of the provision stream, we can see that demand is being amplified as shown in the charts above each storage point. These track the pattern of orders being received over time for a given item. The waves of orders are growing larger and larger at each step up the provision stream in a sort of retail tsunami moving outward from the epicenter of customer demand. Yet demand from customers in the store is nearly level. There is no consumer earthquake precipitating the waves. So why is this happening?

The place to look is the multiple order management systems battling to give orders at every step, even as many managers override the formal, automated ordering systems to deal with perceived abnormalities at their vantage point along the provision stream. (Their actions are shown by the telephone icons and dotted lines representing information flow.) The consequence, in the language of the information technologist, is a low ratio of "signal" (i.e., valid information) to "noise" (i.e., erroneous data). This causes excessive inventories throughout the provision stream (often called "just-in-case" stocks) and a low level of service to the end customer. An amazing achievement, repeated every day across the world.[5]

How Provision Systems Amplify Demand

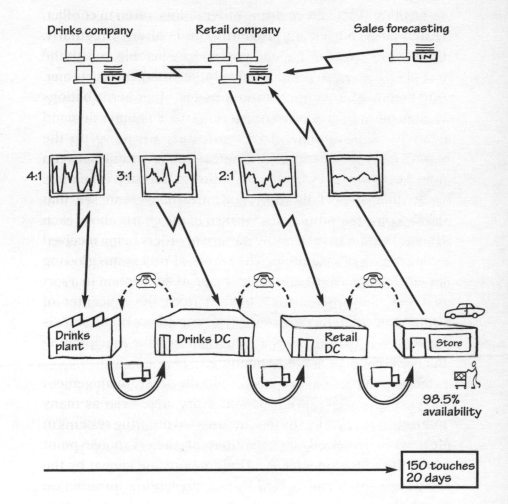

How Lean Provision Can Get You Exactly What You Want and At Lower Cost

Lean thinking solves this problem by reversing all of the traditional logic. The trick is to introduce only one scheduling point in the provision stream, greatly increase the frequency of replenishment at every point, replenish exactly what has just been purchased (unless some special circumstance with well-known demand consequences lay just ahead), and—if at all possible—compress the provision stream to bring manufacturing and distribution activities closer to the point of sale.

In doing this, lean thinkers substitute the pull of the customer for the push of the upstream assets by means of a *reflexive* rather than a *cognitive* information management system. Think of what happens when you put your finger on a hot stove. Does your brain receive signals from the nerves in your finger and process it as follows: "This is a stove. It seems to be on. My finger is on the burner. It is beginning to smoke. This could be very painful. Maybe I should remove my finger?" Or do your reflexes do a better job by simply pulling your finger away from the heat in proportion to its intensity, without any need to consult the central processing unit in your brain?

Obviously we do the latter, and very successfully. Yet information technologists have spent nearly a century now—beginning with schedules produced from punch cards in the 1920s—trying to devise automated, centralized processing systems that collect information from many points within a system. This is the current situation in the provision stream in our grocery example. The hope is to optimize the entire process by means of feedback loops to gain accurate information on current conditions and by use of sophisticated algorithms that permit the central brain to direct every action at every point within the system.

Our exemplar lean company, Toyota, operates the world's highest quality and most reliable production and logistics processes. It also has the most accurate information feedback loops with the least noise. Yet it concluded long ago that centralized management systems never achieve nearly the level of performance their architects envision. Small amounts of noise invariably accumulate and gradually degrade the system. Then, as the instructions sent to each point along the provision stream began to diverge from actual needs, managers began to override the system manually at each point. This causes the performance of the total system to rapidly deteriorate to a much lower base level.

One approach is to push even further ahead, with more sophisticated information collection as a countermeasure—of which RFID is the next step. A better approach is to reduce the need for information and to simplify the decision logic. Ideally, information needs to flow only to the next step upstream, and that step only needs to resupply exactly what has just been consumed by the downstream step.

Making this work depends critically on increasing the frequency of orders going upstream along with the frequency of deliveries coming downstream.[6] This is aided by the introduction of lean logistics in order to permit frequent replenishment of goods (and often of information as well in the case of nearby suppliers) along with the compression of the provision stream in distance and time.[7]

Why haven't more providers done this? A key reason is that firms at all levels of the typical provision stream look at point costs (the cost of an item purchased from a supplier anywhere in the world) and at "chimney costs" (the cost to a particular department for all products purchased) rather than at total costs for each product. For example, a shoe company's purchasing department looks at the cost per shoe and selects a vendor in Vietnam. The logistics department looks at the cost per shoe to deliver from the factory to the retailer and selects sea freight for all shoes in infrequent, large batches. The sales department creates a special departmentwide account for "cost of sales," based on an industry rule of thumb that remaindering costs are acceptable as long as they do not exceed 10 percent of total selling costs. And companies often seem to have no way to count the cost of lost sales and declining customer loyalty due to out-of-stocks.

Yet providers would often be better off to spend a bit more money on the cost per item in order to save a lot more money on inventories, out-of-stocks, remaindering, and lost customers. By doing this they would actually reduce their total provision stream costs for each item while increasing sales and market share.

How Lean Provision Actually Works Through Rapid Replenishment

We are not just describing hypothetical benefits. We have a striking example of what can be achieved, from a company whose progress we have closely examined over a number of years. In our previous book, *Lean Thinking*, you may remember the example of the humble can of cola and its remarkable journey across the world, from raw materials into the hands of the customer on the shelf at a Tesco grocery store in the UK.[8] The total trip required 319 days.

Just for the can to progress from the supplier's can-filling plant to the shelf at the grocery store required 20 days. This included storage in five locations, six order-decision points, and a demand amplification ratio of 4:1. (That is, the variation in demand at the supplier's bottling plant was four times the variation in actual customer demand in the store.) The level of service was 98.5 percent, equaling basket fulfillment of 55 percent if all 40 items in the typical family shopper's basket had the same level of service. (Note this was far ahead of the retail industry's average level of service at that time.)

Shortly after we prepared this example in 1996, Tesco set out to differentiate its position in the grocery industry by providing a higher level of service while reducing its costs. Graham Booth, then the supply chain director of Tesco, approached Dan Jones and his research group at the Cardiff Business School, asking how Tesco could benefit from Toyota's supplier logistics methods to reduce time and effort. As always, Dan suggested taking a walk to examine a typical provision stream, in this case the one for cola. He urged Graham to invite the other functional directors at Tesco—retail, commercial (purchasing), distribution, and finance—along with the operations and supply chain directors of Britvic, the company supplying the cola.

On a cold day in January of 1997 this group set out, walking back through the provision stream for cola from the checkout counter of the grocery store through Tesco's regional distribution center (RDC), Britvic's DC, the warehouse at the Britvic bottling plant, the filling lines for cola destined for Tesco, and the warehouse of Britvic's can supplier. Along the way Dan and his team from Cardiff kept asking simple questions: "Why are products missing from the shelves? Why does a sales associate need to re-sort products from roll cages that have just come off the truck from the RDC? Why is so much stock needed in the back of the grocery store, at the Tesco RDC, and at Britvic's RDC? Why are there huge warehouses of cans waiting to be filled near the bottling plant?" And so on.

The walk was an eye-opener for both companies. When Tesco and Britvic analyzed the map they drew together of the process as they walked, they could see huge amounts of

111

waste at every step along with huge opportunities for saving costs while increasing the satisfaction of the end customer. They also realized that the cost savings and a higher level of service could only be obtained through cooperation between the two companies and among the functions within each company.

What It Takes to Provide What the Customer Wants

As Graham Booth looked at the situation, he realized that practically all of Tesco's existing practices for getting goods from the supplier to the shelf would need to change. The first step was to hook the POS data in the store directly to a shipping decision in Tesco's RDC. This made the end customer at the checkout point the "pacemaker," regulating the provision stream and eliminating the battling scheduling systems.

Tesco then increased the frequency of deliveries to the retail stores. After several years of experimentation, Tesco's trucks now leave the RDCs for each store every few hours around the clock, carrying an amount of cola proportional to what was sold in the last few hours. This saves from one to several days of replenishment time and means the system is responding practically in real time to actual customer demand.

At the RDC, cola is now received directly from the supplier's bottling plant in wheeled dollies. These are rolled directly from the truck arriving from the supplier into the delivery truck to the stores. And once at the stores the dollies are rolled directly to the point of sale, where they take the place of the usual sales racks. This innovation eliminates several "touches" in which employees moved cola from large pallets to roll cages for shipment to the stores and then onto dollies to reach the shelves, where they were handled one last time. (In drawing their provision-stream maps of the original process, Tesco discovered that half of its cost in operating this provision stream was the labor required to fill the shelves in the store.)

In addition, the new method of rolling cola in the same dolly from the receiving dock at the RDC to the shipping dock eliminates the previous practice of taking large pallets of cola to a storage position in a high bay. After a considerable wait in the high bay, the cola was brought down to floor level where the pallets were opened and containers were picked for shipment to each store. (Eliminating the steps of putting the cola into storage, bringing it back from storage, and picking the right amount to send to the store permitted a big labor savings.)

For fast-moving products like cola, the Tesco RDC is now a cross-dock rather than a warehouse, with goods from suppliers spending only a few hours in the building between their receipt and their dispatch to the stores. To guard against sudden spikes in demand, a buffer stock of full dollies is still held aside. But because of the frequency of replenishment, this buffer is very small.

Meanwhile, back at the cola supplier, even larger changes have taken place. Britvic has improved its uptime and the flexibility of its filling lines so it can now make what the customer has just requested in small batches with very high reliability. This means that there are practically no finished goods awaiting shipment in Britvic's filling plant and the product can bypass Britvic's distribution warehouse (originally built to deal with spikes in downstream orders and batch production upstream). Instead, the cola is packed directly on the wheeled dollies at the end of the filling line so they can roll onto Tesco's truck, roll through the Tesco RDC, and roll to the point of sale in the store with far fewer touches for storage and repacking.

The final logistics step is for Tesco's delivery truck to take the dollies several times a day from the RDC on a "milk run" to a series of Tesco stores. At each store it collects the empty dollies and then visits several suppliers to return the empty dollies. At each stop it also picks up full dollies and then returns to the Tesco RDC to restart the cycle. This may sound like a good way to increase truck miles and logistics costs, and many traditional managers, including those at Tesco and Britvic, have assumed it must. However, in practice, these methods substantially reduce the total miles driven along with freight costs while also reducing total inventories in the system.[9]

This all works smoothly because there is only one trigger point for orders in daily operations. This is the customer removing cans of cola from the roller racks and taking them to checkout where the actual order is generated from the POS data scanned from the bar code on the item. From this point back up the provision stream, each step simply replenishes what the next downstream step has removed: if customers purchase four dollies of canned soda in a four-hour period, the RDC gets a signal to put four dollies of canned soda on the next truck. As these goods are scanned onto the truck, the signal is automatically sent to the supplier to prepare four more dollies of canned soda for shipment to the RDC when the truck comes around from the stores with empty dollies.

It would be a mistake to make this system sound perfect. As Toyota concluded long ago, no process is perfect for long, and issues do arise. For example, buyers are still looking for special offers, and suppliers are still tempted to make special offers even though these can be upsetting to the logistics system by introducing sudden spikes in demand or supply.[10] But for the most part the system works well, and it certainly works vastly better than the traditional system it replaced.

By replacing the common-sense system of inventories at

many points managed by sophisticated centralized information management with much simpler but highly refined lean techniques, Tesco has created a vastly simplified provision stream, as shown in the future-state map (*Delivering Fresh Cola*) on the next page.

The consequence, in terms of performance, is remarkable. Total "touches" on the product (each of which requires costly human effort) have been reduced from 150 to 50. The total throughput time, from the filling line at the supplier to the customer leaving the store with the cola, has declined from 20 to five days. The number of inventory stocking points has been reduced from five to two (the small buffer in the RDC and the roller racks in the store) and the supplier's distribution center for these items has disappeared. Demand amplification has been cut from 4:1 to 2:1, and the level of service for this product has been increased from 98.5 percent (already extremely high for the grocery industry) to 99.5 percent.

So far Tesco has applied these techniques to more than half of its fast-moving products as well as to seasonal goods for Christmas, Easter, and the summer. As these methods are progressively applied to every item, "basket fulfillment" for a typical big-store shopping trip increases from 4 percent to 82 percent. This means only one instance of shopping frustration in every five trips, rather than the current industry average of frustration on 24 trips out of 25. And the total cost to Tesco, its suppliers, and its customers—remembering to count the cost of customer time and hassle that is saved in getting everything needed on one trip—will be substantially lower. A win-win-win.

An irony in this outcome is that perishable goods have always been replenished rapidly and frequently in the grocery industry, but at much higher cost using traditional methods. Introducing lean techniques effectively treats every item—

Delivering Fresh Cola

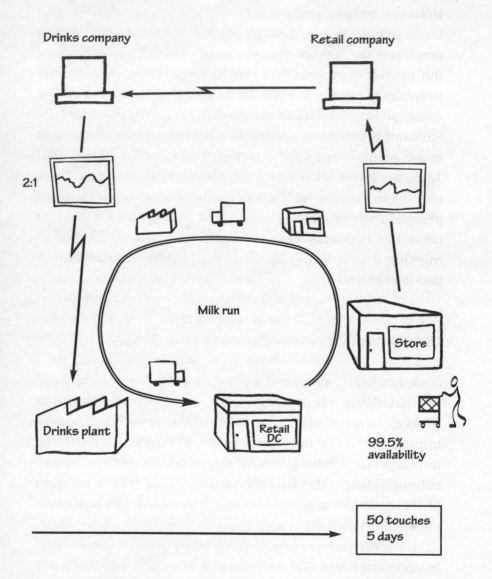

Drinks company

Retail company

2:1

Milk run

Store

Drinks plant

Retail DC

99.5% availability

50 touches
5 days

including the customer—as perishable and actually reduces total costs.[11]

In retrospect, Tesco's approach seems logical and straightforward. Indeed, it's now the new "common sense." However, for any company to make this leap requires real leadership. In Tesco's case, Graham Booth took the lead and employed skillful diplomacy—based on joint assessment of the provision process—to convince the functions and the suppliers to put the interests of the customer at the end of the value stream ahead of narrow organizational interests. Sustaining this new approach required strong support at many points from CEO Sir Terry Leahy, who insisted that Tesco not turn back when problems were encountered. As we will see in Chapter 6, Tesco's relentless focus on leaning its provision streams along with a new approach to providing what the customer wants exactly where it is wanted is marking it as a leader in the global fast-moving consumer goods industry.

Compressing the Provision Process Even Further

It has been popular in business books in recent years to say that distance is dead and that the location of activities in relation to each other and to the customer is no longer important.[12] This may be true of products that can be translated into bytes and sent electronically, such as books, although even in this case the projected date for the triumph of the downloadable e-book to supplant the old-fashioned paper copy you hold in your hand has been steadily receding.

However, the overwhelming majority of products we need as consumers are still molecular. Our colas and cars must move through a number of steps along the provision stream to get to us, and it turns out that where the steps in the provision stream are located is very important if we truly expect to get exactly what we want. Fortunately, if we apply the methods just described to all types of businesses, like the far-flung shoe business examined at the beginning of this chapter, we can discover additional dimensions of opportunity. The key is to *compress the provision stream* by distance and time.

To return to the shoe example, suppose that the shoe retailer, instead of placing one unchangeable order for the season with the contract manufacturer at the top of the provision stream, could stock on the store shelf one pair in each style in each size and then let the customer determine what to restock. The customer would essentially become the single ordering point for the entire provision stream, simply by picking which pair of shoes to buy. This act would automatically generate a restock order that would reach the factory through several fulfillment loops.

For this to work, the shoe company would need to establish a series of distribution centers in North America and Western Europe that could supply each retail point in these regions directly and frequently. Currently, most shoe companies serving these markets from remote production locations have a single distribution center for a whole country or even a geographic region like North America or Europe. This facility breaks down sea containers coming from the contract shoe manufacturer in Asia and repacks the items for onward shipment to retailers. This is often through the retailer's own distribution center, where further time-consuming breakdowns and sorting occur before shipment to the retail point.

If the shoe company established a series of distribution centers to serve retail stores within one day's trucking distance, the need for the retailer's distribution center would be eliminated, just as one layer of distribution centers has been eliminated by Tesco in groceries. This would provide a savings in time and cost.

The shoe company RDCs could operate "milk runs" connecting each distribution center directly with retail stores in densely populated areas and utilize delivery services like UPS in less dense areas. The distribution centers could also ship any order direct to the customer, for next day delivery if desired, if a retail store was out of stock in a given style or size and the customer wanted it immediately.

Back at the distribution center, we would find a small stock of each style and size ready for shipment overnight to retailers or directly to consumers. And in large metropolitan areas, it might even be possible to ship replenishments from RDCs during the day if stores suddenly experienced a surge of interest in a particular model. Seven-Eleven and Toyota in Japan have done this for fast-moving consumer goods and spare parts for many years.

Equally important, we would find a frequent-replenishment system operating between the distribution center and the contractor factories. This would automatically reorder each day what had just been shipped to retailers, with milk-run trucks from the shoe company visiting several contract manufacturer plants to pick up orders corresponding to the items just shipped from the RDCs to the retailers.

At the factories, we would find a highly flexible production process, able to operate very smoothly because of a small buffer of finished items permitting daily shipment of each order without endless changes in the production schedule.[13] Finally, at the receiving dock at the back of the contractor's shoe factory, we would find an equally responsive pull system obtaining the necessary materials from raw materials suppliers, often by milk runs.

We've drawn this whole system, with its associated lead

time, total inventories, and level of service, in the shoe future diagram (*Shoe Future State*). You can compare it with the diagram of the way the shoe business is run today, which we drew earlier in this chapter.

Note that the total lead time from the factory to the shelf at the shoe stores falls from 150 to 10 days, shelf availability goes from 80 percent to 95 percent, and the fraction of goods that must be sold at reduced prices or remaindered because no one wants them at standard retail pricing falls from 40 percent to 5 percent. Also note that when the retail store doesn't have the right style in the right size, the product can be shipped to the customer's home from the shoe company distribution center in two days, meaning that customers willing to wait 48 hours will never need to buy a style they don't really like or leave the store without buying anything.

But there is a problem that traditional thinkers who are at least willing to consider this approach will quickly discover. Rapid replenishment with the customer as the trigger only works if the shoe factory, the distribution center, and the retailer are geographically proximate. Otherwise, rapid replenishment of each demand loop can only be provided—if at all—by expensive airfreight. Yet shoe factories and facilities for many types of manufacturing have been relocating steadily in recent years to the opposite side of the world from their customers in order to take advantage of low labor costs, with goods moved slowly by sea. Would it be cost-effective to reconfigure the system and move manufacturing closer to the customer?

The answer lies in calculating the total cost of a product delivered through a provision stream, not just the cost of a pair of shoes at the factory gate. The total cost is the sum of the cost of the shoes at the point of manufacture, the logistics cost of getting them to the distribution centers and on to the retailer, the cost of operating the distribution centers, the

Shoe Future State

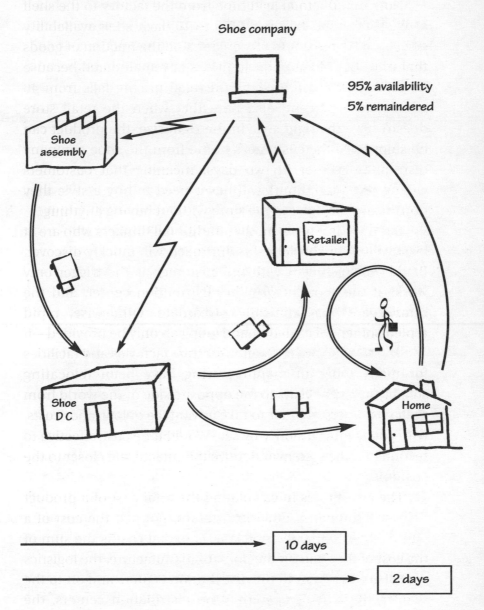

Shoe company

95% availability
5% remaindered

Shoe assembly

Retailer

Shoe DC

Home

10 days

2 days

carrying costs of large inventories, the cost of lost sales due to out-of-stocks, and the cost of price discounts and remaindering of overstocks through special channels at some risk to the brand. And there may be significant additional costs in the form of quality problems (because defects are only discovered by customers months after they occur), management of complex provision streams, and the currency and country risks inherent in placing production in locations far from the point of sale.

The New Lean Location Logic

We have recently spent a good bit of time in the shoe industry conducting interviews about the current company approaches to "location logic" and calculating the total costs of producing products for consumers in given markets.[14] For products destined for customers in North America and Western Europe we find the following "lean" location logic:

Newly launched product types made with new technologies are probably best made near design centers in the U.S. and Western Europe until the technologies mature and the market indicates its long-term interest. This minimizes manufacturing and delivery problems and maximizes the feedback from both manufacturing and sales to the product development team. (It is also important to note that new process technologies may have permanent implications for production location. For example, if a new technology dramatically reduces the amount of labor needed for the traditional stitching required to make the "uppers" of shoes, locating a large fraction of production close to customers in the market of sale may minimize total costs.)

Customized products made to customer order for immediate delivery—for example, through web sites like www.nikeid.com—are probably also best made near company technical centers in high-wage areas. Recent experience shows that customers are willing to pay a premium to customize the colors, materials, and logos on their shoes—that is to get exactly, precisely what they want— but they want the shoes delivered very quickly and are not willing to pay a large premium for airfreight from the opposite side of the world.

This concept is being pursued today by Nike for the customized bags it offers at its Nike iD web site. These items are built strictly to customer order at NuSewCo, a contract manufacturer in Oakland, CA, which receives electronic orders, makes bags in a variety of fabrics and colors for the various panels (as selected by the customer over the web), and embroiders or monograms the buyer's name or special message. These personalized bags are then express shipped to the customer for a total price that is only $10 more, including shipping, than a customer would pay for a standard bag at a retailer. Labor in the San Francisco area costs $15 per hour, including benefits, compared to perhaps 80 cents per hour at shoe plants in China. Yet Nike calculates that the total cost of making customized bags with high-priced American labor and using express delivery is lower than the total cost of making standard bags for American customers from Southeast Asia and selling them through retail.[15] How can this be?

It's possible because sourcing in the market of sale and making only to order permits Nike to leave out a large number of steps in the logistics and sales process:

- Storage of items at the plant in China until there is a full container to take to the port,
- Further storage of the container at the port while shipping awaits a full load for the container ship,
- Customs processes at both ends,

- Storage of the items in the distribution center on the U.S. West Coast and the buildup of containers to send to the stores,
- Entire cost of the retail store,
- Cost of the inevitable overstocks,
- Cost of lost sales due to stocks-outs,
- Revenue loss from reduced-price sales, and
- Cost of remaindering (which sometimes means simply discarding) items produced on forecast for customers who never materialized.

As Nike's cost analysis shows, the "touch labor" is actually a small part of the total cost of producing and delivering these products, despite their labor intensity.[16] Most of the costs reside in the various overheads at Nike, the management of the many handoffs from production sources on the other side of the world, the large inventories at many points, the retailer's overheads, the lost sales from too few goods, and the lost pricing power from too many.

Customized products are usually restricted to the higher-priced end of a manufacturer's range, so standard models with mature technologies selling for moderate prices in retail stores are likely to be a different matter. We calculate that their uncertain sales prospects and their volumes (since they account for a large fraction of the total product line) make them best suited for manufacture at the lowest-cost production point within the geographic region of sale. For North America, this is likely to be the interior of Mexico; for Western Europe it is probably Rumania or Turkey; for Asia is it probably what you might have expected at the outset for all shoes: China.

By locating production within the region of sale, the shoe companies can switch from boats covering long distances—which are cheap but slow—or airplanes, which are expensive but fast (and often necessary when production falls behind), to trucks, which are pretty cheap and pretty fast. For example, shoes could be trucked from factories in central Mexico, where wages are much lower than on the border, to distribution centers anywhere in the U.S. in 12 to 48 hours. The same is true, with perhaps an additional day of travel time, for factories sending products from Rumania or Turkey to central Europe.

This would mean that a shoe bought by a customer today in a U.S. retail store, with the customer acting as the production trigger, could be replenished overnight to the store from the regional distribution center. And the distribution center could be replenished within two days from the shoe factory. Less than a week would be needed to go from factory to store. By contrast, shoes traveling by boat from Southeast Asia to North America and Europe require more than 40 days just to reach the distribution center. This is the sum of the time needed to reach the shipping port by truck and go through customs, wait until the boat arrives and is loaded, sail the vast oceans, unload and go through customs, and travel to the warehouse.

Finally, shoes with mature technologies and highly predictable demand—the basic white sneaker like Nike's Air Force One that has been in production with practically no changes for 25 years—may have the lowest total cost at the lowest-cost global point of manufacture. But even this conclusion is not clear-cut, and we suspect that this is a small and shrinking fraction of total sales.

Based on our discussions with a number of shoe companies, we believe that reconfiguring shoe production, distribution, and retailing as we propose will increase margins for shoe companies by 8 to 10 percentage points, a staggering achievement in this highly competitive business. But we should also be clear that this can't happen instantly.

The biggest problem in relocating shoe assembly from China or Vietnam to Mexico or Turkey is not the assembly operation itself. This requires only simple tools in simple factories with a modest amount of worker training. The real problem lies in the supply base.

Shoes require many different materials, often unique to the industry, and the suppliers of these materials are currently located either in high-wage countries (where they often have their technical centers) or in Taiwan, Korea, and China. What's more they operate facilities requiring significant scale and are not eager to establish new facilities in other regions ahead of established customer demand. However, moving the supply base as well as assembly is the key to creating a rapid response system. Otherwise, response could even slow further if unreliable materials supplied from far away suppliers causes assemblers to stock large inventories.

A simple way to get started on this transition is to establish specialized assembly facilities within each region of sale whose job is to assemble any of a wide variety of shoes whenever it becomes apparent that market forecasts were wrong. These facilities could afford to stockpile a range of raw materials because their ability to practically instantly shift production to the items demanded by the market would be very valuable to shoe companies. In particular, the shoe companies could avoid out of stocks on premier products backed by major advertising campaigns. Then, over time, these facilities could grow to the point that they justified the creation of a nearby supply base. A compressed provision stream would then emerge.

Lean Location Logic for Every Product

The logic we have been describing can be applied to any industry and to all of the basic activities within that industry—product development, production, and customer support and service. For every product supplied to a specific customer at a specific location there is a lowest total cost point to design, manufacture, and support that product. And this point is likely to be considerably closer to the customer than most business leaders currently think. When the product development, production, and customer support processes are all conducted in accord with lean principles, removing waste and its attendant costs of many sorts, the lowest cost design, production, and support location is likely to be still closer to the customer.

However, this point should not be taken too far. We have had extensive experience in the past few years in transferring lean know-how to Eastern Europe, Latin America, and East Asia.[17] We have seen convincing evidence that engineers, production mangers, production associates, and service managers in these regions can rapidly master lean techniques to reduce their total costs dramatically even as wages begin to rise. As a result, we are convinced that a growing fraction of design and manufacturing for the most advanced countries will occur in developing countries. It's just that these developing countries will be in the same region as the advanced country in question, not on the opposite side of the world.[18]

We have now applied the principles of lean provision to two items—groceries and shoes—but the principles work with any type of item from automobiles to yurts.[19] We propose four simple rules to help companies provide everyone exactly what they want:

Create a single point for order entry to regulate the entire provision stream. Lean thinkers often call this point the "pacemaker." Ideally, it is the end customer at the point where the item is obtained.

Signal the need for replenishment frequently with low-noise information technologies—the simpler the better. And whatever you do, eliminate battling Material Requirements Planning (MRP) and Enterprise Resource Planning (ERP) systems located at multiple points along the provision stream. These send contradictory orders to different parts of the system, instructions that are overridden by managers at different points along the provision stream to deal with their immediate problem while making the situation even worse.

Replenish frequently in small amounts at every point up the provision stream from the pacemaker, using the techniques of lean logistics. The common belief that total product costs— from raw materials to customer—are lowered by replenishing infrequently in large amounts is simply wrong. Another mass production idea needing transport to the scrap heap.

Locate production and distribution as close to the customer as possible. The simplest rule for lean location is: (a) Near the producer's technical centers, even in the highest-wage areas, in the case of immature or highly customized products, and (b) at the low-factor-cost (i.e., low wage) location within the region of sale for all but the most standardized, basic, and labor-intensive products with very stable demand.[20] Deciding just where to make what is not a matter of emotion but rather an issue of calculating total cost for each product for each customer, including direct production costs, logistics costs, inventory carrying costs, remaindering costs, and the cost of out-of-stocks.

The Next Challenge: Save Consumer Time and Hassle

We have now tackled the challenge of providing exactly *what* the consumer wants. Remarkably, as providers learn to count the total cost of provision and reconfigure provision systems on a pull replenishment basis with production in the best location, it will be much more likely that consumers can get exactly what they want and at lower costs. In a competitive economy, this should mean lower prices for the consumer as well.

But the consumer's calculation of total cost, as we have noted at many points, goes beyond product prices. It must also include the consumer's value of time and sense of hassle in obtaining the desired items to solve their problems. We need therefore to consider *where* consumers obtain what they need and in what provision format, because these are critical determinants of the amount of time and hassle.

Chapter 6

Provide Value *Where* I Want

If we asked you to name the one place where you should go to get exactly what you want at the very best price, you would probably say, "A 'big box' retailer." For groceries, drugs, personal care items, and utilitarian clothing like socks and underwear—what retailers call "fast-moving consumer goods"—you might try a hypermarket such as Tesco Extra in the UK or Carrefour Hypermarche in France. For home-improvement needs—hammers, plywood, and nails—you would probably go to Home Depot or Lowe's in the U.S. For furniture—both finished and ready-to-assemble—you might try Ikea in Europe or the U.S. And for consumer electronics— from flat-screen TVs to digital cameras—you would probably head for Best Buy or Circuit City. Or, if you were looking for almost everything in a single store, you might try the latest generation of Wal-Mart Superstores in North America. These carry more than 150,000 items (called SKUs for "stock keeping units" in the language of retail[1]) across many categories and are the biggest boxes of them all.

Heading to one of these megaoutlets seems obvious to most consumers because we seem to arrive on earth with preformed notions about scale. If a store is bigger, it must be cheaper to operate due to "scale economies" and must get cheaper goods from its suppliers due to the large volumes in which it buys. And, if a store looks like a warehouse (like Home Depot), with goods stacked to the ceiling, it must be cheap because everyone knows that warehouses are wholesalers who "cut out the middle man." And, if the items come in packs of 24 (at Costco or Sam's Club), rather than one at a time, there must be a cost saving because of additional economies of scale, this time in packaging and handling.[2]

Let's suppose for a moment that all of these big-box retailers take seriously the ideas presented in the last chapter and raise their level of service on single items to 99.5 percent or higher. This would permit a level of service for the entire shopping basket of more than 85 percent for the typical trip to the fast-moving consumer goods outlet along with lowest prices. You would surely think that this combination is about the best the consumer can hope for in combining low prices with high variety. But does it really provide the lowest total cost of consumption?

We can explore this question by drawing a consumption map of the consumer actions required to obtain the items needed at a big box. We will take care to calculate the total cost of consumption, including the consumer's time, not just the price of the items.

The first thing we note is that the consumer spends considerable time and effort to get to the megastore, because there are only a few located in each metropolitan area, typically located on the far periphery in order to find enough land at low cost.[3] For example, a typical shopper at a big-box grocery outlet in the U.S. has driven 25 miles in 50 minutes at a cost of $6 in vehicle expenses. And then, of course, there is the search for a parking space and the walk across the lot into the vast building.

Once inside the store, we find something very interesting.

Based on loyalty card data that some retailers have collected in recent years—and that Tesco has done a particularly good job of collecting because more than 80 percent of shoppers at Tesco stores use loyalty cards—we know that the typical household buys less than 300 different SKUs of fast-moving consumer goods in a whole year of shopping. What's more, many of these items are bought as substitutes when other items on the list of 300 are out of stock.

Because a Tesco Extra carries more than 80,000 SKUs— half food and drink; half household, electrical goods, and clothing—this means that 99.6 percent of the items in the big-box store (which trumpets its wide variety as the centerpiece of its advertising) are irrelevant to the typical consumer.[4] Customers must sort through tens of thousands of items they don't want to find the few hundred they do want.

This activity takes time and, in the case of many shoppers, creates a sense of hassle as well. For example, a visit to a big-box grocery outlet consumes more than an hour inside the store, despite the very efficient checkout process where increasing numbers of shoppers scan their own items. And many shoppers report frustration in trying to locate the specific items they are looking for in the vastness of the big box.

Finally, consumers must journey through the parking lot to find their vehicles and the drive home, requiring another 25 miles, 50 minutes, and $6 out of pocket.

The whole trip takes more than three hours, which is a considerable cost for many consumers given their time constraints. Plus there are significant out-of-pocket costs for travel that are not reflected in product prices. So the big box may or may not provide the lowest total cost of consumption. It depends on the consumer's income, value of time, and need for variety. The total time and travel costs are shown on the consumption map (*The High Cost of Getting the Right Goods at the Right Price*).

There are alternatives, of course. These alternatives will be different for every consumer depending on the basket of goods they are looking for and where they live in relation to each store. We encourage the reader to compile his or her own list of alternatives. Indeed, consumers may evaluate the following choices before heading off to the big box:

They can obtain a limited selection of items at considerably higher prices at a convenience store, a short walk from their office or a short drive from their home. A store like a Seven-Eleven usually carries about 1,500 SKUs.

Or they can go to a traditional neighborhood store in a nearby shopping area for a wider selection at lower prices, which involves a bit more travel and search time. A store like Trader Joe's in an American retail center or a Tesco Metro on a UK "high street" carries 5,000 to 10,000 SKUs.

Or they could select a standard-sized "supermarket" for still more selection at still lower prices but with more travel and search time. American and European supermarkets— such as Kroger and Sainsburys—now carry about 40,000 SKUs, a number that has risen steadily in recent years.

They could also try one of the discount warehouses of the big-box format, like Costco and Sam's Club in the U.S., which carry a narrow range of SKUs (about 3,500 at Costco). In return for buying minimum amounts per item that are larger than consumers need right now (e.g., toilet paper in the 24-roll package) and driving a considerable distance, the customer gets very low prices on the items that are available.

Finally, the consumer could shop from home using the web to access practically all the SKUs in the world with zero personal travel time, but with considerable wait time for items to arrive and with a delivery charge built in to cover the retailer's extra cost of the service. (This could be a clearly stated fee or incorporated in product prices.)

The High Cost of Getting the Right Goods at the Right Price

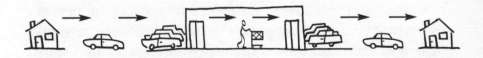

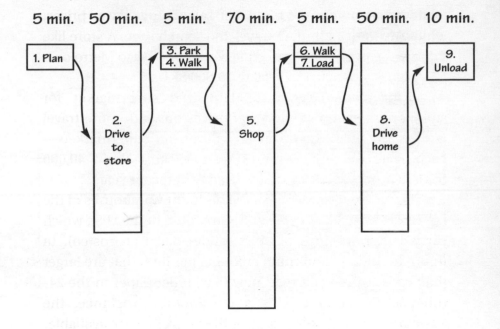

| 5 min. | 50 min. | 5 min. | 70 min. | 5 min. | 50 min. | 10 min. |

1. Plan

3. Park
4. Walk

6. Walk
7. Load

9. Unload

2. Drive to store

5. Shop

8. Drive home

| Travel cost | $12 |
| Total time | 195 min. |

We've drawn a combined consumption map (*Customer Shopping Alternatives*) for obtaining the same basket of grocery items through each of these formats, and have also summarized the consumer's time expenditure, the out-of-pocket costs for travel, and the cost of the basket of goods.

The map and chart illustrate a very simple fact: In choosing between these formats today, consumers must make tradeoffs between product prices, product variety, and personal time and hassle. The biggest store with the lowest prices and the greatest variety is also the biggest consumer of the consumer's time, while the smallest format with the highest prices saves the most time but at the additional price of limited variety.

Customer Shopping Alternatives

	Total time	Travel cost	Product cost
Hypermarket	195 min.	$12	Low
Discount warehouse	160 min.	$12	Very low
Supermarket	95 min.	$5	Low
Neighborhood store	50 min.	$4	Medium
Convenience store	15 min.	------	High
Home shopping	25 min. + delay + delivery	------	Low

Customer Shopping Alternatives

Hypermarket

Discount warehouse

Supermarket

Neighborhood store

Convenience store

Home shopping

Order Delay Receive

The existing range of shopping formats forces consumers to make a time-vs.-variety-vs.-money tradeoff. Most retailers accept this, and seem to assume that consumers settle on one format for most of their shopping needs: The price-sensitive consumer (presumably with lower income on average) will take the time to go to the big boxes while the time-sensitive consumer (presumably with higher income on average) will spend the money to go to the small boxes or to the web. Because retailers seem to think that there are more price-conscious consumers than time-conscious consumers, the bulk of retail investment over the past 20 years has gone toward creating more and bigger boxes. And whatever the wisdom of this logic, large formats have captured an ever-growing share of total consumer spending.

What's more, this same phenomenon has occurred in every product category for fast-moving consumer goods. A few big bookstore chains with very large stores, such as Barnes & Noble, plus web-based Amazon, now account for a majority of book sales in the U.S. A few drug store chains like CVS, using ever-larger formats, now account for the great majority of drug store sales. These trends are steadily pushing out the "independent" bookstore and corner pharmacy.

Indeed, retailers have until very recently been relentlessly pursuing the mass production notion of scale economies toward their ultimate limit—through ever bigger stores and ever bigger buys from suppliers—in an effort to achieve the lowest costs with the widest variety. This mass production logic has been transplanted from old-fashioned factories (which are actually getting smaller today) to create what we will call "mass consumption." The logic seems also to assume that the one cheapest format will drive out alternative formats for the price-conscious shopper. ("Big boxes will win, so do I shop at Sam's Club or Costco?") It also seems to assume that scale considerations will steadily reduce the number of firms offering the dominant format. ("Will it just be Wal-Mart?") The result is a common expectation, held by both critics and defenders of large formats, of the arrival of "Wal-Mart World," an age of truly concentrated, standardized mass consumption. This vision is globalized by the antiglobalizers into a scenario of only a few high-volume providers dominating the whole of world retail.[5]

Curiously, this vision has been emerging even as the manufacturers of the products offered in the big boxes have been converting to lean production methods. Using smaller factories coupled with lean logistics systems, they are able to supply smaller amounts of a wider variety of products reliably and frequently to many locations without a cost penalty.

So is the path to mass-consumption retailing truly necessary, much less desirable? Is there only one viable *where*, at which each of us obtains what we need? And must variety, cost, and the consumer's time always be traded off? The logic of mass consumption says "Yes," but the logic of lean consumption says "No." Let's see why.

The Traditional Geography of Provision

Most companies approach the marketing of products by breaking customers down into specific demographic attributes.[6] How much spendable income do they have? How many members in the household? How many pets? How much education? With these data in hand, it ought to be possible to predict where customers will shop and in what format: The price-conscious shopper at Wal-Mart; time-pressed, higher-income customer at the shops near their home or office or on the web via home shopping; etc.

The lean consumption approach is very different. Rather than focusing on customer attributes, the lean provider looks instead at customer circumstances.[7] When consumers are in a hurry they want to save time; when they are making a big routine purchase of commodities they want to save money; and often they want both but have a hard time finding the right format. Thus, in the case of groceries and household goods, consumers need the occasional trip to far-away Costco for bulk items, the weekly trip to the standard supermarket, the occasional stop at the convenience store for missing items or for prepared meals on the way home, and— during particularly busy weeks—home delivery from the web-based grocer.

Their attributes don't change: same income, same educational level, same number of kids eating dinner. But their circumstances often do change, from week to week and day to day (and even hour to hour), which leads them to seek to buy the same items in different formats. By utilizing not just one, but a range of formats as their time permits (and as their value of time also changes with circumstances), they can minimize their total cost of consumption. This is the sum of product prices plus the value of personal time and effort expended to obtain them.

But here is the really important point: Time is a constraint for most consumers today. It is the signature "circumstance" of our time in history. And practically all consumers would like to obtain the items they need at formats that save time and hassle, if only they were not forced to make a tradeoff between time, cost (reflected in price), and variety. This is where lean consumption can fundamentally change the equation—because the customer can actually obtain the same items cost-effectively through the entire range of formats without being forced to make these tradeoffs. Let's return to Tesco to see how this works.

How Giving You Exactly What You Want and Providing It Exactly Where You Want Work Together

As you have already gathered, UK-based Tesco has been a pioneer in lean provision for more than a decade. In the mid-1990s, as he looked at the opportunities for retailers provided by the emergence of lean logistics, Graham Booth, Tesco's supply chain director (now retired), had a very simple insight: A rapid replenishment system triggered by the customer would work in any retail format. What was more, it would work even better if the same replenishment system, using the same suppliers, cross-dock distribution centers, and vehicles serving many stores could supply every retail format.

Indeed, Booth saw that there might be very little difference in real costs in supplying the same item through any format. This was because the purchase price from the supplier could be negotiated for the whole network, not by format, and the same replenishment system making frequent milk runs to large stores could also stop at small stores to share logistics costs. The cost disadvantage of smaller outlets, due to weak supplier leverage and expensive logistics, would largely disappear.

Using these insights, Tesco set out to create a range of formats, beginning in the UK, so that households could obtain fast-moving consumer goods from a complete variety of outlets as their circumstances changed while staying loyal to the Tesco brand. This has led to tiny Tesco Express convenience stores at gas stations and in busy urban intersections, Tesco Metro stores (at the small end of the "supermarket" range) on busy streets in high-density urban areas, the traditional Tesco supermarkets in urban and suburban areas (now with many nongrocery SKUs), Tesco Extra on the suburban perimeter as an answer to Wal-Mart-type "big boxes" operated in the UK by Wal-Mart's ASDA subsidiary, and Tesco.com for the web shopper.

The strategy has worked quite brilliantly. Tesco has shaken up the convenience store market in the UK by buying several convenience store chains and is now in the process of integrating the replenishment system behind the formats. This has permitted Tesco to establish the lowest-cost position among UK retailers (including ASDA) while posting progressively higher margins and steadily increasing its share in every format. Today Tesco accounts for 20 percent of total spending on fast-moving consumer goods by UK households and more than 25 percent of UK households belong to Tesco's loyalty card program.[8]

Completing the Lean Transformation

But this is just the beginning in tapping the potential of lean consumption for fast-moving consumer goods. By offering households a range of formats for every circumstance and pioneering the use of loyalty cards, which give discounts to frequent shoppers, Tesco (and any other provider who follows this path) is in a position to know everything a household buys during the course of a year at all formats and where and when they buy it. In fact, 80 percent of items currently bought in Tesco stores are bought by loyalty card holders. These loyal customers obtain close to 100 percent of their needs at the range of Tesco outlets.

In addition, because households signing up for the Tesco Clubcard provide some simple information on their characteristics—age, household size and composition, address, special dietary requirements, special interests (babies, toddlers, wine, health foods, etc.)—Tesco is able to create a profile of their cost/variety/time tradeoff and to consider types of new offerings that might be of interest. This is a critical step in converting its customers from mass-market strangers to lean-provision collaborators,[9] a topic that we will cover in detail in Chapters 7 and 10.

The use of a range of formats plus detailed knowledge about specific consumers will progressively permit Tesco, and other providers adopting these methods, to offer each household convenient variety at lower total cost. One way is by tailoring the SKUs offered in each smaller store to what nearby users of that store actually want. In this context, think of the Wal-Mart Superstore as the default option: The store carries virtually everything, so every shopper can find what he or she wants assuming it is not out of stock. But its size means it needs a vast catchment area to operate efficiently, and each geographic region can support only one store. As a result, the average customer must access the store from far away.

Most retailers today develop a standard set of SKUs for a given type of format. It's usually in the form of a "plan-o-gram" showing where every item is stocked in the store in what quantity and how rapidly it sells. Retailers make some adjustments for each outlet on the basis of experience— particularly to remove items that don't sell—but these are generally based more on hunches than actual data. And what they critically lack is information on the items consumers wanted but the store did not stock. The problem is not "out-of-stock" but "could have stocked."

However, by collecting data on what every household buys in a nearby small store and noting what these households are also buying in larger but less-convenient formats, it should be possible to adjust the SKUs in every smaller outlet in relation to the buying preference of every household using that outlet so that more items are available more conveniently for the average household.

Providing More Variety in a Convenient Format

The challenge in a small-convenience-store format is to find a way to provide a wider variety of items without increasing the size of the store. Because its outlets stand on the world's most expensive urban real estate, it's not surprising that the Seven-Eleven convenience store chain in Japan has paid the most attention to this issue. This provider, which owns the 7-Eleven chain in other countries, but seems to have adopted few of its operating practices, has been working on lean logistics and rapid replenishment since Taiichi Ohno (and his deputy Kikuo Suzumura) brought these ideas to the firm's attention in the early 1980s after their retirement from Toyota.[10]

For years, Seven-Eleven in Japan has replenished every item in its convenience stores four or more times a day using a rigorous pull system with milk-run trucks stopping at many stores. In this way the customer has been the scheduling point triggering the replacement of the items just purchased in order to maintain a high level of service with low inventories. In 2004, Seven-Eleven had the lowest OSS rates in Japan and turned its total stocks 55 times. This also means that because the average amount of each SKU on hand is very small, shelves can be very shallow. This, in turn, permits stocking more SKUs in a store of given floor area.[11]

The rapid replenishment process also means that Seven-Eleven can portray itself as the purveyor of the freshest goods available in any retail format because highly perishable items like sushi are prepared only a few hours earlier and delivered quickly and directly to the store.

In recent years, Seven-Eleven has gone further by changing the goods on offer in each store by the time of day and the day of the week. The same truck that replenishes some items every two hours removes other items altogether and replaces them with more timely items. This is in response to the simple observation that some goods are bought much more frequently by certain types of customers at certain times of day as customer circumstances change. A cup of coffee in the morning. An ice cream bar in the afternoon. A bottle of wine in the evening. Soft drinks on weekends.

By closely monitoring customer patterns—for example, the sex and age of every customer is easily entered by the sales clerk using special buttons at the instant of sale and sent instantly to headquarters—and by continually changing the goods on offer in the store by time of day (and day of the week), it is possible to offer an even wider range of SKUs in a small space and to bring more SKUs closer to the customer.

Creating the Ideal Store

The next leap is to combine the virtues of the small, nearby outlet with the variety available from the larger outlet, but without a significant cost penalty. In essence, the idea is to create the ideal store for each household, a market of one.

What would the ideal store for each consumer look like? Our guess is that it would be near the place the consumer will use the goods (sometimes the office but usually the home) and it would carry only the goods actually wanted. Think of it: A nearby store with only the 300 specific SKUs that each household shops for in a year, but actually fewer because there would be no out-of-stocks and, so, no need for substitutes. Plus there would be a few new offerings selected by the retailer as likely to be attractive to consumers based on their current preferences.[12]

This isn't practical today, of course—a store solely for each customer—and it's hard to see how it could ever be fully realized. But there are simple ways to move toward this goal.

For example, what if the local convenience store could obtain exactly the goods consumers want by the time they get there, boxed and ready to go, perhaps without leaving their cars? And what if it could provide them at the same cost as the faraway big box?

This is possible, as long as the consumer provides a bit of notice through a web-based order placed several hours before his or her arrival, perhaps on the way home from work. The trick, from a logistics standpoint, is for the small, nearby format to shop for the customer from larger and more remote formats carrying more variety. The customer's items could then be packed and waiting at the neighborhood retail outlet for pickup.

In fact, this is the way the fulfillment system for home shopping already works at Tesco in the UK. While most new entrants in the web-based home shopping industry—like Webvan in the U.S.—were spending billions trying to construct highly automated, dedicated fulfillment systems from scratch using massive warehouses, Tesco was learning how its employees could shop for Tesco.com customers in the aisles of the nearest standard-sized Tesco store and make money for Tesco in the process.

By eliminating the need for any new bricks and mortar and by using existing store personnel to pick web orders at times when store traffic is low, the costs of this service have been dramatically reduced. As a consequence, Tesco seems to be the only grocer in the world to actually make money off its web-based, home-shopping service while also steadily growing this format's sales as a fraction of total sales—passing 4 percent, and growing at 1 percentage point per year.

However, home shopping still carries an unavoidable cost premium, due to the delivery costs for a fleet of trucks circulating through every neighborhood with significant driving time between stops. Plus there is the problem of requiring the shopper to stay home during an extended delivery window or else finding a reliable way to make deliveries if no one is home. A way ahead, as we suggested above, is to let shoppers pick up their desired items from the nearest convenience store as part of the shopper's daily travel pattern.

The items not carried on the shelves in the convenience outlet would be picked from the shelves of the supermarket. These would then be delivered as a bundle to the convenience outlet using a milk-run delivery truck as shown in the diagram on the next page (*Replenishment through Milk-Run Delivery Trucks*). This would be the same truck that frequently visits the convenience store to restock the items that in-store shoppers had just bought from the shelves.

In this setup, each retail format has two functions: First, a source of direct shopping for consumers with the time and desire to visit the store and pick up items themselves. And second, a type of megastore that provides indirect shopping, by functioning as a warehouse where store employees pick items from the aisles that are subsequently delivered to the end shoppers. This meets the need of shoppers who have a different value time or a different taste for in-store shopping.

Water Spider for the World

At our exemplar lean company, Toyota, a sophisticated materials handling system was devised many years ago in its factories to bring all of the necessary parts and raw materials to every work station on assembly lines or in fabrication cells. These deliveries occur every few minutes and are conducted by an employee, known popularly as the "water spider,"[13] who drives a small tugger pulling carts of parts and raw materials through the plant. The water spider stops at every work station and supplies all material needs.

Replenishment through Milk-Run Delivery Trucks

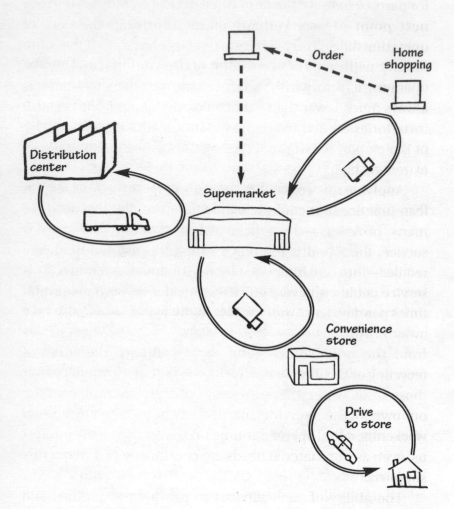

The consequence, and a useful one for Toyota, is that production employees never need to stop their work to look for parts or to move the items they have just completed to the next point of use. Perhaps more surprising, the cost of operating the delivery service is not large because of the route density, with stops at every point of use. And the total cost of operating a factory with this materials management system is always much lower than with conventional methods because inventories are slashed to the minimum and the productivity of the employees working directly on the production tasks is extremely high.[14]

Applying this concept to provision suggests a final leap in lean practice that could hook together the delivery needs of many providers—the grocer, the post office, the courier service, the laundry, the office supplies store, the hardware retailer—into one integrated loop with one water spider. This service could visit every office and residence, perhaps several times per day. This "water spider to the world" could also take away finished goods— for example, completed documents from the home office—and even waste in the form of recycling or the dirty laundry. The consequence would be that those of us who currently spend our valuable time running our own logistics services, particularly in the evening and on weekends, could spend our time on things that really interest us, even as our material needs are continually and frequently supplied.

The ability of such services to provide every office and household with all of its material needs might justify expenditures on storage lockers to hold the goods when no one was home, in much the way roller racks are used in factory environments to supply goods to production areas while taking away finished items and waste, without needing to bother anyone in the production process. And the density of the route networks, dropping items at practically every residence and office on every trip, would reduce the cost per item just as they do in lean factory operations.

We are unaware of any current implementation of these methods. But as energy prices increase, traffic congestion grows, and recycling becomes more comprehensive, this approach is the simplest and cheapest way to provide wide variety at low cost without any expenditure of time by the office worker or householder. Perhaps some reader will wish to tackle this challenge as an entrepreneur.

Instrumental vs. Experimental Shopping

When we present our logic to audiences, we often find a concern that our prescription for lowest total-cost provision means that only massive retailers, i.e., those able to create a full range of formats backed by a sophisticated lean fulfillment system, will be able to survive. Stated another way, they hear us saying that the biggest problem with Wal-Mart, Home Depot, and Best Buy is not that they are massive influences in the shopping world but that they try to force consumers into a single, large format when most of us want a range of formats, which they could also provide. And this is true.

But what about the neighborhood bookstore that knows us personally? And the corner pharmacy where we get personalized advice? And small, independent shops of many types where we are more than a credit-card number? Are these all doomed?

Our answer is that they face a limited future if they are only going to serve our instrumental shopping needs. By instrumental we mean our desire to get routine items in a way that minimizes our total cost, particularly our time. For toothpaste, paper clips, page-turner novels, and jars of pasta sauce our objective is usually just to get the goods, at an attractive price, with as little thought and time as possible.

However, for other types of items, that's not what we want at all. One of the authors has the unusual choice of living within easy walking distance of a massive chain bookstore and a small bookseller, where you can often find the owner. Prices are somewhat higher at the latter, but we always buy there nonetheless. Why? Because when we want a well-known book in a hurry with no hassle, we can just go to the web and pay for overnight shipping. But when we are looking for something different to jog our thinking, we want to be "hand sold" (to use the language of independent bookstores) a title we would not have considered otherwise. We want to shop in a familiar and personal setting, where someone has selected a thoughtful and surprising range of books that will appeal to us. We want to be able to ask their advice. And we want to shop with other shoppers with the same interests. In simplest terms, we care about our shopping experience just as we care about the goods we ultimately obtain. What's more, we are willing to pay a bit more. This same desire drives us to shop for gifts at fancy boutiques with knowledgeable staff and to occasionally go to dinner at fancy and unique restaurants. These choices are for what might be called "experiential" shopping, where the experience is as important as the isolated objects we obtain.

What we don't know is how the desire for instrumental vs. experiential shopping is spread across consumers. Just how many of us are willing to pay extra for special treatment or a really interesting selection of goods? While many consumers say they are when responding to surveys, their preference may go no further than theory, just as survey respondents often say they are "green" and therefore concerned about the environment yet then proceed to buy large cars and commute great distances.

Nor do we know what types of fulfillment arrangements might arise to reduce the cost of goods to independent stores. These stores currently face a significant cost disadvantage when obtaining standard items from the same suppliers that sell to high-volume formats because they buy and ship goods in volumes too low to take advantage of the cheapest shipping or to qualify for the biggest discounts. But, as we have seen, the advantage of independent outlets will never be in providing the standardized items that are also available from high-volume formats. The real issue is how cost-effectively they can fulfill the unique items where they have an advantage so that their pricing does not need to be too high.

What we do know is that lean fulfillment systems should reduce the amount of time all of us need to spend on instrumental shopping. This should free up time for experiential shopping—the type we would label pleasure rather than unpaid work.

The Emerging Lean Geography of Provision

We have argued that the cost of an item and of a bundle of items is largely determined by the brilliance and scope of the fulfillment system, including the delivery system all the way to the consumer. We also have argued that time is a growing constraint for all of us. It follows that the mix of formats that consumers use for obtaining routine items will shift toward convenience in the years ahead and that new delivery systems will emerge as well. This doesn't mean the end of the Wal-Mart-style big box. But it does mean a greater mix of formats and a steady move toward bringing the items we need closer to us in space and travel time so we conserve our personal time.

If the Wal-Marts of the world grasp this logic, they may

well become the leaders in the shift from mass to lean consumption by developing a range of formats for every consumer circumstance and converting their customers from strangers to partners. However, leaps of this type are always hard for established players with large installed asset bases. In this case, shifting formats is likely to drain at least some customers away from the most expensive asset (the big box), yet the most important metric for financial analysts of the fast-moving consumer goods industry is annual increases in same-store sales. At a minimum, some explaining is going to be necessary for financial analysts to understand the need to change.

However, if the current leaders in mass consumption don't make the leap, we believe they are likely to be supplanted by operators of smaller formats expanding their scope or even by logistics services, such as UPS, FedEx, and DHL. Just as Henry Ford, the originator of mass production, was supplanted by lean producers, these merchants of mass consumption will be supplanted by other, leaner providers with a different and better understanding of customer needs.

When Do We Want What We Want?

However this turns out, our discussion to this point has made an implicit assumption that we now need to address: We have been assuming that consumers want what they want where they want it and exactly *when* they want it, with when always meaning "right now." If this is true, it means that providers must always stock some amount of finished goods somewhere in their systems in order to truly serve consumer needs right now. But does "when" necessarily mean "right now?" Are finished goods really needed for many types of products? Probably they are for many of the fast-moving consumer goods we have been discussing in this chapter—the many small items needed to solve myriad small problems that are typically "built to stock" in advance of indicated consumer desires. But in many cases we think not, and in particular for the larger and more complex items needed to solve our larger problems, which can instead be built to order. We will turn to this question in the next chapter.

Chapter 7

Solve My Problem *When* I Want

We have now looked at lean provision methods that reduce total cost for providers while getting customers exactly *what* they want *where* they want. And we have seen how new provision formats backed up by common fulfillment systems reduce total costs for providers and consumers. But we still have a leap to make. We need to explore a new approach to consumption where consumers and providers work together as collaborators, rather than as strangers to reduce total costs for the consumer and for the provider to an even lower level— one that is far below anything currently accepted.

The place to start is by asking "when?" Most of us have been conditioned to think that consumers decide what they want in an instant and then expect to obtain it in the next instant. This is certainly the tone of most appeals by providers, who tell consumers: "We have a great deal for you, but you need to decide right now." This is the appeal of buying items off the rack rather than taking a bit of extra time to order something that is exactly right.

But is instantaneous response always the consumer's true desire? And do consumers really make most of their

155

consumption decisions on the spur of the moment? Let's consider the thought processes most of us actually go through when obtaining the items to address our major needs.

When did you last decide you needed a new car? Was it the moment that you were driving down the street past the dealer and saw a particularly attractive model out of the corner of your eye? Or was it the moment you saw the ad announcing the launch of the new Belchfire III? Perhaps it was one Saturday morning, when you finally had enough time and energy to deal with the dealer. Or was it the day you heard that rebates on the model you had been interested in would expire at the end of the week. In short, was your decision sudden, even impulsive? Equally important, did you need to receive the product immediately?

Or did you formulate a plan. And could you have been equally satisfied receiving the product at some point in the future, particularly if that point was certain and you could reduce your total cost of consumption while getting exactly the product you wanted by collaborating with a provider on the decision process?

In our case—and we are probably typical—we don't think very far ahead about the mundane items, such as those carried by the retailers discussed in the preceding chapters. We trust that a toothbrush with the right stiffness in the right color will be available in the store when we go, and we go whenever it fits our schedule.

But most of us think far in advance about big-ticket items like cars, home appliances, personal computers, and entertainment systems, not to mention the repair and upgrade decisions on personal capital goods, like our cars and homes. A decision-making algorithm is always grinding away somewhere in the back of our heads, even if not in full consciousness, and we know some ways in advance what we are going to ask for and we will ask. However, in today's consumption process, consumers have no one to talk to until the actual moment of commitment to a specific product at a specific price. Instead they are constantly barraged by advertised "deals," which are inevitably designed to get them to obtain or repair or upgrade their products at a time most convenient to the provider. This time is almost always *right now*, because the items in question have already been produced and are accumulating inventory-carrying costs.

This consumption process is not lean. Imagine, instead, going into a car dealer and saying that you will need a new midsized SUV of a given description with the following color and equipment about a year from now, when your current vehicle reaches an age and mileage that makes you worry about its reliability. And imagine further that you offer to make a commitment right now—with some flexibility on the delivery date to suit the manufacturer's production capacity—in return for a significant discount. To whom could you talk? Possibly the security guard, after you are labeled an unstable personality. Certainly not to the salesman. No car dealer is currently geared to talk with you about the long term. They are focused completely on making the immediate deal with what they have on hand or nearby.

As you begin to think about it, you will probably discover that this same situation holds true across almost all of your major consumption experiences. You probably consider an upgrade of your home for several years before you actually sign the contract, but talk to contractors only at the moment that you are ready to make a deal.

You are always thinking ahead about what your next computer, phone, PDA, and copier/scanner/printer/fax should be, but no provider knows what you are thinking until the instant you go to the web and order. And you've had your eye on large, flat-screen TVs for some time now and have set a price point when you are likely to enter the market, but no provider knows your price threshold for sure.

This is not to say that we always plan even for large expenditures. If our cars are totaled or our houses suddenly develop major structural problems, we've got to have another car or a major home repair right now. So we go straight to the dealer and take what's available or go with the contractor who has the capacity to do the job now. And a small but significant minority simply enjoys spontaneous decisions and doesn't want to plan. We really do swerve into the dealer when we see the attractive model out of the corner of our eye. And with a good bit of luck—remember the waiting at the car dealer in Chapter 4—we might even drive out with it.

Given these realities, any provision system that truly meets consumer needs must be able to deal with customers as their circumstances change and they switch from "plan-ahead" to "got-to-have-it-now" consumers and back again. One of the fundamental tenets of lean consumption is that one size—one way of consuming—doesn't fit all consumers. Indeed, it doesn't fit most consumers all of the time.

The Temporal Bias of Current Provision Systems

If most of us are thinking ahead most of the time, why don't provision systems think ahead with us? And why do they instead try to make us impulsive buyers by presenting a constant barrage of special offers and deals to obtain items immediately?

This is a particularly interesting question because more and more consumers want to specify the exact features of their products, and the cost of responding instantly to the customer on a make-to-order basis is actually very high unless there is some ability to plan. To see why, let's look at Dell.

Dell's approach to the consumer is direct sales: avoiding retailers entirely by providing exactly what customers want, made to their specific orders, within just a day or two of receiving their requests, typically via the web.[1] But actually doing this implies one of two things: Either the flow of orders is very steady and the mix of models and options is very predictable, so Dell can have enough production capacity and just the right parts on hand to do the right job right now, or Dell must have remarkably flexible suppliers and maintain lots of excess production capacity in order to deal with spikes in total demand and sudden shifts in the model mix and options that customers are requesting.

The real answer, in the real world, is that neither condition can be met.

Dell's orders from large corporate customers are somewhat predictable. More importantly, they come in batches that are often scheduled for production and delivery over a considerable period because the customer isn't prepared to receive and install the whole order at one time. But its "retail" customers—ankle biters like us in our roles as home computer users and small-business operators—order very unevenly, with frequent spikes. For example, we are likely to go on the web on weekends, when we have enough time to get the order placed, and we are even more likely to order at the end of the month or quarter, when we or our businesses have a bit of cash to spare. In addition, retail customers tend to follow trends, placing sudden waves of orders for items that are hot, and to swing unpredictably from fully loaded to simple configurations and back again.

Dell assembles its computers, servers, and other products within the region of sale, at assembly complexes in Texas, Tennessee, Ireland, Brazil, Malaysia, and China. But a large fraction of the electronic components used come from a small group of independent manufacturers in Taiwan and

Singapore. Using low-cost sea transport means these suppliers take weeks to respond to sudden shifts in demand. In fact, rapid response is only possible by means of expensive airfreight. Even worse, the suppliers also serve Dell's competitors and may experience spikes in demand from many customers at once, straining or exceeding their total production capacity and making it impossible to respond quickly even by air express.

So Dell asks its suppliers to store considerable amounts of each part number in massive warehouses operated by third-party logistics firms and located across the road from Dell assembly sites.[2] Even with this arrangement, some airfreight is still necessary, and Dell is, in fact, a major user. But the great bulk of the parts assembled comes from the warehouses across the road, called "revolvers."

Dell does maintain assembly capacity that is higher than long-term average demand. This is cheap for the actual assembly cells but expensive for the test cells, which consume the great majority of assembly time and capital investment. So Dell only can afford to maintain a small amount of extra capacity in relation to swings in customer demand. Because the short-term spikes in demand can be several times long-term demand and extra capacity is very costly, it is not practical for Dell to maintain enough capacity to respond instantly to every swing in the market.

So what does Dell do to respond to its make-to-order customers rapidly at reasonable cost? The answer is to steer customer demand by frequently changing the prices on options and whole units and by stretching or shrinking promised delivery times. For example, we recently inquired on the web about a Dell computer system with a given specification and found the pricing for options so unusual that we asked to talk to a service representative. The representative seemed to have a very strong feeling that what we really needed was a much larger hard drive for the system, and noted that a special offer was in effect on the largest hard drive fitting the computer being considered.

This seemed like a curious coincidence—between our alleged need for the largest hard drive and Dell's low-priced offer for the same drive. So, as process thinkers, it was natural for us to ask additional questions of the service representative about what was really available, price aside.

As it turned out, Dell had run out of stocks of the smaller drives offered on its web site for our proposed system and could only have obtained them with expensive airfreight even if the supplier had the capacity to provide them.[3] A better path for Dell was to offer the component it did have at a special price. And, after some consideration, we took the offer, thinking the bargain was a good one on balance.

But then we had to deal with the next problem, which was that the delivery date was considerably further out than the "make it instantly and ship it" proposition we had expected. Further inquiry showed that there currently was a surge in demand, and we would need to wait for this system. So we ended up with a better system than we expected (or needed) at an attractive price, but at a loss for Dell because it was installing the more expensive drive for pennies more than the price of a small drive. And we had to wait much longer than expected of the new computer, at some cost in the form of inconvenience in getting work done. After all, we had thought Dell could supply it right away, but the reality of the situation was that it couldn't.

We are not telling this to criticize Dell. The company is the best in the world and probably the best in history at trying to cost-effectively supply exactly what its customers want. Our point is that there is a logical disconnect between what Dell wants to do for its customers and what Dell—or any other firm in this situation—can actually do for them cost-effectively given the gyrations in their demand in combination with Dell's capacity constraints and far-flung suppliers.[4]

The Three-Day Car

Even with the challenges we have cited, Dell and other electronics companies have a major advantage in customizing products to consumer order. This lies in the modular nature of their product designs.[5] A computer, to take the most common example, has a standard chassis with standard fit points for the hard drive, the board holding the central processing unit, the power management module, the disk drives, etc. All hard drives fit in the same space on the chassis, so it's easy from an assembly standpoint to provide small, medium, or large. But this is much less true with other products that are far less modular and for which the challenge of customization to customer order is much greater. Let's take the case of cars.

In the past few years there has been an enormous amount of discussion in the global auto industry about how to get away from large, finished-unit inventories on the one hand and from lengthy and unpredictable waits for specially ordered vehicles on the other. Taking inspiration from Dell's stated practice of making just what every customer wants just when it is wanted, practically every automaker has embarked on a "three-day car" or a "five-day car" car initiative to discover how to make what consumers really want quickly to confirmed order and to deliver it exactly on the promised date.

The reward for the companies would be twofold: They could firm up actual transaction prices—what the customer really pays for the vehicle—by eliminating pervasive rebates designed to move unpopular models and option combinations that have already been built to forecast. And they could eliminate the carrying cost on the 60 days of new vehicles on dealer lots (currently worth about $60 billion) that has been a constant in the North American motor industry for more than 80 years.[6]

What do the companies have to show for their efforts? Very little. With current designs, car companies must add more than 1,000 parts and components to each vehicle as it comes down the final assembly line. (Dell, by contrast, adds only about 15 major items to the chassis of its PCs in final assembly.) What's more, the number of copies of a given model that car companies are able to sell each year, even into global markets, continues to shrink. So manufacturers have found it necessary to run several completely different vehicles down many of their assembly lines to achieve scale economies. Each of these vehicles comes in several body styles, with many options and several trim levels, and in a wide range of colors. This creates a multitude of choices for many of the 1,000 fit points on each vehicle and greatly complicates getting the right materials to the right assembly station at the right time.

As a result, even a lean producer like Toyota has discovered that to make the assembly process work it must lock its schedule in place 10 days in advance of actually building a specific car. Car companies must add to this delay the time it takes to get an order from a customer through the dealer to the car company and worked into the production schedule,[7] which is usually several weeks. And they must also add the time required to get the vehicle from the factory to the dealer (for "preparation") and on to the customer cost-effectively, which is about a week. Some simple math shows that it is not possible today to promise a customer delivery of a custom-ordered vehicle in less than a month even when it is manufactured in the region of sale. And if the vehicle must travel by boat between regions, it is necessary to add two to four more weeks.

At least Toyota is likely to deliver the vehicle on the promised day because of the rigor with which the company manages its order and production process. By contrast, the typical European luxury-vehicle manufacturer doesn't offer custom-order vehicles in markets outside of the region of production and only delivers made-to-order vehicles to customers on or before the exact date promised—typically six to eight weeks after the sale—about 20 percent of the time.[8]

Progress likely will continue to be made in compressing the scheduling process, and we hope that suppliers will gradually relocate closer to assemblers within the region of final assembly. As a result, the total time required from customer order to delivery will surely shrink somewhat in the years ahead. But the prospect of making every vehicle to confirmed customer order and delivering it within three or five days—commonly assumed to be the amount of time a customer is willing to wait rather than just buying a less than perfectly specified vehicle off the dealer lot in response to a price discount—is practically nonexistent at any time in the foreseeable future.

And the same can be said for most of the major goods and services that we need to obtain, maintain, repair, upgrade, and recycle. Our varying demands, arriving with no warning, will continue to present a major challenge for capacity-constrained, slow-response provision systems.

The Default Options

In the absence of progress toward making exactly what the customer wants and delivering it instantly, whether in consumer electronics or motor vehicles or white goods or any other complex product, we can expect to see a continuation of the tactics providers have always used to move merchandise made on a forecast or to an unrealistic delivery schedule.

The salient characteristic of all such systems is that they either produce too much (because the financial analysts says to keep fixed assets working) and then steer customers to items they don't really want by offering discounts, or they wait for customer orders and then make unrealistic or unreliable delivery promises, hoping customers don't cancel orders when they discover how long they actually must wait or when the ordered item doesn't arrive on time. In either case, both the consumer and the provider lose. The customer makes compromises on product specifications in return for price reductions that cost the provider significant revenues. Or the customer accepts a long wait as the provider struggles to get the job done quickly at higher cost.

Fortunately, there is a better way. Our discussion to this point has prepared us to look for it.

A Hint from a Dismal Industry

The airline industry provides a very simple product—a passenger seat flying through the air. But it has two unusual attributes:

First, the product can't be held in inventory and sold later. Every time an airplane backs away from the gate, any empty seat on that flight provides no revenue for the airline. Poof. It's gone.[9]

Second, the people using the seat to fly through the air tend to fall into two categories. They may be very concerned about the price of the seat but much less concerned about the exact timing of the trip or the total travel time. Indeed, they may be willing to book far in advance to get a low price. Or they may be very concerned about the exact timing of the trip and the travel time. And they may be unable to book far in advance because the plans of the party they are planning to meet may change. But they are much less concerned about the price of the trip.

Some individuals are always in one category or the other. But most of us go back and forth between these categories, depending on our circumstances. For discretionary trips that we are paying for ourselves, we often look for a low price, even with a less than perfect departure time, a longer trip, and a need to book far in advance. For business trips, where our employer or the client is paying or where we hope to turn travel into revenues, we often look for exactly the right departure time, the shortest trip time, and the ability to book up to the last minute, even if this means a high price.

Since their earliest days, airlines have pondered the problem of the empty seats and how to price seats in relation to time of purchase so that the maximum revenue is recovered as all seats are sold. Starting at about the time of industry deregulation in the U.S. in 1979, the airlines were able to take advantage of the growing crunching power of computers to start dynamically setting prices for seats. The method that almost everyone adopted was to change all fares frequently as market conditions changed and to price seats in relation to how far in advance they were booked. This meant offering much lower fares for advance booking, especially when the travel dates could not be changed without a penalty.

Most carriers did this in discrete jumps. They offered one price for a 21-day advance purchase, a higher price for a seven-day advance purchase, and a still higher price for purchase close to the time of departure.[10] At the same time, they adjusted all the ticket prices frequently to maximize their "yield," the term used by airlines for the revenue received per seat mile flown.

Recently, new-entrant carriers, led by easyJet in Europe, have adopted truly dynamic pricing in which a flight is opened perhaps three months ahead of departure at a very low price per seat. (But not always with the same price at the beginning because a weekday flight is likely to have more demand than a Saturday flight, a flight to a city holding a big convention three months later is likely to be more heavily booked, and so on.) Then prices increase as sophisticated algorithms in the reservation system continually evaluate the pattern of bookings. The objective is to maximize revenue on every flight while filling every seat so long as it can be filled at more than marginal cost, which in the airline world is the food plus fuel needed for each additional passenger.

Business travelers, who often can't book ahead, sometimes criticize this system. We have even uttered critical words ourselves when we discovered a last-minute travel need that we couldn't get anyone else to pay for! But this approach to pricing does deal with the practical problem of the inability to inventory the product. And it also deals with the needs of travelers flying through the air in the same seat between the same cities but in two different circumstances: Price-sensitive but able to plan vs. time-sensitive and unable to plan. By sharing their plans in advance, the price-sensitive travelers can get an attractive trade of fixed schedule for low price while those who have to go right now can usually find a (high-priced) seat.

The latter condition can often be met because airline computers can predict with some accuracy how many passengers are likely to book at the last minute. So they can set prices for these seats high enough so that a few seats are likely still to be available right up to the time of departure. This is important for business travelers with the potential to make high revenue on their trip if they can just get to the client or customer in time and builds business traveler loyalty to a given airline if its computer system assigns scarce seats first to frequent flyers.

Because of the dismal financial history of the airlines in recent years and a common-sense view that the same seat ought to cost the same amount for the same trip no matter when booked,[11] it seems a bit odd to advocate a demand-management model they have pioneered. However, with a bit of modification, the airline model provides an interesting approach to the plan-ahead vs. get-it-for-me-right-now problem facing consumers and providers of a wide range of products.

Reversing the Temporal Bias of Provision

We have seen that a pure get-it-right-now-for-everyone model can't work very well at anytime in the foreseeable future for complex products. How could a modified pricing-by-time model borrowed from the beleaguered airline industry make things better, where "better" means moving consumers toward a lower total cost of consumption and producers toward higher margins, in a win-win collaboration?

Let's start with three physical facts—realities that apply to many providers of goods and services.

First, production systems can deal with small amounts of get-it-for-me-now demand, provided that production slots for last-minute orders are *planned*[12] and don't exceed a certain fraction of production.

Second, getting these made-to-order products to the customer *quickly* will still cost the provider more, no matter how well production is planned. This is because of the need to juggle the schedule, expedite missing parts from suppliers, and expedite the finished product to the consumer.

Third, making all other products to order and getting

them to the customer *slowly* will cost the provider less because the provider can carefully plan its output and arrange for supplies at just the right time.

This will make it possible for providers to practice what Toyota calls *heijunka*, which is leveling demand by both total volume and mix over extended periods. As a result the whole production process can run smoothly at a steady pace rather than responding continuously to sudden shifts in aggregate demand and mix. Continuously changing both the total level of output and the mix of products causes all sorts of costs, including overtime, "just-in-case" inventories, excessive equipment wear (because there is no time for preventive maintenance), and excessive capacity on average in order to meet the spikes in demand. These costs can be largely avoided with some simple leveling.

Now let's make the leap from current practice, taking cars as an example:

Suppose car dealers had no finished units. None, that is, but a "demonstrator" for each type of product on offer, and a few "loaner" vehicles, perhaps low-mileage used vehicles coming back on trades.

And suppose they offered customers two choices, A or B:

A: Specify exactly the car you want for delivery some ways ahead, with the price going lower the further ahead you are willing to plan. (Just as airline seats get cheaper the further ahead you are willing to plan.)

B: Specify exactly the car you want for delivery as quickly as possible, perhaps within the long sought three or five days, with a price that is considerably higher than the plan-ahead customer will pay for the same vehicle. And, if you can't wait for even a few days for a vehicle (perhaps your current vehicle has been wrecked), take one of the loaner cars until your vehicle arrives.

In this arrangement the delivery point for both types of

orders is specified in advance—maybe three days, maybe six months—and the price moves in relation to how far ahead you set the delivery point from the current date. As we have just noted, the ability to plan produces major savings for the provider on those vehicles and doesn't inconvenience the customer, so long as the new vehicle arrives when promised and a loaner vehicle can be provided if the current vehicle suddenly ceases to work in the meantime.

Equally important, this slot system—with plan-ahead and immediate delivery slots moving through the same provision system—permits the provider to satisfy both got-to-have-it-now and plan-ahead customers. It can do this without the customer steering, special deals, unrealistic delivery dates, and expediting that get-it-for-me-now companies like Dell currently face by offering their customers only one option. What's more, it permits the provider to build *every* product to customer order while saving large amounts of costs by level scheduling its production facilities and getting parts without need for expediting. This solves the two issues Dell chronically faces with its current practices and that car companies would face if they custom-built more than a tiny fraction of their vehicles.

The airline practice we are modifying involves firmly setting the delivery point—the date you actually travel—and varying the price by how far in advance you inform the carrier of your plans. For most other products, it makes more sense to vary the delivery point—the time you are willing to wait—in relation to product price. But the fundamental concept is the same: Consumers share their plans in advance with providers in return for lower prices.

If this approach was fully implemented in the car industry, everything would be built to order and there would be no finished-unit inventories (with $60 billion of carrying costs). There would be no rebates on vehicles no one wants. Perhaps most refreshing, there would be no pushy sales force trying to convince you that you don't really want what you think you want—the Belchfire III with purple paint with the smaller engine—and that you really do want what you don't want, which is whatever the dealer happens to have on the lot.[13]

And in the case of most other products the effect would be the same: The shoe store with no inventory—just demonstrator models—that takes orders for a given shoe, from one price for delivery to your home tomorrow, to lower-priced for delivery in a few weeks. The big-box electronics retailer with no inventory of DVDs, flat-screen TVs, notebook computers, etc. Just demonstrators and a range of prices based on your value of time vs. cost. The kitchen remodeling contractor who prices a given remodeling in relation to your planning horizon, with a few slots held open for immediate work at typical current-day pricing and a lot of capacity in the future for the same kitchen makeover at a lower price. Even the medical center that can perform elective surgery right now at one price or help you plan for surgery at a lower price.

Creating a Channel for a Different Type of Provision Stream

As you consider this concept, you will no doubt be able to think of problems. But the major issue, as we see it, is not with the customer. What can be the problem with a system that provides exactly what customers want either right away for one price (at or below current prices) or at some time in the future—to allow for planning—for a still lower price?

The problem is with the provider, if the firm in question is either a traditional retailer or a traditional producer of goods and services. And the specific problem is the traditional division of labor and use of human effort along the provision stream.

Current-day retailers see their role as squaring the circle by convincing customers to buy what they may not want, from inventories bought on forecast and now owned by the retailer, while making an adequate margin. This means an emphasis on sales techniques to "close deals" and lots of promotional activities through advertising and special offers.

And current-day producers of both goods and services see their role as making their best guess about what consumers actually want, fully utilizing their production assets to make these products, and pushing off the task of reconciling demand with supply onto the retailers situated between them and the consumer. This means an emphasis inside the provider on meeting sales forecasts, often through special incentives to the sales organization, and through special offers to retailers.

But in the world of lean consumption these tasks are no longer required. For big-ticket items, there aren't any inventories of finished goods at the retailer and the provider is adjusting pricing some ways in advance to regulate demand on its assets. Thus, both retailer and producer must change their mindset and behavior. Indeed, they must work together as collaborators with the end customer.

To see how this might work, let's return one more time to the car dealer, now converted to a new way of doing business. The sales person who, earlier this chapter, didn't want to talk to the customer about obtaining a new SUV a year from now, suddenly wants to listen. But it can be a brief conversation because none of the usual motivations of the sales person are in play.

Customers simply want to drive the demonstrator to make sure the vehicle is right for their purposes. Then they need to specify the exact options wanted, consult the manufacturer's price list (not under control of the dealer), and sign up for delivery on a given day. It should only take a few minutes, and it ought to be a friendly encounter. The customer and the dealer now share the same interests because the timing and commission on the arrangement are independent of the way the service representative—no longer a "salesman"—manages the customer's request.

But there may be a problem convincing dealers beyond our hypothesized lean dealer to embrace this new approach. The sales person doesn't have much to do in the new arrangement, and the dealership doesn't need to perform most of its traditional jobs either: Shuffling inventory, offering special incentives on models with too much stock, trying to maximize the dealer revenue out of every transaction by convincing you that you really need service contracts, dealer-installed options, and even the fabled "undercoating."[14]

So what does the dealer do instead? One approach is to get out of the way of progress and accept the notion that retailers in the future will spend their time simply taking orders and reselling used vehicles, with fewer employees, less real estate, and lower investment. Transitioning from current dealerships would require a one-time adjustment in head count and the assets deployed, probably freeing a large amount of cash for investment in other purposes. All change is painful in some way, and this change might be quite wrenching, but once done the consumer will be better off, those involved in traditional retailing will have found a better use for their time, and assets will be redeployed in better ways. Society as a whole will be a clear winner.

An alternative approach that would be much easier for existing dealers is to redeploy assets to a lean service process, as described in Chapter 4, that would cause most customers to stick with a dealer for the life of the product rather than defecting to independent repair outlets as commonly happens now. This could create a long-term relationship between collaborators that would also greatly increase the odds that subsequent products would be obtained through the same dealer. What's more, by applying the same lean service process to certifying, upgrading, and reselling used vehicles (as GSF has done), the new car dealer could continue a relationship with many vehicles through their useful lives under a succession of owners.

Getting Consumers What They Really Want

We have now shown how consumers can obtain exactly what they want when they want where they want even as providers are better off and employee work lives are better. But this is only true if managers in real businesses make it happen. So we now need to shift our focus from the principles of lean consumption and lean provision to the challenge of creating lean provision streams. In particular, we need to look at the role of managers and strategists in creating the smooth-flowing value stream that both providers and consumers need.

Chapter 8

The Challenge of Lean Provision: The Role of the Manager

Let's assume that as providers we really want to do the right thing for the consumer. That is, we want to get consumers exactly what they want, where they want it, and when they want it, so as to completely solve their problems without wasting their time. Let's further assume that in doing this we are going to create successful businesses and be rewarded in the market with ample profits and a growing share of the consumers' spending. All we need to do is to create smooth-flowing consumption streams matching up perfectly with smooth-flowing provision streams. These can create more value on many dimensions for the consumer while saving costs at every turn for the provider.

But just how can we make this happen?

Process Thinking as the Essential Complement to Strategic and Financial Thinking

Despite much talk about using cross-functional teams

and matrix management to address customer needs, most businesses today are decidedly inward-looking and highly functional in their actual operations. They organize knowledge, assets, and careers by tightly bounded departments such as sales, marketing, product development, finance, personnel, operations, information technology, quality, and, sometimes, more. And all of these are oriented vertically toward the CEO and COO at the top of the organizational chart.

By contrast, the processes required to listen to the customer and to deliver the desired value run *horizontally* across departments and functions. And they often run far beyond individual firms, through a number of independent organizations. These include the retailer, the distributor, and the manufacturer in fast-moving consumer goods; the HMO for primary care, the giant medical center for specialized treatments, and the equipment and drug suppliers in healthcare; and the airline, the outsourced maintenance organization, the airport operator, the aircraft manufacturer, and the rental car and limousine companies for long-distance travel. As we have seen, it's very hard for functions, departments, and firms to work together horizontally with consumers to truly solve their problems.

That we haven't made much progress in addressing this issue is not hard to understand when we look at the leaders of today's value-creating organizations. We have interacted with many CEOs and COOs in recent years as part of our research, and we usually find that the senior leaders are most at home as either strategic thinkers or financial thinkers. In either case, they find it easiest to look at the problem from the standpoint of their own organization.

Senior leaders as strategic thinkers ask what customers can be serviced profitably with a firm's existing assets, knowledge base, and geographical configuration. They often spend the bulk of their time selling assets—including managers and business units—no longer viewed as useful. Or they buy assets—including new managers and new businesses—likely to be needed for future initiatives. They often treat the actual value-creating processes used by the organization to solve the consumer's problem as mere details best left to the functions to handle.

Alternatively, senior leaders as financial thinkers ask how the firm's resources can be deployed to the right uses within the business units, functions, and departments. In recent years, the creation of performance metrics to ensure that good use is being made of the resources allocated has been a top priority. But again, the precise definition of customer value and the actual processes that create value are treated as matters for functional experts. The senior leaders feel that their work is done after putting in place a scoreboard to show that every asset is being properly utilized.

In our visits to companies we often ask how better metrics can create better value-creating processes. For example, how do inventory turns, as a proxy for flow, or customer complaints, as a proxy for product quality, improve performance? In particular, how are these metrics going to improve performance when employees can't see the consumer (who is one or more firms away), can't see the consumption and provision processes (which run across many functions and departments), and have no principles to guide improvement? Rarely do we receive satisfactory answers.

In short, what's missing in most organizations is a "chief process officer"—someone at the top who can employ process thinking to take responsibility for the definition and continuous improvement of the key value-creating processes. This means working backward from the customer's complete specification of value, and it often involves rethinking the efforts of many firms.

When we say this to senior managers, we usually hear that their organization already has a process improvement function, thank you very much. It's called the Quality Department or the Process Improvement Office. It conducts the ISO and Six Sigma campaigns or the lean initiative or, more recently, the combination of lean with Six Sigma. But then we observe what these entities actually do. It turns out that they conduct point interventions when isolated process steps are particularly faulty. And they typically evaluate their efforts in terms of money saved divided by money spent. They rarely look at the consumption process from the standpoint of the end consumer and at the entire provision process. Instead they make isolated interventions in defective process steps. The frequent result is little or no payoff for the end consumer or the business as a whole, and gains that can't be sustained for any length of time if they are achieved.

Our experience in observing many instances of this situation in companies around the world has led us to propose a very different path.

Lean Leadership for the Lean Transformation

In simplest terms, the definition and maintenance of a firm's core provision processes are too important to delegate. Someone at the very top needs to take a leadership role to make sure that the total process is defined, sustained, and steadily improved. Who might this be?

It could be the chief executive officer. Indeed, we hope that in the future CEOs will have a more finely developed ability to think about processes. But CEOs are busy. They have strategy on many dimensions to think about, boards and stockholders to deal with, and succession plans and executive development to consider. We've seen a few CEOs, like Paul

O'Neill when he was at Alcoa, who were able to take direct responsibility for this task. But it may not be practical for the typical CEO to also function as a chief process officer.

More promising is the chief operating officer since "operation" and "process" should be much the same thing. And we truly hope that the COO of the future will learn to see every value-creating process in his or her business in order to ask the right questions and put in place the right rewards for management actions. However, COOs are also busy people. They must think about the creation of strong business units in business unit organizations. They must create strong functions in centralized, functional organizations. And they must oversee the relationship between the business units and between the functions in any type of organization. Although the COO is often the best person to initiate the transformation to a process-focused organization, he or she will usually need to put in place some new leaders and change mechanisms to help.

We believe that the most promising approach for the firm wishing to embrace lean provision in support of lean consumption is to create a small, offline team. It should be led by a high-potential manager a step below the CEO and COO who has shown an aptitude for process thinking. This lean leader will evaluate the organization's core value-creating processes from the standpoint of the customer, asking how consumption and provision can be smoothly linked. Note that to get the right answer, this person must listen carefully to the customer. And, at least initially, the lean leader may need to ignore all received wisdom about how the organization does business. Every relationship with external retailers and service organizations down the provision stream plus suppliers further up the stream may need challenging, along with assumptions about traditional methods for conducting internal procedures.

This is a highly strategic task, because the lean leader's conclusion may well be that the structure of the firm and its place in the total provision stream must change. To modify Alfred D. Chandler's famous phrase, "strategy precedes structure,"[1] in a lean world "strategy precedes process, and process precedes structure." In other words, define value first. Then define a process that provides the desired value. Then create an organization able to operate the process.

To take a specific example, remember how Tesco—using a small, offline team of the type described—began to rethink its core process of getting customers exactly what they want when and where they want. It soon concluded that it should restructure its business to create a complete range of retail formats and an integrated provision system to support all of them. This decision entailed buying a large number of convenience stores to fill one gap in its formats, creating mid-sized Metro stores to complete its range of retail formats, and experimenting with web-based home shopping to make it cost-effective. The decision also meant changing Tesco's relations with its suppliers. They were asked to produce goods almost instantly to fulfill Tesco orders generated directly by its consumers. This was in striking contrast to long-standing industry practices of storing large batches in warehouses in response to complex scheduled forecasts.

How does the lean leader given responsibility for this task proceed?[2]

First, he needs a staff, but only a very small staff. We are always amazed when CEOs, COOs, and Vice Presidents for Strategy hire armies of consultants to conduct complex strategic exercises. Instead, a strong team leader with full access to the senior managers and a small team of helpers with process-thinking skills and no allegiance to the old ways of doing things can figure out pretty quickly how things currently stand and what the alternatives are.

Second, in firms with different provision streams for different products or different types of consumers, the lean transformation leader will probably need to assign a responsible person for each of the different streams. In the most successful instances we have seen, these are also "high-potential" executives one step below the lean leader, currently with functional or departmental responsibility. They are either given the additional responsibility for leading the process evaluation team while also performing existing tasks, or they are placed on special assignment for a brief period to lead the analysis. It is important to make someone responsible with the instruction that this is an important career test that must be met. This makes clear to the senior executives and to the rest of the organization that this activity is important.

The Lean Transformation Method

How can the team leader, with a bit of staff support, get the job done? The key step is to create a map of the existing process—including both the consumption stream and the provision stream—as it actually functions. And the only way to do this is to take a walk along the entire process, talking with consumers and with those in every function, department, and firm who touch it. As we have noted earlier at several points, the most effective walk is one in which all of the managers touching the provision stream in different functions, business units, and external organizations are participants from start to finish.

What does this process look like? While individual cases may appear slightly different, there are several common and fundamental characteristics:

- Clearly state the *purpose* of the process. It's what the customer wants to receive in the way of value. And it's what the firm needs to achieve in the way of return on its investment in order to survive and prosper. To endure, every provision process must achieve this combined purpose.

- Develop measures of performance that capture whether the purpose is being served. For example, measure the ability of the current process to provide exactly what is needed when it's needed—such as the likelihood that the product desired is on the shelf in the store every time it is desired. Or measure the degree to which the process solves the problem completely: How many calls to the help desk and how many service calls are needed to get the customer the desired value? Or measure the total throughput time and inventories in the process that are needed to provide a given level of service. These are a good indicator of the wasted time of employees and total cost of the process. Finally, measure the degree to which the cost of the process matches the consumer's willingness to pay. Then note the gaps between acceptable and unacceptable performance.

- Record every step in the process, both for the consumer and the provider, from start to finish. The trick here is not to record what is supposed to be happening, but to *record what is actually happening, based on direct observation*. In every organization there is some gap between a process as it is supposed to be and a process as it actually works. But often the gap is huge and highly enlightening. Writing down what is supposed to be happening, rather than what is really happening, is worse than useless for rethinking the process.

- Evaluate each process step to determine whether it actually creates value for the consumer and the provider. Use the findings to devise summary statistics of the ratio of value-creating time to total time in the process, value-creating work to total work, value-creating expenditures to total expenditures, and so forth, as appropriate.

Writing down the purpose of the process in a few words, devising a few simple measures of current performance compared with consumer and provider needs, and drawing a simple map that makes the current state of the process visible to everyone at a glance are essential first steps. Yet the true purpose of these actions is to fundamentally improve the process—not just characterize it. The question is how.

For this we need to consider an additional dimension complementing purpose and process: people. There is, of course, a long history of attempts to improve processes in organizations, the most famous era being in the business-process reengineering (BPR) movement originating in the U.S.[3] In retrospect, this campaign in the early 1990s was almost entirely a failure. Few processes were actually reengineered, and those that were reengineered quickly regressed to their prior level of performance once the process improvement team left.

The problem with most process improvement efforts is simple. The people who perform the value-creating steps in a process do their tasks well only when three conditions are met: when they can see the whole process, when they understand the logic of the whole process and the need for change, and when they believe in the virtue of the new process. The only way to achieve these three conditions is to involve the people actually touching the process in the analysis of the current process and the design of a better process.

But this is not always easy. Often, many steps in a process need to be eliminated, even if the basic contours of the process are retained. Equally often, fundamental revisions in the entire process running across many organizations are needed to truly achieve customer purpose. In either case, process revisions are disruptive of existing jobs and organizational boundaries.

To deal with these issues, management must make some simple and profound decisions at the outset: How will excess people be treated? How will work be rethought and explained? How will organizational changes be implemented and explained?

While every senior management team must make its own decisions on these matters, we believe that any organization and society will be best served with the following approach:

- Use cost and effort savings whenever possible to grow the business so excess resources can be absorbed. For example, when we examined the effort of Jefferson-Pilot, an American life-insurance company, to rethink its process for customer claims and appointing agents, we found that the improvement in response to customer purpose generated substantial new business—70 percent in one year. The growth in sales meant that the new, more-efficient process absorbed all of the employees needed to operate for the previous, inefficient process.[4]

- If this is not going to be possible and the survival of the business depends on rapid cost reductions, tell this truth at the outset. In any case, never lie. Don't engage in drip torture in which employees are let go a few at a time as the process is improved, with the implication that each round of job cuts is the last. Employees react to this approach with subtle sabotage that gradually degrades the performance of the new process. We always remember that the comic strip *Dilbert*, whose alienated characters avoid responsibility for anything, grew rapidly from obscurity to universal acclaim as the reengineering movement proceeded in American businesses in the early 1990s. No organization with a collection of *Dilbert* characters for its bosses and employees can succeed for long in achieving customer purpose through brilliant processes.

- A similar approach is needed with other firms sharing a value stream. It may be possible to keep everyone in his or her current position. Perhaps existing firms can perform their current tasks, but perform them better. And this is fine. But if an analysis of the value stream reveals that much better ways can be devised that eliminate great blocks of effort and even whole firms (and we will see some striking examples in the final chapter), this truth must be acknowledged.

With the purpose, the process, and the people addressed, it's time to rethink the value stream to provide what the customer actually wants at a lower cost for the provider. How to do this? Obviously, by reference to the principles of lean consumption in combination with the familiar principles of lean production.[5]

- *Solve the consumer's problem* completely.
- *Minimize the consumer's total cost* (including time and hassle plus price) *and the provider's total cost* as well.
- Provide exactly *what* is wanted.
- Deliver value *where* it is wanted.
- Offer value *when* it's wanted.

Do this by:

- Identifying the *value stream* providing the value and removing all wasted steps.
- Putting the remaining steps into continuous *flow*.
- So the customer can *pull* value from the system
- While pursuing *perfection*.

The objective, in simplest terms, is to evaluate the entire process to achieve these objectives, reconfiguring the process as necessary to do so.

Applying the Method to a Sample Provision Stream

Let's make this method concrete by describing in detail how a lean transformation team can proceed. We'll take the hypothetical case of a fast-moving consumer goods firm in the home-improvement category. We'll call it Big Box. This is a firm like Lowes or Home Depot in North America or B&Q in the U.K. But please understand that this is an example designed to demonstrate a method; it's not a prescription for any specific company.

After years of steady success, Big Box has suddenly started to lose market share and to see its margins decline. The CEO and the COO conclude that the firm is reaching the limits of its current business model and decide to do a clean-sheet rethink of the business. As a first step, they remove one of the most promising vice presidents from his line position and give him the three-month task of conducting an analysis of the firm's consumption and provision streams.

The first step for this "value-stream leader" and his small team is to actually experience the consumption process by shopping. And so they conduct a field test. They buy typical baskets of items in the firm's stores as well as at the stores of competitors with the same format. They then shop small neighborhood stores (e.g., True Value and Ace) that dominated this category before the arrival of the big boxes. They also buy baskets of items from the web sites of Big Box and all its competitors. In addition, the team asks advice of sales personnel in the stores and consults help lines to see whether they can actually help.

The team then talks with customers in all types of formats, including those of every type of competitor, asking them what problems they are trying to solve and how well a given firm and format is meeting their needs.

Not surprisingly, the team finds that the same customer has very different circumstances over time. Shoppers at the neighborhood hardware outlets typically value time more than money at the instant of shopping and are particularly attracted to the personal attention and knowledge of the shopkeeper about the specific problem they are trying to solve. Shoppers using the web are even more time-conscious as they make their purchase. By contrast, shoppers driving to the big-box format are more cost-conscious, more knowledgeable about the right items to do the jobs at hand, and tend to buy more items to address more consumption problems on each trip.

As we have noted, these are not just distinct types of consumers—high income vs. low, homemaker vs. wage earner, young vs. old. They are often the same consumers in different circumstances—relaxed, hurried, or even frantic. Most shoppers, it turns out, utilize all three formats at least occasionally.

It is also not surprising that the complete shopping habits of customers for this category of items are unknown to each firm because most firms have only one type of store (small or very large). And, even if a firm has been experimenting with different types of formats, their frequent shopper cards are used only to a significant degree by one group of customers. These are small contractors, who use the same store frequently to obtain all of the items needed for that day's or that week's job. In short, the current situation is largely a matter of strangers buying from strangers.

With the value desired by customers in different circumstances clearly in mind, the team can easily specify the provider's purpose. This is to grow sales while continually growing margins, in contrast with the current situation of stagnating sales and falling margins.

Once consumer and provider purpose are summarized, it is time to map the existing consumption and provision processes through each format and to measure the performance of each format in terms of meeting customer desires. The team chooses a simple mapping method in which the steps for each encounter are listed horizontally, from the start of the encounter on the left to its completion on the right (see *Home-Improvement Consumer Alternatives*).

Looking at the summary boxes for the three maps reveals the pros and cons of the three shopping alternatives:

Home-Improvement Consumer Box Score

	Total time	Total cost	Available	Range	Advice
Big Box	52 min.	$45	80%	60,000	Poor
Neighborhood store	20 min.	$55	90%	10,000	Good
Web shopping	17 min. + delay	$45 and $5	85%	60,000	Good

Home-Improvement Consumer Alternatives

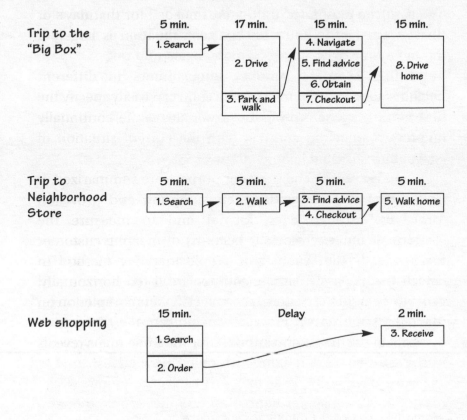

Trip to the "Big Box"

| 5 min. | 17 min. | 15 min. | 15 min. |

1. Search → 2. Drive / 3. Park and walk → 4. Navigate / 5. Find advice / 6. Obtain / 7. Checkout → 8. Drive home

Trip to Neighborhood Store

| 5 min. | 5 min. | 5 min. | 5 min. |

1. Search → 2. Walk → 3. Find advice / 4. Checkout → 5. Walk home

Web shopping

| 15 min. | Delay | 2 min. |

1. Search / 2. Order → 3. Receive

Total time	
Big Box:	52 min.
Neighborhood:	20 min.
Web:	17 min. + delay

It is easy to see that a shopping cycle for a given set of home-improvement items takes the least time and is more likely to provide useful information on the web, but this route also costs the most if the products are to be received quickly. By contrast, the trip to the big box costs the least money and the most time, with low scores on advice and out-of-stocks but a high score on product range. Finally, the small, neighborhood shop is in the midrange on price, and is the best for time spent, out-of-stocks, and advice. But it is weak on product range.

Making the Lean Consumption Leap

Because the team wants to serve all kinds of customers— this is clearly the key to growing sales and share in this category—they ask a simple but profound question: "How can our firm serve customers in every circumstance while making a good return in every circumstance?" This is the opposite of the mass consumption question previously asked in the do-it-yourself industry, which is "How can we find a 'category killer,' a single format that can make money while making every consumer happy?" It was this simple thought process that led to the age of the big box.

The CEO and COO are intrigued with the question but know that its implications may be upsetting to many parts of the organization. For example, if this big-box firm is going to diversify its range of formats, won't this threaten the bulk of managers who have been raised in a big-box environment? And won't it be upsetting to the financial thinkers as well, whose most important metric of success is ever-higher sales in individual stores open more than a year? After all, trying new formats is almost bound to draw some consumers from existing formats. It would take a true optimist to think that the new customers would come only from direct competitors' stores rather than Big Box's own stores.

To deal with the inherent conservatism of mature organizations, the CEO and COO decide to keep the analysis offline until the full range of options can be specified. They direct the team to specify options for each customer circumstance and to evaluate these from the provision side. The question to answer is, "How can the firm provide the value desired by every customer while increasing its overall sales and margins?"

Leaning the Big Box

When the team looks at Big Box's current format for price-conscious customers in light of the findings in the consumption map, it is clear that these customers want more advice and a higher level of goods in stock at no increase in price. How can the provision stream be improved to make this possible?

As the team draws a simple provision map (*Trip to the Big Box*), looking at the actions currently required to get the right goods to the consumer with the right advice, some simple insights jump out.

First, the store's practice of receiving goods directly from suppliers at two-week intervals means that large amounts of each item have to be stocked in the store in the high bays, far above shoppers. And this means in turn that newly received goods need to be put away at night, when "falling inventory" cannot harm customers. In addition, the firm's practice of storing goods in any high-bay location that is available means that many out-of-stock items are actually in the store but impossible to locate. And so the store staff spends much of its time during selling hours looking for missing items rather than giving advice to customers.

Second, there is a uneven pattern of shopping activity each day—with 80 percent of sales concentrated in two two-hour windows, one in the early morning, the other in the evening. To address falling margins, store managers recently have cut labor costs converting from straight shifts, often using retired skilled trades with impressive product knowledge as sales personnel. Now the sales associates are mostly part-time workers, often quite young with no product knowledge, who work a few hours at a time to cover the demand surges. This means that while the stores are saving money on personnel, they must consider the cost of the many shoppers frustrated with the lack of useful advice who are rethinking their loyalty to Big Box.

The team can easily see an alternative approach. Each store can be restocked from a distribution center multiple times each day (like Tesco). The restocking signal can be based on what customers have just bought, as signaled by the scanners at checkout. The traditional weekly schedule can be eliminated.

Doing this requires a shift from direct shipments by suppliers, from their distribution centers to each store. Instead, Big Box will create its own distribution centers and arrange to pick up many items directly from supplier factories or from the docks where imports arrive. It will cross-dock them in its distribution centers and deliver directly to a series of stores on each delivery loop.

This dramatically different approach will require Big Box to make major expenditures to overhaul its logistics systems. However, the result will be vastly lower inventories in the store with the elimination of the high bays and a higher level of service because each item will have a specific location and more frequent replenishment. Even better, demand on the

Trip to the Big Box

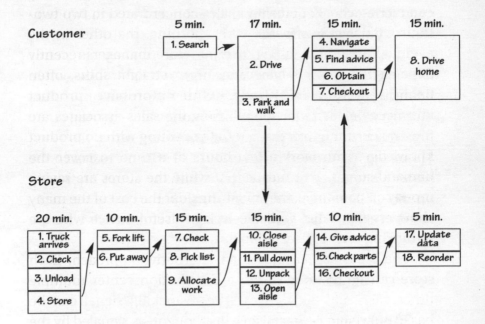

Customer

5 min.	17 min.	15 min.	15 min.
1. Search	2. Drive / 3. Park and walk	4. Navigate / 5. Find advice / 6. Obtain / 7. Checkout	8. Drive home

Store

20 min.	10 min.	15 min.	15 min.	10 min.	5 min.
1. Truck arrives / 2. Check / 3. Unload / 4. Store	5. Fork lift / 6. Put away	7. Check / 8. Pick list / 9. Allocate work	10. Close aisle / 11. Pull down / 12. Unpack / 13. Open aisle	14. Give advice / 15. Check parts / 16. Checkout	17. Update data / 18. Reorder

Total time
Customer: 52 min.
Store: 75 min.

store work force will be smoothed by cycling knowledgeable employees, now working two standard shifts, between the equally important tasks of giving advice to customers, conducting checkout during the peaks, and replenishing the shelves during the offpeaks.

In short, the big-box format will remedy its major deficiencies—poor advice and high out-of-stocks—while financing better-trained labor and new distribution centers through a drastic reduction in inventories and carrying costs. Big Box currently has five annual inventory turns, requiring $16 billion in inventories to support $80 billion in sales. In the future it should be able to increase turns to about 24, freeing up $12 billion in cash inventories, which is sufficient to finance regional distribution centers with some funds left over.

Leaning Neighborhood Stores

This finding is promising, but it is not an answer for customers in more time-conscious circumstances because the inherent nature of big-box formats is that they will be far apart due to the large catchment areas needed to justify their scale. This will always mean a considerable drive for the average shopper and suggests a continuing role for the convenient, neighborhood format. However, as conventionally operated, these neighborhood stores face two problems. They have higher costs (meaning higher prices), and their range of available items is limited, often too limited to solve a given consumer's problem. The next question for the team is: How can the provision stream for small, nearby formats be leaned to serve the needs of time-conscious customers at a reasonable price?

The team now draws a provision map of a typical neighborhood outlet, including its replenishment stream. This suggests a number of innovations worth investigating.

Trip to Neighborhood Store

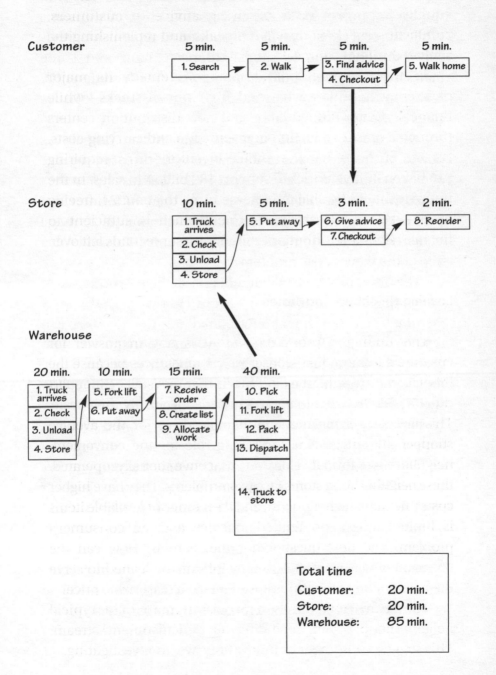

Customer

5 min.	5 min.	5 min.	5 min.
1. Search	2. Walk	3. Find advice / 4. Checkout	5. Walk home

Store

10 min.	5 min.	3 min.	2 min.
1. Truck arrives / 2. Check / 3. Unload / 4. Store	5. Put away	6. Give advice / 7. Checkout	8. Reorder

Warehouse

20 min.	10 min.	15 min.	40 min.
1. Truck arrives / 2. Check / 3. Unload / 4. Store	5. Fork lift / 6. Put away	7. Receive order / 8. Create list / 9. Allocate work	10. Pick / 11. Fork lift / 12. Pack / 13. Dispatch / 14. Truck to store

Total time
Customer: 20 min.
Store: 20 min.
Warehouse: 85 min.

The most important point is that the cost difference between the neighborhood store and the big box is mostly in the cost of purchased items and getting them to the store. While the cost per square foot to operate small urban stores is slightly higher due to more expensive land and some inefficiencies in labor utilization, most of the cost differential is due to the superior bargaining power and lower logistics costs of the big-box operator.

This simple insight suggests that if the bargaining power of the big box and its lower logistics costs—by use of a combined delivery system—can deliver items less expensively to the neighborhood store, the two formats can offer nearly equal pricing at comparable margins on the range of items the small store has the space to carry. This will solve one of the consumer's problems.

The other problem, which remains, is the narrow range of items the small outlet can stock. However, if the new distribution arrangement envisioned for the big box can replenish the small store daily or even more frequently with exactly the items just sold, it may be possible to drastically reduce the amount of each SKU held in the store and to gain shelf space in order to carry a wider range of SKUs. This will go some way toward solving the customer's second problem with small outlets.

The team therefore decides that there is a synergy rather than an inherent conflict between the operation of different store formats as long as there is a common purchasing and distribution system. And, in addition, this analysis suggests that there is room for experimentation with a range of store formats between small-but-convenient stores and large-but-far-away stores to determine the best mix for satisfying customers while increasing average margins for the firm.

Leaning Web-Based Shopping

But what about the truly time-pressed consumer willing to pay a higher price to get just the items as soon as possible without traveling at all? Big Box, like practically every retailer in the world, experimented with the web in the 1990s, but failed to find a formula that generates many sales or any profits. Might it be possible to do better by mapping the current provision stream for this format, which supplies goods to customers by delivery vehicles operating from a large dedicated warehouse in each metropolitan area that receives goods from suppliers?

As the team draws the provision map for the current web-based shopping alternative, it becomes apparent that the biggest problem is the long distance between the warehouse and the average customer (which is why projections of profitability with this approach always assume an unreachable level of "shopping density" to make delivery runs efficient). This approach burns too many resources driving long distances between widely scattered customers, and the cost of the warehouse itself is primarily due to the many handoffs for storing and picking the necessary items.

Looking at the provision maps for the big-box format, the neighborhood stores, and web-based shopping gives the team a simple idea that provides advantages for all three approaches.

Why not replenish the neighborhood stores from the big-box outlets at times when the shopping demand is low? And why not give shoppers an additional web-based choice of ordering from the web on day one and picking up all of the items on day two at the nearest neighborhood store for no delivery fee? Similarly, if a shopper in a neighborhood store finds that some needed items are not carried or are out of stock,

Lean Solutions

Web Shopping

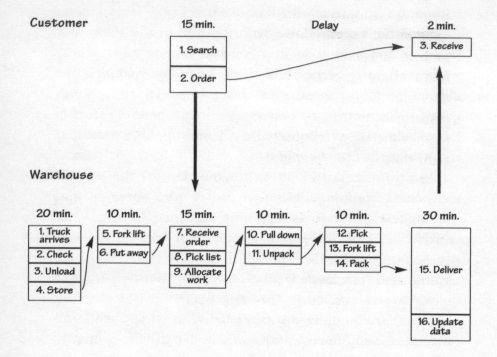

Total time			
Customer:	17 min. + delay		
Warehouse:	95 min.		

the store can order them from the replenishment system for delivery on the next run, possibly even the same day.

An additional advantage that also emerges from this analysis is that loyalty cards will now work much better because customers can do all of their hardware and do-it-yourself shopping from one of the company's formats, *picking a format as their circumstances dictate*. Using the frequent shopper data collected can provide an additional and significant advantage in showing the firm where consumers live in relation to what they are buying and where so that the right items can be assigned more closely to the right stores.

Home-Improvement Provision Box Score

	Total provider time	Total cost	Supplier delivery	Total inventory	Reorder cycle
Big Box	75 min.	$25	90%	2 months	2 weeks
Neighborhood store and warehouse	20 min. 85 min.	$35 --	95% 95%	1 month 1 month	1 week 2 weeks
Web shopping	95 min.	$25	90%	2 months	2 weeks

From Insight to Action

As the team looks at the results of this simple analysis, it is apparent that a large number of new ideas have been generated and that many of these are worth trying:

- Replenish the big boxes from regional distribution centers, responding several times a day based on the items just bought.
- Replenish regional distribution centers from supplier factories rather than supplier warehouses, with many items produced to order.
- Eliminate the high bay and random storage locations in the big boxes. Use only low-bay and fixed locations.
- Use the same, more knowledgeable store personnel to stock goods, give advice, and check out customers, with assignments shifting with the level of demand.
- Buy or build neighborhood stores to give consumers a wider range of formats.
- Replenish neighborhood stores from big boxes during off hours.
- Fulfill web-shopping orders for delivery from big-box formats during low-demand hours to eliminate the need for a separate warehouse and staff.
- Fulfill orders for items not carried in neighborhood stores from big-box formats with frequent delivery runs (the same runs restocking the small stores).
- Enhance frequent-shopper programs to encourage consumers to make all purchases from the same firm, to create problem-solving partners rather than strangers.

However, it is also apparent that these ideas fall in four categories based on likely payoff in sales and margins on one dimension and difficulty of implementation on the other.

Difficulty vs. Payoff Matrix for Lean Transformation

Degree of Difficulty for Big Box to Implement

	Hard	Easy
Large	Establish neighborhood store format Reconfigure big boxes to eliminate high bay Redefine store work with flexible, knowledgeable staff	Replenish big boxes from distribution centers Fulfill small stores from big boxes
Small	Convert suppliers to make-to-order	Fulfill web orders from big boxes Enhance frequent shopper program Supply small-store shoppers with extra items from large stores

*(Left label spanning rows: **Payoff for Big Box**)*

Some of the highest-payoff concepts are also the most difficult to implement, while some concepts with modest payoffs look like an easier place to begin, as shown in the table.

In our experience, most companies encounter this challenging set of decisions when trying to convert mass consumption businesses to lean. Some prioritizing is in order. In general, we believe that as a firm gets started, achieving some visible measure of success is more important than the magnitude of the success, so it's generally best to start with a few changes that are not violently resisted by the organization in order to show the benefits of a new way of thinking. More challenging changes with bigger payoffs can then be tackled progressively.

Similarly, changes that can be conducted entirely within your own organization are generally easier than changes requiring other firms to change their habits. Thus, the Big Box team decides that getting suppliers to manufacture to order and ship directly to the distribution centers rather than replenish stores infrequently from supplier warehouses will be a big challenge, particularly given the lack of trust in Big Box's traditional relations with its suppliers. This initiative is in fact judged the hardest of all and kept until last.

Creating Lean Consumption Streams

With their analysis completed, it is time for the Big Box team to transition from analysis to action. How can the ideas emerging from the consumption and provision maps be put into practice? The best approach is to create a different type of team, led by a responsible person who will see that the entire process is implemented.

In the case of fulfilling web-based orders from the big boxes rather than the existing warehouse, this means picking a new leader for the web-based option and asking this person to create a detailed map of the new value stream, based on careful consultation with everyone who would touch it, including a sample of customers. To repeat a key point we have made several times: Sustainable process improvement requires that those consumers and providers participating in a process can see it, understand its new logic, and actually believe in it. The real test of a lean leader is the ability to create these conditions.

Note also that this leader is the business head of Big Box at Home, the web-based operation, and also the chief process thinker. It is always best when these two roles can be combined, and in this simple business they can be. However, you may find in your own business that the business itself is too complex for one leader to wear both the business-leader hat and the process-thinker hat. It's a matter of judgment and you need to be clear who is wearing which hat.

Fortunately, the transformation of the web-based option at Big Box succeeds, and this creates momentum to expand the ideas of lean consumption further into the business. The logical next step, although a step with a much higher degree of difficulty, is to transform the operation of the large-format stores. This requires more careful preparation of consumption and provision maps by the transformation leader. It's the process thinker rather than the business-line leader in this case. And it will require an extended implementation process over two years.

With success from this initiative there will be widespread support in Big Box for expanding the range of formats and bringing the fulfillment system operating behind the scenes into a new configuration that can support all formats, including a new "City Store" format halfway between the neighborhood store and the ex-urban big box. This is the final leap in the lean transformation. A reasonable completion date is four years after the initial analysis.

Sustaining Lean Leadership

We now have looked at the dramatic transformation involved in introducing lean consumption in mass consumption businesses. This corresponds to the *kaikaku* (revolutionary) phase in production system transformations we talked about in *Lean Thinking*, and it can be deeply satisfying to consumer and provider.

Most of life, however, is about evolution rather than revolution. And the sad story of evolution in most consumption and provision streams is that it quickly becomes a regression toward the original level of mass consumption performance. It's not hard to see why: No one has any responsibility or mindshare for the mundane but vital task of continually sustaining and improving each consumption and provision stream.

To deal with this natural tendency we need to introduce another new role to go with the process analysis team and the transformation team. This is the lean enterprise manager assigned to every important consumption and provision stream on a continuing basis. This person might be the business-line executive for that product—the ideal solution— as assisted on technical issues by the process improvement department. Or it might be someone in the process improvement department assigned to keep a continuing eye on each value stream.

In either case, the essential task is to continually walk along the consumption and provision streams, noting changing consumer needs, updating and posting the map of the current state, and measuring and posting performance. Periodically it will be time to lead a process evolution team involving everyone touching the process. The team's task is to restore the stream to its original level of performance or, much better, to move it to a higher state. In short, someone should have the job of maintaining a "plan for every process" just as managers at Toyota have a "plan for every part" going into Toyota vehicles,[6] and a "plan for every employee" working in the organization.

A vital tool for achieving this is the A3 Report, pioneered many years ago by Toyota, in which the management team determines the most important problem facing the provision and consumption stream, based on taking a walk and producing a map of the current state that incorporates everyone's input. The challenge is to take the statement of the problem, the current state of the provision process that is causing the problem, the envisioned future state that will correct the problem, the specific tasks assigned to each individual to create change, and the precise date the tasks will be initiated and completed. All this information is then boiled down to one sheet of legal-sized (A3) paper that can be posted for everyone touching the process to see.

We've done this on the next page for the auto service example we looked at in Chapter 4.

This, of course, is but a visual version of Deming's famous "plan, do, check, act" cycle,[7] which Toyota has modified slightly to "analyze, implement, reflect, adjust." However, there is one vital difference: The current state and the plan for improvement are not the secret knowledge of a quality or process expert. Instead, they are community knowledge, both because they were developed by observing the current process together and because the plan for improvement was worked out with everyone present and is equally visible to everyone as improvements proceed.

A3 report

Lean After-Sales Value-Stream Improvement

Background
- In after sales, the ability to deliver serviced and repaired cars to customers RFTOT is currently low (55%). Customers are inconvenienced and the company can improve profitability by introducing lean thinking—improving flow throughout the after-sales value stream, saving 50% of customer time while reducing dealer cost by 30%.

Current Situation
- Customer fulfilment = 55% (Quality = 85%, Delivery on time = 65%).
- Booking lead time: Drop off = 5 days, Collection = 8 days, Loan car = 8 days.
- Time required to complete job: 50% on the day, 25% in 2 days, 25% over 2 days.
- Productivity (hours sold/hours worked, measured only as average for workshop) = 88%.
- Hours sold = 15,000.

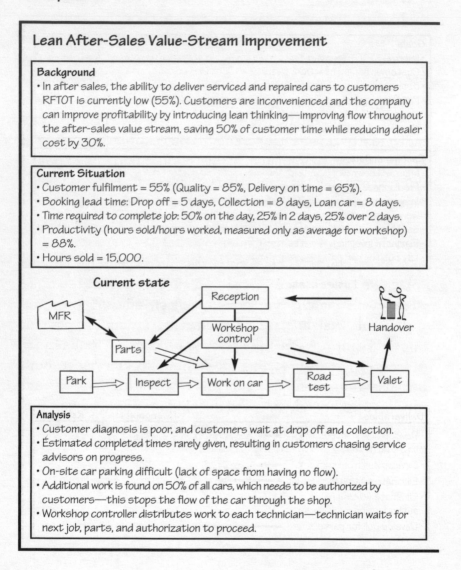

Current state

Analysis
- Customer diagnosis is poor, and customers wait at drop off and collection.
- Estimated completed times rarely given, resulting in customers chasing service advisors on progress.
- On-site car parking difficult (lack of space from having no flow).
- Additional work is found on 50% of all cars, which needs to be authorized by customers—this stops the flow of the car through the shop.
- Workshop controller distributes work to each technician—technician waits for next job, parts, and authorization to proceed.

Goals
- Improve RFTOT for after sales while improving profitability of after sales.
- Customer fulfilment = 90% (Quality = 100%, Delivery on time = 90%).
- Booking lead time: Drop off = next day, Collection = 3 days, Loan Car = 3 days.
- Productivity (measured by work type) = straight services 0-2 hr. 140%, service and repair 2-4 hr. 110%, repairs/breakdowns 95%.
- Hours sold (potential) = 20,000.

Recommendations
- Improve known work content through improved booking process.
- Prediagnose work before cars enter shop.
- Implement takt time on 0-2 hr. jobs. Base the pace of work through workshop on customer demand.
- Establish pull system for parts and delivery to eliminate technician waiting.
- Eliminate invoicing errors to smooth handover process.
- Lay out the car-parking site for improved visibility and flow.

Future state

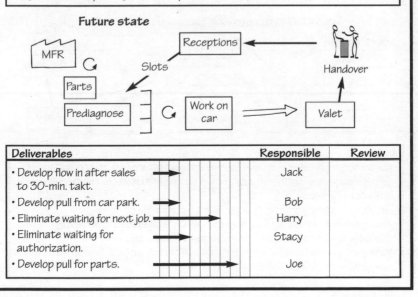

Deliverables		Responsible	Review
• Develop flow in after sales to 30-min. takt.		Jack	
• Develop pull from car park.		Bob	
• Eliminate waiting for next job.		Harry	
• Eliminate waiting for authorization.		Stacy	
• Develop pull for parts.		Joe	

From Simple Problems with Easy Options
to Complex Problems with Missing Options

We have now explored the role of the lean manager, whose job is to listen to the consumer, discover the value truly desired, and then create new consumption and provision processes that jointly provide the desired value. This may even be easy within an organization with relatively simple problems, although in most cases it requires significant will and commitment.

But who will take the lead when complex value streams for complex problems flow across many organizations? In these situations, assets are under separate control and may be doing the wrong things in the wrong places. And who will create totally new options for consumers, possibly involving new business models, when none of the existing options actually solves the consumer's problem? We'll search for the answer in the next chapter.

Chapter 9

Get Me the Solution I *Really Want*: The Role for the Lean Entrepreneur

The consumer problems we have been considering have in many cases been straightforward. They could be solved by obtaining and using one or a few items or a simple service. The right pair of shoes at the right place at the right time. The complete basket of groceries. The hassle-free car repair. The new computer or car when you actually need it.

But many problems are more complicated, and the solution requires a bundling of a number of items. These problems are often more challenging because they require many assets, often located in different organizations, to be combined in order to meet the consumer's need. Indeed, because they are much more challenging, we often observe that the solutions consumers seek don't seem to exist. No one has stepped forward to offer the option we really want.

In highly dynamic economies, and this seems a fair characterization of the world's market economies today, we tend to assume that if there is a real consumer need an answer will be forthcoming. Yet we observe situations every day where this is not true. Providers all too often have failed to offer a complete range of options to solve common problems. So we have devised a way to think systematically about what consumers really want. We call it the solution matrix, and will describe it in a moment. By starting with true consumer desires, and working backward to create a provision process able to serve them, it is almost always possible to envision a better way to solve a given problem. But who is going to act on this insight?

In the previous chapter we assigned this task to managers within organizations. Listening carefully to customers' desires and then creating better processes to serve them is one of the most useful things managers can do. But what happens with more complex problems when organizations and assets are shared across many enterprises and aren't in the right place to get the job done?

Even worse, what happens when the existing asset holders, instead of stepping up to the challenge, do just the opposite and try to make the world safe for their assets by actually thwarting the desires of the customer? We see this, for example, when car dealers enter the political process to obtain legal protection for the existing (and truly awful) dealing systems, as they have done in practically every developed country. Even when consumers and automakers complain, it's a great challenge to find a way around the impasse.

The true solution may in fact require a new player to pioneer a new path. This, of course, is the entrepreneur, whose most striking and useful feature is that he or she has no respect for the existing assets blocking progress. In fact, entrepreneurs delight in Joseph Schumpeter's fabled "gales of creative destruction" that blow away assets doing the wrong things in the wrong places. What the lean entrepreneur needs is a way to think about the opportunity space between unhappy customers and existing assets. So this chapter provides guidance for the lean entrepreneur just as the previous chapter was focused on the lean manager.

The Solution Matrix

To see how an entrepreneur can pursue lean solutions for the benefit of the entrepreneur, the employees in the provision process, and the customer, let's return to the principles of lean consumption.

- Solve my problem completely.
- Don't waste my time.
- Provide exactly *what* I want.
- Provide value *when* I want it.
- Provide value exactly *where* I want it.
- Reduce the number of problems I need to solve.

We can write these across the top of our solution matrix. Then we write the existing options along the left-hand side to see how well each option addresses each principle.

Solution Matrix

	Solve my problem	Don't waste my time	Get me			Simplify solutions	Cost
			What I want	Where I want	When I want		
Current option A							
Current option B							
Current option C							

If it turns out that an existing option gets consistently high scores, we can end our search. While the manager can perfect the process delivering the best solution, there is nothing more for the entrepreneur to do. And yet, we often find that none of the existing options does very well. Then it's time to think about new options by relaxing all the usual constraints—existing assets, existing organizational configurations, existing market structures. Freeing the mind to produce a clean sheet solution often reveals startling opportunities the entrepreneur can seize to make both consumers and providers better off.

The best way to demonstrate what we have in mind is to take a couple of examples, look at the existing options, and search for something better. Let's start with the vexing problem of business travel, particularly air travel.

The Long-Distance Travel Problem

Suppose that we need to take a business trip between two midsized cities we'll call Scylla and Charybdis, the mythical danger spots Homer tried to avoid in the Odyssey but which many of us feel we often need to visit.[1]

We can refine the principles of lean consumption for this problem as follows:

- Solve my problem *completely* means getting there safely, on time, and with my luggage.
- Don't *waste my time* applies to trip preparation time and total door-to-door travel time, not just cruising speed in the airplane.
- *What* I want means the right combination of seating and amenities to accomplish my trip purpose.

- *When* I want means frequent departures, ideally precisely customized to my precise time requirement.
- *Where* I want means traveling from an airport near my departure point to an airport near my precise destination.
- *Simplify my decisions* means bundling all the trip arrangements—air reservation, rental car, hotel—into one simple package from one touch point.

With the principles refined, it's time to look at the organizations and assets involved. It's a formidable list: One or several air carriers (including their ground staff and maintenance organizations), several airport operators, a security system, an air-traffic control system, one or several aircraft manufacturers, providers of ground-side travel complements such as rental cars, and—if you don't want to do the work yourself—some type of travel agent to put all the elements of the trip together into a complete package. Note that in today's world these assets, often very large and expensive, are controlled by different sets of managers in independent organizations. It's hardly surprising that their combined efforts often fail to solve the problem.

So what are the existing choices, as offered travelers by the current-day air travel system?

Hub-and-Spoke

The default option for most of us has been the traditional hub-and-spoke airline: American, United, Northwest, Delta, Continental, and US Airways in the U.S. and national flag carriers such as British Airways in Europe.

The logic of hub-and-spoke is quite consistent with mass-production and mass-consumption thinking. The major airlines fly large airplanes from commercial airports in smaller cities (Scylla and Charybdis), in pulses about two hours apart, into a massive sortation center (hub airports, typically near a major city). There the large batches of passengers and freight are cross-docked before final shipment out the spokes to the destination cities at the outer rim of the network.[2]

The public justification for this concept, when it was pioneered at the end of airline regulation in the U.S. in 1979, was that it would maximize aircraft utilization and minimize the cost per mile of travel. It used large planes—argued to be inherently more cost-effective—while increasing departure frequencies from small cities. The private argument, quietly offered inside the hub operators, was quite different. "Fortress hubs" (in Dallas, Cincinnati, Atlanta, and a dozen or so other cities) and the new yield management systems pioneered at the same time (Sabre and Apollo) would permit each airline to establish a stable sphere of influence around each hub. With the market under control, carriers could hope to make money in a deregulated environment where there was a constant threat of new entrants "cherry picking" the highest-margin routes.[3]

The glaring problem with these hub-and-spoke systems has been that they actually have poor asset utilization (for reasons to be examined in a moment) and high provider costs. What's more they usually require long door-to-door times for travelers because of the need to take two flights (one into the hub and a second to the end of the spoke) to get to a destination. This also doubles the chance for delays, lost luggage, and hassle on every trip.

When we write down the process steps for our Scylla to Charybdis trip via a hub-and-spoke carrier, it's easy to see how the "legacy" or "network" carriers operating this concept have been losing money while travelers wallow in misery.

We can turn this step list into a consumption map (*The Long Grind of Hub and Spoke* on the next page spread). Note that the actual value-creating time—the time you are actually going somewhere—is shaded and amounts to less than half of total travel time.

"Turning" the airplane at the hub—that is, taxiing in from landing, deboarding the inbound passengers, cleaning and servicing the plane while the passengers shuffle to their next flight, boarding the outbound passengers, taxiing out, and waiting in the queue at the end of the runway—requires more than hour. This is because the logic of hub-and-spoke requires that all planes arrive and leave at roughly the same time, emptying the airport between the pulses and overwhelming it during the peaks.

As a result, during the five pulses each day the average plane spends more than five hours on the ground in a hub airport. And, every other flight segment is effectively only repositioning passengers who wanted to go from A to B but had to stop at C on the way. These twin evils drastically reduce the availability of expensive aircraft to do things that actually earn money. It also means that hub employees are poorly utilized on average because of the spikes in demand through the day.

But the biggest problem with hub-and-spoke for passengers is not on the cost side. It's on the price and service side. And it lies in the fact that these systems mix up travelers in two completely different circumstances. Discretionary travelers, for whom money usually is more important than time, are provided practically the same product as time-sensitive business travelers—for whom time is often more important than money. Airlines have tried to address this business traveler's problem with clubs in the hubs and with frequent-flyer benefits (including upgrades to "first class"), but the reality is that the product is nearly identical for travelers in both circumstances.

Consumption Steps and Time for the Traveler

Steps	Consumer time
1. Drive to airport in Scylla	15 min.
2. Park in large car park	5 min.
3. Walk to terminal	5 min.
4. Go through boarding process in terminal	30 min.
5. Wait in secure area (in proportion to extra time needed because of incapability of the boarding process)	20 min.
6. Board large airplane and wait for full passenger load	20 min.
7. Taxi to runway	5 min.
8. Wait in queue at end of runway	5 min.
9. Fly to Timbuktu hub airport	45 min.
10. Taxi to terminal	5 min.
11. Deboard large airplane	10 min.
12. Walk through terminal to departure gate	10 min.
13. Wait for departure	20 min.
14. Board large airplane and wait for full passenger load	20 min.
15. Taxi to runway	5 min.
16. Wait in queue at end of runway	15 min.
17. Fly to Charybdis	45 min.
18. Taxi to terminal	5 min.
19. Deboard large airplane	10 min.
20. Walk through terminal to baggage claim	5 min.
21. Collect bags	10 min.
22. Walk to rental car counter	5 min.
23. Take bus to remote rental car storage area	5 min.
24. Pick up rental car	5 min.
25. Drive to final destination	15 min.
Total trip time	**5 hr. 40 min.**

The Long Grind of Hub-and-Spoke

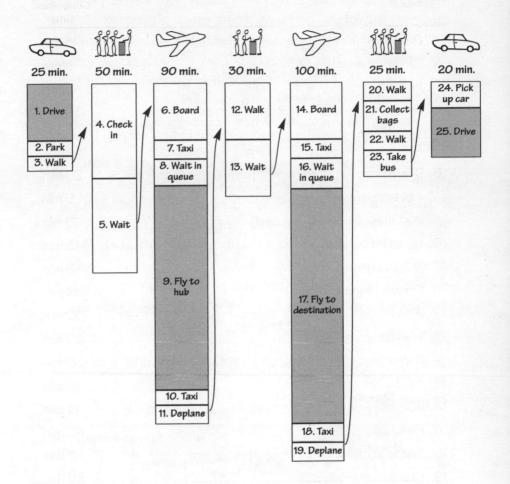

This is bad enough, but it turns out that yield management systems have been highly effective in targeting business travelers. Because they often must make their reservations close to the day of the flight and can't stay over the weekend at their destination, they pay much higher fares for a product that fails to address their most important value consideration, which is their time.[4]

Let's give this option a box score by writing down its performance on our solution matrix.

With this box score, it's not surprising that the hub-and-spoke systems have been unpopular with business travelers from the beginning. However, the cost of breaking into a mature airline industry where nationwide connectivity is important has meant that although the number of hub operators has steadily fallen (as they have merged in pursuit of greater efficiencies), the emergence of entrepreneurs to challenge them with new travel options has been very slow.

Solution Matrix

	Solve my problem	Don't waste my time	Get me			Simplify solutions	Cost
			What I want	Where I want	When I want		
Hub-and-spoke							

Point-to-Point

Point-to-point commercial airlines have been the emergent option, as exemplified by Southwest, founded by entrepreneur Herb Kelleher in 1971. After years of steady success, it recently has been joined by carriers such as JetBlue, AirTran, America West, and Frontier in the U.S. and by easyJet and Ryanair in Europe. These carriers, most of which are still associated with a founding entrepreneur, fly most of their passengers point-to-point.[5] And they do save business travelers some time, as shown in the step list for the same trip from Scylla to Charybdis.

We also can show this trip in the form of a consumption map (*Getting There: A Better Trip via Point-to-Point* on the next page spread), noting that the fraction of value-creating time to total door-to-door time is considerably higher even as total trip time shrinks by almost an hour.

However, current point-to-point service is hardly optimal for business travelers. Because they have followed the mass production logic of scale as the most important factor in cost-per-seat mile, these carriers have standardized their fleets on 150-seat narrow bodies, notably Boeing 737s and Airbus A320s. And because they understand that frequency is important to business travelers, they only serve city pairs which have large enough volumes of travelers to fill 150-seat planes four or five times a day.

These decisions in combination mean the number of city pairs suitable for this type of service is limited. Even when this concept is fully deployed and hub-and-spoke service accounts for a much smaller fraction of total air travel, passengers will still need to use hub-and-spoke operators to

Consumption Steps and Time for the Traveler

Steps	Consumer time
1. Drive to airport nearest Scylla	45 min.
2. Park in large car park	5 min.
3. Walk to terminal	5 min.
4. Go through boarding process in terminal	30 min.
5. Wait in secure area (in proportion to extra time needed because of incapability of process)	20 min.
6. Board large airplane and wait for full passenger load	20 min.
7. Taxi to runway	5 min.
8. Wait in queue at end of runway	5 min.
9. Fly nonstop to airport nearest Charybdis	60 min.
10. Taxi to terminal	5 min.
11. Deboard large airplane	10 min.
12 Walk through terminal to baggage claim	5 min.
13. Collect bags	10 min.
14. Walk to rental car counter	5 min.
15. Take bus to remote rental car storage area	5 min.
16. Pick up rental car	5 min.
17. Drive to final destination	45 min.
Total travel time	**4 hr. 45 min.**

Getting There: A Better Trip via Point-to-Point

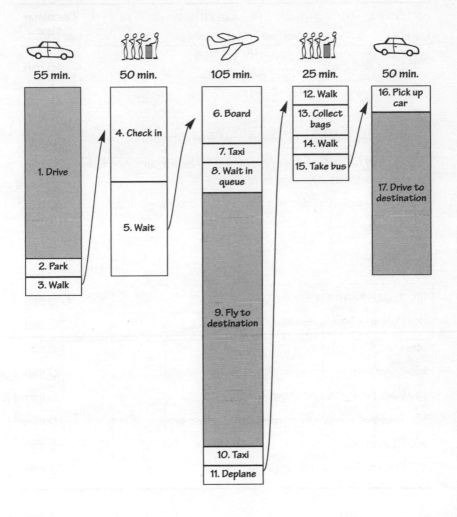

reach many city pairs or will need to drive considerable distances to airports with the correct point-to-point service for their trip. Finally, because they are focused on price-conscious travelers, current point-to-point operators minimize the bundle of amenities offered—especially legroom between seats—and operate from conventional airports with large terminals.

This means that the environment for the business traveler is spartan.[6] Moreover, point-to-point airlines, as they grow, become more and more subject to the same airport delays, both in the terminal and on the taxiways, that degrade equipment utilization and travel times for their hub-and-spoke competitors.

Solution Matrix

	Solve my problem	Don't waste my time	Get me			Simplify solutions	Cost
			What I want	Where I want	When I want		
Hub-and-spoke							
Budget point-to-point							

Dedicated Private Plane

There is, of course, a truly attractive alternative for business trips. This is a *dedicated airplane* that waits for us, then goes precisely where we want to go precisely when we want to go, and is totally private. Because of its high cost, it's a nonstarter for all but a vanishing small portion of business trips. But its performance attributes are provocative when we think about lean alternatives. So let's take a moment to list them.

This concept uses the small private airports near your home and your final destination instead of the big commercial airports on the periphery of most cities. You walk directly from your car or taxi to the small plane parked only a few feet away. You get in and are underway in minutes or even seconds. You fly nonstop to the small airport nearest your final destination. And you find a vehicle waiting next to the plane for the trip to the final destination.

Compared to the same trip on a hub-and-spoke operator or the commercial point-to-point operator, our sample trip takes only 30 to 40 percent of the total time and is largely effortless and hassle-free. Yet note that the airplanes used fly at the same speed. The difference lies in leaving out the second leg on the hub-and-spoke alternative and the groundside travel and airport wait time for both options.

We can show this option on a consumption map (*Dear Dedicated: Costly But Nearly Perfect Travel* on the next page spread), noting that value-creating time when the traveler is actually in motion is now three-quarters of total travel time

This option is truly the product, the *what*, that most of us want. The problem, of course, is its fundamental cost. The small airports and tiny terminals involved are cheap to operate. But the typical corporate jet comes with a multimillion dollar price tag and flies only about 300 hours per year, so the capital cost per seat mile is very high. And the

Consumption Steps and Time for the Traveler

Steps	Consumer time
1. Drive to private airport in Scylla	15 min.
2. Park in parking area near airplane	5 min.
3. Walk through small, fixed-base operator to airplane	5 min.
4. Board airplane	3 min.
5. Taxi to runway	3 min.
6. Fly nonstop to Charybdis	60 min.
7. Taxi to FBO	3 min.
8. Deboard airplane	3 min.
9. Enter waiting car near plane	2 min.
10. Drive to final destination	15 min.
Total trip time	**1 hr. 54 min.**

Dear Dedicated: Costly But Nearly Perfect Travel

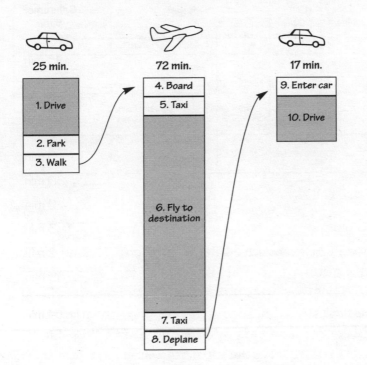

Solution Matrix

	Solve my problem	Don't waste my time	Get me			Simplify solutions	Cost
			What I want	Where I want	When I want		
Hub-and-spoke							
Budget point-to-point							
Dedicated jet							

airplane needs an experienced flight crew plus ground staff that usually outnumbers the passengers and is typically underutilized between trips. Even though it's not a practical option for most trips, let's list it in our solution matrix for purposes of comparison, now adding one additional column to our matrix for the cost of the trip. (Note, as always, that cost is determined by the nature of the process and the cost of each input to the process. Price is determined by the market.)

In the chart *Solution Matrix for Current Air Options*, we have given a value for each criteria. The bars extending below the line are "bad" and the bars extending above the line are "good." Then we've summed the results for each option. The simple conclusion is that the choice that gets the highest scores for consumer time and convenience—the dedicated airplane—spectacularly flunks the cost criteria (cost to customer). By contrast, the option that is most cost-effective—commercial point-to-point—gets poor scores on every other indicator. And the currently dominant but rapidly

Solution Matrix for Current Air Options

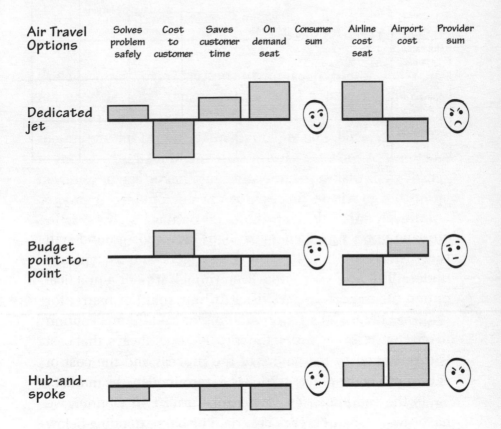

fading alternative—hub-and-spoke—does poorly on every criterion. Surely there must be something better. Let's search for it by doing a bit of scanning against the principles of lean consumption and provision.

Imagining Lean Air Travel

What alternatives might better solve the traveler's problem for getting from Scylla to Charybdis safely, in the least total trip time with the least hassle, yet do this cost-effectively while making an adequate return on investment for the operator? We always start our thinking by asking if costly steps that waste time and cause hassle can be removed from the provision process for current options. If process improvements by lean-minded managers in existing organizations can do the job, we don't need to call for the entrepreneur.

Enhanced Hub-and-Spoke

In looking at hub-and-spoke, we see that it can never be time-effective for the business traveler, no matter how it might be modified. That's because it will always need an intermediate stop for passenger self-sortation. Nor can it be asset-effective for the operators due to poor aircraft, staff, and airport utilization. And, as the recent airline crisis has shown, it's extremely lumpy with regard to investment. The monument hubs, with their massive fixed costs, are extremely sensitive to a loss of volume and have limited ways to respond when this occurs. Indeed, the most likely "innovation" in these types of services in the period immediately ahead will be a nonstop flight to bankruptcy in which employees will be forced to take permanent wage cuts as stockholders lose practically all of their investment.

However, there will still be a need for "network" carriers who can provide connectivity between far-flung cities of medium or small size, destinations that will never generate enough trips to justify nonstop, point-to-point service. It's hard to imagine any air travel concept that can offer frequent nonstop service between Portland, ME, and Portland, OR, or between Aberdeen, Scotland, and Athens, much less between either of the Portlands and Aberdeen or Athens. The best solution available probably will be to substitute smaller but longer-range aircraft for more frequent trips into smaller hubs for passenger transfer and to speed turns in these hubs, for example by smoothing flight timing and boarding planes from the front and exiting from the rear. This is a great task for lean managers and we wish them every success.[7]

Enhanced Point-to-Point

Rapidly expanding point-to-point service in its current form suffers from the need for most travelers to cover a long distance on the ground to reach the minimum-sized cities that can generate enough traffic for point-to-point service using today's 150-passenger aircraft. And it increasingly suffers from the personal activity burden and hassle required to make reservations and negotiate large airports on either end of the trip.

One way ahead is to use aircraft smaller than the current 150-passenger models to permit point-to-point travel between many additional city pairs.[8] For example, the squadrons of 35- to 90-passenger commuter jets now feeding hubs from smaller cities every two hours could be shifted to flying nonstop between smaller cities on similar frequencies, leaving out the detour to the hub and speeding up turn times at both ends. This approach is an easy one for lean-minded managers inside established airlines to implement because it requires no shuffling of assets, no rethinking of aircraft designs, and no changes in airport operations. Point-to-point operators like JetBlue have recently placed orders for jets smaller than the 150-passenger standard used so far, and we anticipate that these practices will spread widely.

Business Point-to-Point

Even with these improvements, the two dominant options are still less than optimal for the business traveler. They require long processing time in large terminals that are further than desirable from the traveler's start point and end destination. And they still use larger aircraft operating infrequently that are slow to load and unload. The result is more than twice the amount of trip times than those of the dedicated airplane and a modest likelihood that there is service precisely when you want it. What's more (or less), they offer amenities en route, particularly in baggage handling and seating, that most road warriors find exasperating: Inadequate luggage space in the cabin, long waits for checked luggage, and tiny seats with no leg room surrounded by passengers (often young and noisy) with different trip purposes. In short, they are still mixing up travelers in different circumstances, giving both the same product. How can lean thinking permit a leap to something better?

One approach is to stop wasting business-traveler time in large airports. Why not use the hundreds of small airports in the U.S. and Europe that are often closer to both residences and business destinations than big commercial airports and which are currently largely empty? And why not use the existing fixed-base operators (the small hangers you taxi by on the way to the commercial terminal) at these airports to service flights? And why not deal with reservations and security issues by carrying only passengers who have joined the carrier's "club" and passed a background check? (Carrying passengers without preflight screening is unacceptable. But flying only well-known "partners" rather than strangers will make the security task faster and easier.)

Those are approaches to high-cost, time-wasting airports. But what about the airplanes, another big cost in air transport? Why not use smaller airplanes, suited for smaller airports, that are fitted with the appropriate amenities? Current designs for 35- or 50-passenger commuter jets could easily be reconfigured to provide business-class accommodations for perhaps 20 to 35 passengers with adequate storage space in the cabin for luggage. With better designs in the next generation—for example, putting luggage bins under each seat and adding doors to load from both ends of the cabin—these planes could be turned much more quickly with much less ground staff to raise the utilization of expensive aircraft while reducing the amount of human effort required.[9]

If turns could be reduced to 15 minutes from landing to takeoff (vs. one hour for the hub operators and at least 30 minutes for today's point-to-point operators), if most passengers could travel nonstop from origin to destination, and if the capital requirements of traditional terminals could be reduced, it should be possible to reduce costs below the current prices for full-fare coach tickets, to provide higher frequencies, and to cover many more city pairs (lessening ground travel time) at ticket prices within the reach of most business travelers.

Finally, why not simplify the operation of aircraft so that no cabin service is needed and the two-person flight crew can

Consumption Steps and Time for the Traveler

Steps	Time
1 Drive to private airport in Scylla	15 min.
2. Park in parking area near airplane	5 min.
3. Walk through small, fixed-base operator to airplane	5 min.
4. Board airplane	5 min.
5. Taxi to runway	3 min.
6. Fly nonstop to Charybdis	60 min.
7. Taxi to FBO	3 min.
8. Deboard airplane	3 min.
9. Walk to rental car lot near airplane	2 min.
10. Obtain rental car	3 min.
11. Drive to final destination	15 min.
Total travel time	**1 hr. 59 min.**

Fly Me with No Waste: Business Point-to-Point

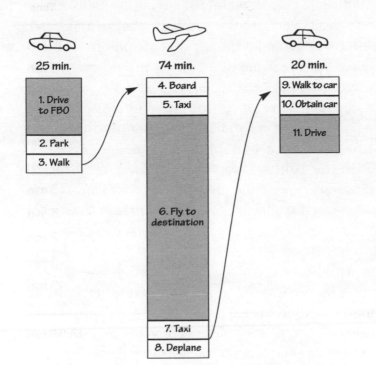

handle groundside tasks as well as flying the plane? If passengers carry their own bags, pick up any needed meals and drinks from a caterer's cart at the gate, and swipe their ID cards and boarding passes to quickly get through security, terminal staff could consist mainly of a security guard. And if aircraft were designed for quick preflight checks and quick refueling—the way you refuel your car at the pump—the first officer could ready the plane while the pilot prepared for the next flight segment.[10]

We can list the steps for this option and easily see that total travel time could be the same as for the dedicated private plane at a fraction of the cost.

By drawing the consumption map (*Fly Me with No Waste: Business Point-to-Point* on the previous page) we can also see that the value-creating time is now also a very high fraction of total travel time. With no prospect for supersonic travel over short to intermediate distances or a helicopter jet to take the traveler from his front lawn to the roof of the meeting site, this option is nearly perfect in terms of what is technically possible for the foreseeable future.

But perhaps it could be even closer to perfection. Recently a number of aircraft manufacturers have announced plans to introduce very light jets (VLJs) that can carry five to nine passengers at vastly lower capital and per-seat-mile operating cost than traditional jets. Four projects have been announced so far and others may emerge.[11] These planes can be used as dedicated aircraft like other corporate jets, and their substantially lower capital costs should mean that a larger fraction of executives will be able to afford either their own plane or a "fractional ownership" aircraft share with other users.

More interestingly, several potential operators are now proposing to use VLJs as point-to-point "air taxis" for business travelers. For example, DayJet proposes to deploy a network of 309 Eclipse 500 jets by 2008. A second entrant is, of all people, Robert Crandall, the retired chairman of American Airlines who at the end of the 1970s invented the hub-and-spoke concept (Dallas-Fort Worth and Chicago), yield management (Sabre), and frequent flyer (AAdvantage), the low-grade drug that keeps miserable passengers hooked on one carrier. Crandall and his partner, Don Burr, the former chairman of one of the early low-cost, point-to-point carriers, People Express, are proposing to operate hundreds of five-passenger Adam Aircraft A700 jets as Pogo air taxis.

The idea is for the traveler to go to the web, express his or her desire for a nonstop trip at a specific time between specific points, and get the best match of consumer desire to provider availability. The aircraft would operate from the same FBOs used for our proposed business point-to-point service and in a shared configuration, unless a passenger wanted to buy all of the seats available on a given trip to accommodate a group or to ensure privacy.

The additional attraction of this concept is that travelers might be able to set precisely their desired trip time and to travel between almost any airport pairs in North America no matter how low trip density is between those points.

Of course, this option will succeed only if enough passengers sign up to produce acceptable load factors and utilization rates. And that presumes in turn that passengers will accept the notion of going up in the sky in a small plane with a single pilot. Other imponderables are that the Eclipse and the other VLJs under development can operate reliably at their projected costs per hour over extended periods with little maintenance in a much more demanding environment than normal corporate jet use (1,500 flight hours per year vs. 300). Because the steps and time involved are the same as for the enhanced point-to-point option we have just outlined, we won't repeat the step list or the consumption map.

Completing the Solution Matrix

We now can fill in the solution matrix with the two new options as shown, adding them to the three existing options. A quick glance shows that both options are far better than the two currently dominant options and are worth serious consideration by both travelers and entrepreneurs.

Are these all of the possible options? Of course not. Another might be scheduled rather than on-demand air taxi service using VLJs. And surely there are still more.

Are we predicting that these options will triumph and that entrepreneurs will do well for themselves while doing good things for business traveler? Absolutely not. This is not the point of the exercise. We are presenting a way of thinking about future options that is rigorously structured and driven by the principles of lean consumption and lean provision. We are trying to be constructive and provocative rather than predictive.

What is clear is that creating a fast, low-effort, low-hassle, cost-effective, secure solution to this consumer problem involves simultaneously rethinking assets (airports and airplanes), operating practices (airline staff), and operating systems (security and air-traffic control). The complexity of the problem and the need to push existing assets out of the way clearly make it a job for the lean entrepreneur who can pull all the pieces together, including those which will never be under the direct control of the airline providing the service.[12]

That being the case, does this method provide insight for entrepreneurs on how to proceed with a wide range of consumer problems? We think it does. Let's test this hypothesis by looking at another common problem, diagnosis and treatment of a typical condition in healthcare.

Solution Matrix: New Air Options

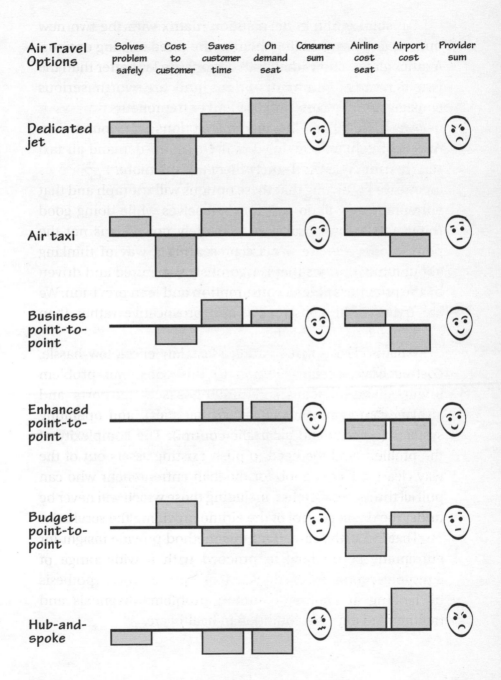

Toward Lean Healthcare

Consumers have concerns about their health from time to time and many have actual health problems in need of treatment. So about four times a year, the average American goes to his or her doctor or to a medical center to go through a diagnostic process, followed by a treatment process if necessary. How should we analyze the options for solving this two-step problem?

The principles of lean consumption can be applied as follows:

- We want our healthcare problem solved *completely*, meaning we want an accurate diagnosis with no mistakes and the best treatment.
- We want to minimize our total cost. Because most of us don't pay the full cost directly, we in particular want to *avoid wasting our time*.
- We want to obtain a diagnosis and receive treatment precisely when we want, without long waits for an appointment or at inconvenient hours.
- We want to obtain a diagnosis and treatment *where* we want, which would ideally be close to our home, school, or place of work.

So what are the choices, as offered by the current-day healthcare system? Let's create a matrix of healthcare choices. This time the task is easier, because the great majority of consumers (patients) currently follow the same steps through a very similar process.

Conventional Diagnostic Path

Let's suppose a consumer has a simple problem: chronic hoarseness and throat pain, particularly at night. While many materials are available on the web and a medical dictionary suggesting likely diagnoses and treatments, most of us reach a point from time to time when we suddenly feel the need for expert advice. "This might be something serious, even life threatening. I'd better go to the doctor."

The typical first step is to call the primary healthcare provider to make an appointment. In the U.S. today, this usually takes place through some type of HMO connected with an insurance plan.

The initial action, already described in Chapter 4, usually necessitates several calls and callbacks, with the receptionist or nurse doing the frontline screening of the patient's inquiry. Then several more calls and callbacks are needed to arrange a visit to the HMO's throat specialist. Because of the fixed schedules for specialists, who have not been converted to open access in most practices, this is usually some days away and at a time that is not convenient.

At the appointment, after a considerable wait, the doctor often concludes that a definitive diagnosis and treatment recommendation will require a visit to more specialized specialists at a large medical center.[13] Because of the medical center's expensive equipment and expensive specialists and the desire to keep these assets fully occupied with billable tasks, a lengthy queue for this service is maintained, necessitating a considerable wait for the first appointment. In addition, the several appointments that may be necessary are often scheduled at inconvenient times to the patient. Finally, the vast medical center is itself inconvenient, being many miles from the patient's home and work. It also presents a significant challenge to find parking and to navigate through

Patient's Steps and Time

Steps	Time
1. Call HMO to discuss problem (including hold)	5 min.
2. Call back from HMO to discuss problem	5 min.
3. Call to HMO throat specialist (including hold)	5 min.
4. Call back from HMO throat specialist	5 min.
5. Drive to appointment	10 min.
6. Parking	5 min.
7. Walk to office	2 min.
8. Wait in office	20 min.
9. Meeting with specialist	20 min.
10. Return home (walk/exit parking/drive)	17 min.
11. Call medical center for appointment (including hold)	5 min.
12. Call back from medical center with date	5 min.
13. Drive to medical center	45 min.
14. Park	5 min.
15. Walk to appointment	10 min.
16. Wait for appointment	30 min.
17. First appointment	30 min.
18. Return home (walk/exit/drive)	60 min.
19. Call medical center for second appointment	5 min.
20. Drive/park/walk to appointment	60 min.
21. Wait for appointment	30 min.
22. Appointment	30 min.
23. Walk/exit parking/drive home	60 min.
24. Call specialist for findings	5 min.
25. Discuss findings with specialist	10 min.
Total time	**8 hr. 4 min.**
Actual diagnostic time (value-creating time)	**1 hr. 30 min.**
Total steps	**25 steps**

Provider's Steps and Time

Steps	Time
1. Answer patient's call	2 min.
2. Call patient back to discuss problem	5 min.
3. Answer patient's call	2 min.
4. Call back to discuss problem and schedule visit	5 min.
5. Retrieve medical records in preparation for visit	10 min.
6. Check patient in for visit	10 min.
7. Specialist meeting with patient	20 min.
8. Specialist write-up of case details	10 min.
9. Answer patient's call at medical center	2 min.
10. Call patient back to set date	5 min.
11. Confirm date with scheduling system, order records	10 min.
12. Check patient in for visit	10 min.
13. First doctor diagnostic procedure	30 min.
14. Write-up of findings	10 min.
15. Answer patient's call and set appointment	5 min.
16. Check patient in for visit	10 min.
17. Second doctor diagnostic procedure	30 min.
18. Write-up of findings, diagnosis, and proposed treatment	10 min.
19. Talk with patient about findings and treatment	10 min.

Total staff time expended	3 hr. 16 min.
Actual diagnostic time (value-creating time)	1 hr. 30 min.
Total steps	19 steps

241

the vast complex of buildings to the right wing, floor, and office.[14]

Eventually the expensive doctors using the expensive equipment report some good news. There is no cancer or internal bleeding. The problem is moderate acid reflux that can be controlled with diet, proper breathing, and some simple medications. The diagnostic process in a situation where no continuing followup and treatment are necessary still involves many steps, much of the patient's time, a lot of the medical system's time, much expense for the medical system, and a lot of inconvenience. We've summarized this process with a list of the steps and time involved, first for the patient, and then for the provider.

By stacking the steps and drawing a consumption map (*Please Wait: The Consumption Process for Diagnosis*) on top of a provision map and shading the steps that actually create value, we can easily see that fully three-quarters of the patient's time and half the provider's time is wasted. And, we can now translate this information into the format of our solution matrix (*Solution Matrix: Diagnosis*).

Solution Matrix: Diagnosis

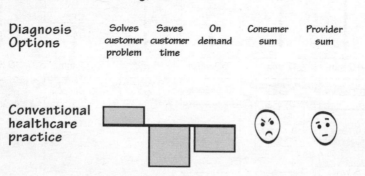

Diagnosis Options	Solves customer problem	Saves customer time	On demand	Consumer sum	Provider sum
Conventional healthcare practice					

Please Wait: The Consumption Process for Diagnosis

Consumer time
= 484 min.

20 min.

1. Call HMO
2. Answer call
3. Call specialist
4. Answer call

74 min.

5. Drive
6. Park
7. Walk
8. Wait
9. Meet specialist
10. Return home

10 min.

11. Call
12. Answer call

180 min.

13. Drive to medical center
14. Park
15. Walk
16. Wait
17. Appointment
18. Return home

5 min.

19. Call

180 min.

20. Drive to medical center
21. Wait
22. Appointment
23. Return home

15 min.

24. Call specialist
25. Discuss findings

24 min.

1. Answer call
2. Call back
3. Answer call
4. Call back
5. Retrieve records

40 min.

6. Check in
7. Meet specialist
8. Write notes

17 min.

9. Answer call
10. Call back
11. Order records

50 min.

12. Check in
13. First Diagnostic
14. Write notes

5 min.

15. Answer call

50 min.

16. Check in
17. Second Diagnostic
18. Write notes

10 min.

19. Discuss findings

Provider time = 196 min.

243

Imagining Lean Alternatives to Better Solve the Problem

What alternatives might better solve the patient's problem by providing a diagnosis and the appropriate treatment at the lower total cost? As we noted with business travel, let's not call in the entrepreneur to drastically overhaul the system if lean-minded managers can address the current problems.

Enhanced Conventional Diagnosis

In looking at the conventional diagnostic path through the HMO and the large medical complex, it's apparent that much of the time expended by the patient and the staff involves the initial contact and the scheduling system. (Think of this as the healthcare system's equivalent of the help desks we encountered in Chapter 3.) The general practice has been to position the least knowledgeable employees at the point of first patient contact and then to send patients to higher levels of contact as appropriate. (These are the call and callback loops shown on the map.) The consequence is many callbacks, much lost information, and much mutual frustration.

The problem of initial touch is compounded by the scheduling system, which typically tells patients to arrive promptly for appointments that are unlikely to take place at the time scheduled. This causes patients to take the scheduled times casually and the whole system to gradually degrade in performance. Not to be dismissive of the special aspects of the medical enterprise, but the situation is identical to that of the car repair process we examined in Chapter 4.

One way forward, therefore, is to rethink patient touch

and scheduling by moving the highly knowledgeable nurse directly into the frontline and giving this person the information to instantly decide what diagnostic path to follow. Doing this means making patient records instantly accessible electronically and providing a clear set of diagnostic paths that don't require thought or confirmation from a higher level of oversight.

A second step is to transition from rigid scheduling to "open access," as described in Chapter 4. Patients with a demonstrated need can come in whenever they find it convenient and then flex the resources of the provider to deal with variable demand.[15]

A bit of simple analysis shows that if we simplify patient touch at every step in our healthcare consumption stream, we can remove four steps in the call/callback scheduling loop for the patient and four for the medical system. The patient would need to make two calls, one to the HMO and one to the medical center. Because decisions would be made instantly on what to do and when, the providers would respond to two calls as well. In addition, we can shorten the one hour and 20 minutes of wait time the patient expended (by showing up on time for appointments that started late) by asking the patient to pick a time to show up and flexing the resources of the system to respond without delays.

These steps are a good start, and can be performed by right-minded managers without fundamental restructuring of the diagnostic system. But they don't deal with the larger issue of the remote and massive regional medical center, which consumes most of the time and resources in this diagnostic process. Let's look at the problem from the standpoint of the entrepreneur.

Dedicated Diagnostic Path Option

Large medical complexes are the most complicated and disorienting structures constructed by society for good reason. They are built to share expensive equipment and expensive specialists by means of complex buildings and expensive scheduling systems. They comingle many different diagnostic and treatment streams, each making claims on the expensive equipment and specialists through the intermediation of the scheduling system.

To the lean thinker they bear a striking resemblance to the traditional mass production factory in which activities are segregated by department. All welding is done in the welding department. All painting is done in the paint shop. All assembly is done in the assembly hall. The parts (patients in this case) travel from activity to activity along the treatment path, frequently encountering queues en route. Many traditional factories also have "central stores" where parts are taken between steps to await their appointment at the next step. These resemble nothing so much as the towers of rooms that modern hospitals use for patient storage while awaiting the next step in the process.

One of us recently had a direct experience with this phenomenon when an elderly relative developed symptoms necessitating a trip to one of these large medical complexes. As an interested reader of our previous writing, the relative suggested that we keep a time and steps log as we accompanied him through the diagnostic process. In the end, more than 100 steps were required over four days, including three nights in a patient room high above the city. Of the 96-hour elapsed time from arrival to discharge with a specific diagnosis, the patient was involved only in four diagnostic steps (e.g., blood work, CAT scans) consuming a total of two hours. The rest was queue time for use of complex equipment and more queue time waiting for the specialists to interpret the results of the tests. The total bill, as charged to Medicare and supplemental insurance, was more than $12,000. (Incidentally, the first doctor to make a physical examination—of about 10 minutes' duration—made the same diagnosis as the elaborate testing system. Thus, the four additional days and most of the $12,000 went to verifying the initial diagnosis.)

Needless to say, with all this movement and the need to coordinate complex equipment, an elaborate centralized scheduling system is essential.

In the factory world, lean thinkers have made great progress by disaggregating the "process villages" housing different types of activities and reconfiguring the equipment and technical expertise in "process sequence" in various types of cellular configurations. These permit the item being manufactured to proceed directly and instantly from one process step to the next, ideally in single-piece flow with no waits and no inventories between steps. This also permits the factory to be broken up, with different product families being moved closer to the customer in smaller facilities.

Doing this in healthcare is not so easy as in manufacturing and truly does demand the entrepreneur. This is because the operating economics of the large medical center, like the hub airport, are such that draining off revenues for a few diagnostic and treatment paths may threaten the economics of the whole. Thus, the one thing that is certain is that the established centers will stoutly defend their claim to continue doing all of the things they have done traditionally and to resist the creation of independent, dedicated diagnostic and treatment paths.

But how else are we to eliminate the long trips and long queues with their attendant costs for patients and providers in order to make diagnostic and treatment processes patient-focused rather than provider-focused? And how else are we going to make healthcare a more competitive industry as primary care doctors gain a choice of dedicated diagnostic and treatment paths to recommend to patients with cost/price as an important consideration?

Let's suppose that this is done, that all steps are lined up in sequence with a direct handoff from the HMO to the dedicated diagnostic process nearby. We can see the potential savings by listing the new steps required for the simple diagnosis we have been using for our example.

By translating this information into consumption and provision maps and shading the value-creating time (which is the actual diagnostic time), we can see that the fraction of value-creating time for both patient and provider is now nearly 75 percent (*Lean Process: Dedicated Diagnosis*).

This looks simple as presented but would actually require many difficult actions. Equipment would need to be repositioned and, wherever possible, right-sized to make it easier to operate and maintain in a dedicated diagnostic path. Record-keeping would need to be simplified and handoffs speeded between the referring HMO and the dedicated diagnostic and treatment team. And medical personnel would need to be multiskilled and more flexible so that a few staff members could perform a range of steps compared with the current-day medical complex where staff members can be dedicated to each step.

Because of the predictable resistance of the existing managers and the threat to existing assets in the system, this is likely to be a task for the entrepreneur rather than the traditional manager, no matter how committed that person might be to lean methods. But entrepreneurs have already started down this path for conditions that don't interact with the whole body—laser eye surgery, hernia operations—and it is only a matter of degree to extend the concept to more challenging conditions.

Patient's Steps and Time

Steps	Time
1. Call HMO to discuss problem and arrange appointment	5 min.
2. Drive to appointment	5 min.
3. Park	2 min.
4. Walk to office	2 min.
5. Meet with specialist and make appointment	20 min.
6. Drive to dedicated diagnosis site	15 min.
7. Park	2 min.
8. Walk to office	2 min.
9. Diagnosis, with continuous flow between steps	30 min.
10. Discussion of findings and next steps	5 min.
11. Walk/exit/drive home	20 min.
Total time	**1 hr. 48 min.**
Actual diagnostic time	**55 min.**
Total steps	**11 steps**

Provider's Steps and Time

Steps	Time
1. Answer patient's call and make appointment	5 min.
2. Retrieve medical records in preparation for visit	1 min.
3. Check-in and meeting with specialist	25 min.
4. Write-up of case details	10 min.
5. Preparation and diagnostic procedure	40 min.
6. Discussion of findings and next steps	5 min.
7. Write up findings, share records with referring HMO	10 min.
Total staff time expended	**1 hr. 36 min.**
Actual diagnostic time	**1 hr. 5 min.**
Total steps	**7 steps**

Lean Process: Dedicated Diagnosis

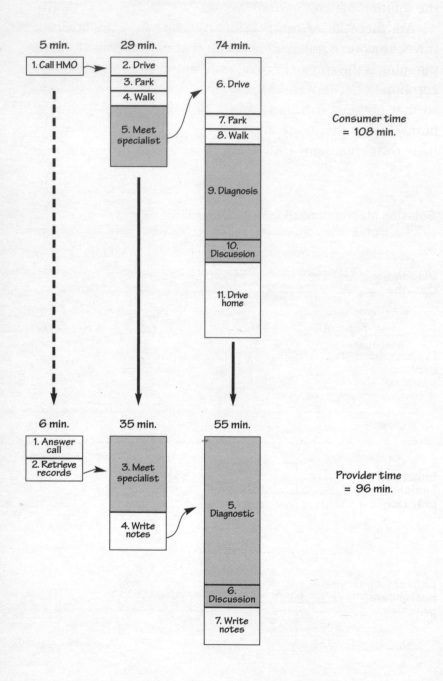

We can summarize this situation with our final reference to the solution matrix (*Solution Matrix: New Diagnosis Options*).

Are these all of the possible options? As with business travel, of course not. Another path that many innovators are pursuing is the spread of right-sized personal capital goods in combination with web-based information and expert systems so that patients can increasingly do their own diagnosis at home (using the many kits now being offered) followed by their own treatment (including home-based application of

Solution Matrix: New Diagnosis Options

Diagnosis Options	Solves customer problem	Saves customer time	On demand	Consumer sum	Provider sum
Decentralized healthcare practice					
Enhanced healthcare practice					
Conventional healthcare practice					

251

complex procedures like dialysis). And surely combinations of dedicated diagnostic paths and home-based healthcare are possible as well.

As with air travel, the objective of the process maps and solution matrix is not to predict which options will work, much less which will triumph. Instead it is to provide a rigorous and consistent method for searching for new options. Whenever this method is used, we guarantee that options worthy of serious study, if not of immediate adoption, will quickly emerge.

Solving a Smaller Number of Problems on a Continuing Basis

We've now explored the principles of lean consumption and lean provision and described the role of the lean manager and the lean entrepreneur in solving many consumption problems. But note that most consumer problems don't need solving only once but on a continuing basis. And even if the leanest methods are applied to each type of problem, many consumers will still face a bewildering variety of problems. We will tackle this issue in the final chapter by asking how many problems can be reduced to a few and how consumers and providers can work on a continuing basis as partners to solve these few big problems. We'll call the result a "solution economy."

Chapter 10

Solve My *Complete* Problem *Permanently*

Up until now, we've been talking about consumption as a matter of obtaining a wide variety of individual goods and services at the lowest total cost, including the consumer's time. We see this as a big step ahead from what most providers offer today. But another leap is possible, if we ask a simple but crucial question: What is the fundamental unit of consumption that consumers will seek in the 21st century? What combination and configuration of goods, services, and capabilities do they really want to obtain?

In the course of economic history, consumers have bought an ever-wider variety of ever-more-sophisticated objects. Oxcarts, donkey carts, horse-drawn carriages, Model Ts, SUVs—things that were made useful by purchasing a growing range of ancillary items and services, such as ox feed, donkey feed, gasoline, financing, insurance, spare parts, maintenance, and repairs. The average consumer's job has been to stitch together a range of goods plus services from an ever-growing vendor base to solve his or her problems. And, as we have noted, the combination of steady growth of available goods and services coupled with no growth whatever in available time in the day threatens to overwhelm consumers with too many decisions and too little time as society moves ahead. And this is true even if lean thinkers succeed in reducing the total cost of each consumption element, including the consumer's time.

The wealthy few, of course, have always obtained something else. Instead of isolated goods and services, they achieve comprehensive solutions to their basic consumption problems. They do this by employing personal attendants to combine goods and services into satisfying wholes on a continuing basis, as needed. In simplest terms, Bill Gates, Warren Buffet, and the Sultan of Brunei don't think much about how to buy a new car, why their e-mail won't work, or whether there is anything in the fridge for dinner. Their problems are solved—at a high but perfectly acceptable cost in staff time—through a process that might be called "craft consumption." Their personal consumption managers fit together many goods and services to create complete solutions.[1]

But let's imagine a different approach. We believe that average consumers can work together with providers in new ways to solve their basic problems by combining many goods and services into a few bundles on a continuing basis to reduce time, hassle, and cost for all parties. In fact, a convergence of technologies (to be described) and value-creation techniques (described in preceding chapters) should make it possible, progressively, to change the fundamental unit of consumption. Consumers and providers can shift from focusing on isolated objects and services, obtained one-at-a-time and usually from strangers, to complete solutions to life's major problems, obtained from only a few providers on a continuing basis with lower cost and hassle. Such a world is possible. That's why we believe we are now ready to move toward what might be called a solution economy.

Hassle-Free Information and Communications Management

The place to start is by asking what are our basic problems. What fundamental issues in our lives as consumers do we need to address?

One that leaps to mind as we write this book is information management and communication. We have an enormous need to communicate with the world, both to learn things we need and want to know and to tell the world what we have learned and what we will need next. It sounds simple, except in practice.

To see the magnitude of the problem for today's consumer, let's look at just one of our households. Like many homes today, it is also a production site for the husband's book-writing business and the wife's small publishing business. When we take a gemba walk in the house, we discover four land lines for phones (family, home-office number one, home-office number two, and fax line); four cell phone numbers (one per parent and one per teenager); four different long-distance providers for the land lines and cell phones; a high-speed data line shared through the house from yet another service provider; and a cable hookup with various entertainment channels.

To use this capability we need six e-mail addresses (one per household member, and two used only for ordering over the web so as to avoid being bombarded with spam on our four personal e-mails). These are provided by four different Internet service providers.

We also need hardware and software: phone handsets (14 at last count), computers (six for sure, but maybe the one in the basement still works), lots of operating systems and applications software, printers (four), a fax (old-fashioned but still occasionally useful), scanner/copiers (two), modems (in every computer), wireless transmitters for the high-speed data link (in the basement and on the top floor), network connections, a hard drive to back up all the other hard drives, and a curious device living in the basement known as the master bus that periodically needs to have its current taken away and then restored so it will start making sense again.

Finally, let's not forget Josh, who fixes the household software (getting rid of irksome spyware just today), Fred who fixes the hardware (mostly all that wiring in every room plus the transmitters for the wireless system), and the help line and service technician from one of our businesses that tends to both the hardware and the software in our house belonging to the business (tending to a disk failure just last week).

But this is just today. As we write, we are completing the transition from chemical to digital photography so that all of our pictures, from the electronic cameras—including the ones in the cell phones—will soon go to grandparents over the web rather than through the mail. (If only we can get the software to work.) And within a few years practically all of our home entertainment equipment will be completely digital and interconnected with our communications infrastructure so that our TVs (with the DVD players plus the old VHS) and our audio systems (including, of course, the iPods) will be part of one big communication system.

These capabilities are all wonderful or otherwise we wouldn't seek them. But who designs the master system? Who supplies all the equipment? Who researches and obtains all the service contracts for equipment, software, and data transmission? Who does the preliminary diagnosis of problems? Who lines up the service team to fix them? Who takes care of recycling superannuated equipment while continuously searching for better equipment and better service contracts? In short, who creates and implements the master plan to solve our information, communications, and entertainment problem on a continuing basis in a time of rapidly changing technology?

The answer is that we do, for no pay. And we hate the job. For example, recently both of us tried to rationalize our telecoms providers and make sure that we are obtaining the best combination of price for service with our many vendors. And … we gave up. It was simply too complicated and time-consuming. Doubtless we are paying too much and getting too little, but we've decided to be satisfied with satisficing.[2] There just aren't enough hours in the day to do better, particularly if we are ever going to get this book finished.

Why can't we deal with just one party to solve the whole problem? Why can't we do this by going to just one computer screen to describe our communications problem—needs and wants—and our budget? And why can't this one party just take care of our problem on a continuing basis without our needing to invest any time and mind share? Ideally, we wouldn't invest any money in hardware or software either. Instead, we would simply be provided with everything we need—hardware, software, support services—as we need it in return for a fee per amount used.

A Solution for Every Core Problem

The rapid pace of technical change and the interconnectivity of many of the technologies might suggest that information management, communication, and entertainment are, in combination, a special problem that particularly benefits from a solution approach. Perhaps most consumption problems are inherently small and unsuited to bundling? We think not. Indeed, we believe that the great bulk of the multitude of current-day problems that consumers are trying to solve can be reduced to only six core problems.

Shelter

Everyone needs a place to live. Each of these abodes is a complex mechanism crammed with goods and services. The structure itself and all the equipment—as you have already guessed—needs obtaining, installing, maintaining, repairing, upgrading, and recycling on a continuing basis.

Many consumers live in apartment houses and condominium arrangements whose principle attraction is that care of the property is done professionally by a dedicated service organization, although often not to the resident's satisfaction. But the fraction of residences that are owned rather than rented and the fraction of these that are standalone units continue to grow in practically every developed country as ownership becomes the norm and residential densities fall. One of the consequences is that the problems of the property all pile up on the consumer's desk.

Many owners spend considerable time learning to fix things—which for some becomes a satisfying hobby and pastime that shouldn't be disturbed. (Except, of course, to reduce out-of-stocks and to provide a variety of venues for shopping—as we described previously—so that just the right items for home repairs can be obtained easily.) But many consumers own their abodes despite their lack of skills and construct a network of favored service providers to keep things running.

In our own situations we have found it necessary to identify an electrician, a plumber, a heating and air-conditioning expert, an arborist/yard service, a chimney sweep, a carpenter/handyman, a cleaner, a roof and gutter expert, and several appliance repair services to keep things running in a steady state. (We've already assigned another group of helpers, frequently on the property to troubleshoot the telecoms and computing systems, to our communications problem.) And we have both undertaken significant upgrades or major structural repairs in recent years involving a separate set of contractors and subcontractors.

Assembling and managing this team is time-consuming and frustrating, particularly given the habit in the building trades of never showing up when promised and rarely getting the job done right on the first try. But the current alternative, in the form of management firms taking the whole problem in hand, carries a prohibitively high price tag when it is available at all. So we continue to manage our supply base ourselves.

Why can't we instead just go to one computer screen to share our current problems and future needs and to work out a plan for our shelter problem so that maintenance is done right the first time, at the right time, and at a cost below what we are currently paying for breakdown maintenance? And why can't this "solution provider" keep the records on our homes as well—accurate blueprints showing the configuration of all systems, modifications, appliance models, repair records?

This would enable the provider to calculate the best time to make repairs and upgrades in the context of life-cycle management while dispatching the repair team with the right tools and parts so callbacks aren't necessary. For example, we always wonder if it makes more sense to replace the roof before or after it starts leaking. A shelter provider could make it its business to gather experience-based data and determine the right answer. Just on our own, deciding what to do about this and many other life-cycle problems is hopeless.

Healthcare

Years ago, when doctors didn't know much and tended to be small businessmen themselves, patients went to their general practitioner for evaluation and were only sent to the appropriate specialist for treatment as necessary, often to an expert sharing referral fees with the primary care physician. It was a one-touch relationship and usually remained so as long as the patient lived in the same place.

Then, as doctors learned more, medical practices were turned into vast HMOs and patients began to move more frequently, things got a lot more complicated. Faced with a series of vast bureaucracies, the customer was forced to adopt a whole new set of skills to maneuver within these systems.

Now, under the pressure of cost containment, this maneuvering is getting more complicated, especially as the big healthcare organizations are beginning to break up into independent specialists who treat specific problems but have no sense of the whole.[3] What's more, medical records are often a mess, which makes them hard to transfer when patients decide to shift doctors or HMOs. Given the mobility in modern society, this means that most consumers of healthcare now deal with a series of primary care practices and specialists in different cities and even different countries during their lives, and that records and knowledge often get left behind.

But this is only part of the healthcare dilemma when defined as a consumption problem.[4] Consider the billing nightmare. Most healthcare is insured in some ways. Managing the insurance paperwork—particularly the maddening errors—has become a major task for many consumers, particularly the elderly who lack the energy and often the acuity to tackle all of the problems they encounter. As middle-aged children of aging parents, we've become well-versed in the tangle of billing systems connected with private and government health insurance, and we have no illusions that we will ever really understand them. For our parent's generation, mastery of these details is completely hopeless.

Why can't patients have a single long-term touch point for medical care, specifically an organization with a stable staff where they can make a plan for their health (including the ability to specify what they are really looking for in healthcare) and maintain lifetime records to support them along the way wherever they may move and whatever health problems they may encounter? This organization would have case managers paired with a doctor with direct knowledge of each patient's needs and expectations and would provide one-touch service for lining up whatever expertise and information patients need at the moment while handling all problems with finances and records.

This organization would need to specialize in information management and to assign knowledgeable staff to front-line positions directly facing the consumer. Logically they should also gear their fees to things that might go wrong with the patient's health rather than the number of problems the patient actually calls about, a concept that should sound familiar from our discussion of the failure industry in Chapter 3. There we learned that lean-thinking firms understand that assigning people with a lot of knowledge to directly address the root cause of problems through direct contact with customers is a lot more effective than asking people with little knowledge to mechanically interact with consumers after things go wrong, gradually moving them to higher levels in the system as problems worsen. This is particularly true in healthcare, where neglected conditions cost much more to remedy later, if they can be treated at all.

Mobility

In Chapter 7 we talked about better ways to obtain the vehicles consumers need for personal mobility, and we hope that many of these methods will be available in the years ahead. But buying the vehicles and finding a competent repair option (as discussed in Chapters 1 and 4) is only part of the problem. Consumers still need to search for, finance, register, insure, inspect (for safety and emissions), routinely maintain (e.g., the oil change and the new windshield wipers), and dispose of each vehicle, and most also feel the need to line up some type of emergency service. This means more relationships and more time spent on unpaid work.

Why can't consumers instead have a single touch-point for their mobility needs? Why can't a single organization accessed through a single screen supply all the information needed about different vehicles and put just the vehicles desired in the driveway just as they are needed, doing this with no hassle and no waste of time and at lower total cost to both the consumer and the provider? And why not use the same touch-point to order and pay for taxis, limos, and even public transport, as consumers need different types of mobility?

Note that consumers wouldn't need to own anything, although some might want to legally possess a specially valued vehicle and would only want the mobility provider to provide insurance, registration, inspections, maintenance, and emergency service. Consumers would normally just use goods and services as needed for as long as needed. These would be provided by an agent the consumer could stick with no matter how their circumstances changed and no matter where they moved. This is provided, of course, that the agent continues to do a good job, an issue we will discuss further in a moment.

A similar concept could be employed for the other aspect of personal mobility, the need to travel great distances. In the previous chapter we looked hard for missing options for long-distance travel, such as the point-to-point business airline focusing on road warriors or the on-demand air taxi for the same purpose. But even if the full range of these options existed, consumers would want to use a combination of products—which we will call solution elements—as their circumstances change. This would involve many relationships, and throwing in the need for hotels and rental cars would add many more.

Combining all these solution elements into a comprehensive whole that completely solves the traveler's problem over time is the real challenge. For a while, it appeared that the web would be the perfect way to do this. Services like Expedia and Travelocity survived the bursting of the e-bubble to offer instant bookings, often with special prices when airlines and hotels had excess capacity. Yet the full promise was never realized.

In fact these services are actually quite limited. They work well for simple trips such as the round trip between two major cities with nonstop flights on the same carrier. But when consumers try to put together complex itineraries—and our itineraries always seem to be complex for both business and pleasure trips—it is usually hopeless, and always requires a large amount of unpaid work. Business travelers in particular often end up going back to traditional travel agents who know their preferences, have real-time knowledge of what others are reporting about the different solution elements, and who provide a familiar voice the traveler can actually talk to (and commiserate with) when something goes wrong.

But now, of course, consumers pay directly for this service because airlines, car rental companies, and hotels have eliminated agent commissions in an effort to force consumers to use their own web sites containing information only about their own services.

What seems to be happening is that local travel agents are moving toward the role of solution providers by forming global networks to serve consumers anywhere. At the same time they are automating as much of their routine service as they can in order to work together with the traveler to minimize the time and effort of both parties. And automated web-based services like Travelocity and Expedia are hiring real humans to deal with complex problems and beginning to look more like travel agents. As this continues, it's a natural progression to full-blown mobility provision.

Financial Management

Perhaps the most exasperating new consumption problem for many consumers is the need to manage personal finances in a time of deregulation, frequent job changes, vanishing employer paternalism, and rapidly proliferating product options. Our fathers never thought about their pensions or insurance—the issues were taken care of by someone at their employer. But we devote substantial mindshare to our retirement funds, our insurance (life and disability), and our surplus funds that must be invested somewhere. Plus, we must figure out how to file the tax forms, how to pay all of those bills that come with all of our goods and services, and how to file all the documents that flood in as a consequence of routine transactions. (A quick check shows that one of us has 51 active vendors in the "payees" list on the bank web site designed to make bill paying effortless.) The debate over "privatization" of Social Security in the U.S., whatever the merits of the proposals, raises the prospect of another set of decisions for consumers to make late at night.

It would seem that at this point in history all of the information needed could be marshaled on one screen where consumers could talk it over with one advisor for a modest fee and make all of their decisions with a few keystrokes and clicks. But this seems not to be the case. Just transferring funds from personal to business accounts in the same bank is a struggle, and the idea of getting Fidelity, Schwab, Scudder, Northwestern Mutual, Bank of America, and one's financial advisor and/or accountant to put personal data on one combined screen so consumers can see where they stand in real time at a glance is still a far-off dream.

Nevertheless, rapidly maturing technology will soon make it possible to create a single touch for consumers' financial lives, one that can be accessed without a change in relationship no matter where in the world they work or live. The actual solution elements—the insurance policy, the short-term bond fund, the bank account—may still come from different vendors. And, as we will see, it will always be best if there is a choice of element vendors and solution providers. But when these vendors and elements are combined into a single touch-point, the unpaid work in consumers' lives can be reduced dramatically.

Instrumental Shopping (or Personal Logistics)

The final problem in our list of major consumption challenges pops up frequently in dinner conversation with friends, but doesn't have a common name. While everyone understands that personal mobility means moving your person through space as necessary, hardly anyone seems to understand the terms "instrumental shopping" or, more accurately, "personal logistics" when we propose them. By this we mean obtaining all of the mundane things consumers need to run their lives and to successfully deliver them through space to their point of use.

To begin to see what we are talking about, ask yourself what you do most evenings and every Saturday. You get in your car and run errands. You shop for food at a Tesco, pick up hardware for your home at a Home Depot, go to a Wal-Mart to get sundry items, drop off and pick up the laundry, pick up the videos for evening entertainment, visit a bookstore to pick up a book (perhaps this book?), and quite possibly go by the office to get work items you meant to bring home but forgot. None of this is shopping for pleasure. It's unpaid work in which consumers perform instrumental shopping for routine items and run a personal logistics service to do so.

In some areas this situation is improving. For a growing number of items, like the book ordered from Amazon, the provider arranges with a shipper like UPS or FedEx to get the item to the consumer's home or office. And for other items like home grocery shopping, the retailer sends its own vehicle.

We believe that many of these can and will be done better. For example, Tesco has learned how to steadily grow its volume of home shopping profitably by rethinking its picking and delivery process, and we believe that every grocer will copy these methods over time. But the consumer still faces the need to make many trips and to wait at home at the right time for others. We use home grocery shopping perhaps once a month, but would use it more frequently if it weren't for the irritating two-hour delivery window when someone must be at our home receiving dock to await the goods.

In Chapter 7 we suggested one way ahead, based on Toyota's water-spider system of materials delivery in the factory. Translating industrial methods into personal practice would mean for each of us to contract with a logistics firm to fetch for us the things we need while taking away things we are finished with (including the recycling). At the same time, this service could deliver the items we want others to receive from us. The idea would be to eliminate many personal trips that consume time, as well as deliveries from many logistics firms sent by suppliers at irregular intervals to the home or office. Instead, we could benefit from a periodic pickup and drop-off, probably using a specially provided pass-through by the front or rear door to hold the outbound goods and receive the inbound products without our needing to be there.

This approach would save energy and reduce congestion because a few vehicles, making stops to drop off and pick up large numbers of items every few houses, would replace much of the current driving by each of us operating our personal logistics operations.[5] And it would save our time as well, providing more leisure time to pursue the shopping we actually enjoy once the problem of routine shopping is solved.

This solution is certainly possible from a technical standpoint, if only the existing logistics operators—including the post office—can change their thinking about who the customer is. Right now it's the shipper, who pays the bills. But it should be the recipient. In fact, this is one of the most important things that Toyota learned many years ago as an industrial consumer. If a company like Toyota "pulls" needed materials from its suppliers, frequently and in the exact amount needed, everything runs smoothly. (We saw in Chapter 6 how Tesco is now doing this with its suppliers by sending trucks to pick up its needs directly from supplier factories.) By contrast, if Toyota or any other industrial consumer depends on providers to ship goods at the suppliers' discretion, jam-ups and shortages result. If we can only enlighten a few logistics firms to take the lead on personal logistics, a dramatic transformation might be possible. Then if we can just figure out a way to package the children, so they can be picked up and dropped off by the personal logistics provider, we will really take a whack out of unpaid work!

Solution Migration: From Small Problems with Small Solutions to Large Problems with Large Solutions

When summed up, these six simple but large problems— information, communication and entertainment, shelter, healthcare, mobility, financial management, and mundane shopping—constitute a large fraction of the consumer's daily needs and of total household spending, in both money and time. What's needed now is for providers to come forward to solve these large problems on a continuing basis.

A good way to start is by adding a final principle to the concept of lean consumption:

• Solve my *complete* problem *permanently*.

What's needed to do this is a partnership between the consumer and a series of *solution providers*. A communications facilitator. A shelter manager. A healthcare partner. A mobility agent. A single financial touch-point. A logistics operator. Their objective would be to simplify life by providing complete solutions at lower cost. Ideally, these providers would work for consumers on an exclusive and continuing basis, thus enabling them to build a knowledge base about the consumer's circumstances and desires. This would improve the provider's level of service while reducing total cost for consumer and provider.

The solution provider would do well, of course, to simplify its own life by enlisting the help of a series of object and service providers for the individual elements of each solution. For the communications provider these would include the hardware manufacturers, the software providers, the service technicians, and the help-line operators. For the shelter provider it would include the multitude of skilled trades and materials retailers, distributors, and manufacturers. For the financial problem solver these element providers would include insurance companies, banks, funds traders, accountants, and investment advisors.

Following this logic, the element providers would also do well to simplify their own lives with the aid of a group of component or part providers. And so on, all the way to raw materials. Each layer of providers up the value stream would solve the problem of the customer immediately downstream.

The concept of reducing the number of suppliers is already widely practiced in industry. Leading-edge firms are increasingly reducing their supply base by forming lasting partnerships with a smaller number of more knowledgeable suppliers solving larger problems at the next level of the value stream.

Today it's only consumers who are still trying to solve problems in atomistic markets where strangers buy from a multitude of strangers in one-off interactions. For example, many airlines no longer buy either airplanes or the jet engines that power them. Instead they go to leasing companies like GE Capital Aviation Services (GECAS) or International Lease Finance Corp. (ILFC) to provide the planes, changing out their fleets as operating conditions change. And GECAS and ILFC in many cases don't buy or maintain the jet engines on their planes. Instead, they obtain "power by the hour" through agreements with Rolls-Royce, GE Aero Engines, and Pratt & Whitney. These firms supply the engines, arrange for periodic overhauls, and conduct emergency maintenance for a set fee per hour of engine operation. The airlines simply provide crews and receive bills for the number of hours the airplanes and engines are used. Their problem is solved.

We are certain that providers can solve the big problems of millions of individual consumers, but only as providers rethink their definition of value and the fundamental organization of value creation. During the bubble economy of the 1990s, the promise of e-commerce created a widespread willingness to rethink the business models needed for new definitions of value. In our view, this was the bubble's one lasting contribution to economic progress. Unfortunately, providers largely missed the point as to the real problems to be solved. Thus they often ran aground introducing complex services to push brilliantly optimized goods onto overloaded consumers and businesses

The Architecture of Solution Provision

To fully understand how solutions might be provided, let's take one last look at the short-range mobility problem, a challenge that we've already examined from several angles.

Suppose consumers could sign up with a new solution provider, Mobility Inc., to place the vehicles they need in their driveways as they need them on an open-ended basis. This would mean that consumers would never need to think about the vehicles themselves. Obtaining, maintaining, repairing, insuring, registering, inspecting, replacing, or even fueling them would cease to be a concern, let alone a problem. They would pay their provider by time and mileage. The relationship with Mobility Inc. would be permanent—so long as the provider continued to solve the problem cost-effectively. Motorists would no longer need to devote mindshare or time to the complex consumption and provision streams needed to solve their mobility problem. The provider would assume the burden of identifying and supplying the solution elements needed for each consumer's specific solution.

In order to achieve this, Mobility Inc. would maintain relationships with all motor-vehicle manufacturers to obtain new vehicles as needed. This would be essential because customers might be indifferent about the image of their mobility provider but they will probably have important feelings about the image and features of the motor vehicles they use every day. To make the full range of consumers happy, the mobility provider would need to fill every customer's driveway with the right objects at the right time with the right image.

Some consumers, of course, wouldn't feel the need to have any dedicated vehicles in their driveway. They would be happy with shared car services like Zipcar, or with cabs and limos, and consumers needing only those options wouldn't need Mobility Inc. But most consumers, as the circumstances change, would probably need a combination of vehicles assigned exclusively to their use and vehicles shared with other users (like taxis and limos). Mobility Inc. might therefore want to add these element vendors to its complete solution.

The mobility provider would also need to create a service network for vehicles, perhaps involving traditional car dealers or rental car companies in a new role. Such a service system, directed by the provider, would provide customers a high degree of reliability without any hassle or drain on their time.

In addition, the mobility provider would need to develop relationships with financing sources and insurers, who probably would own and insure the vehicles being provided. However, these sources would be different from the current leasing industry that focuses on individual vehicle transactions, churns its fleet, and often suffers from miscalculating residual values. The mobility provider would have little need to churn its fleet under management because older vehicles could be placed with more price-sensitive users. As a result, the vehicles themselves could stay with the same owner—the financing company or with Mobility Inc.—from the time it leaves the auto factory to recycling. As we will see in a moment, this is an important advantage of the solution concept in the world that lies ahead of us.

Finally, the mobility provider would solve the problem of recycling. We are moving rapidly from a world where goods could simply be abandoned when worn out—where dilution is the solution to pollution—to a world where most objects will need to be recycled. Mobility Inc., as the controller of the physical objects, would therefore face this final problem in collaboration with a recycler. Fortunately, the information on the product that Mobility Inc. would receive from the manufacturer and the additional information on the product gathered during its useful life will make it possible to more cost-effectively solve the recycling problem, as we will see in a moment.

An obvious candidate to take on the task of mobility provision would be the large mega-outlet car dealers, like AutoNation, that have developed in recent years. They would simply change their role. Instead of facilitating transfers of vehicle ownership from car manufacturers to new-car buyers and from new-car buyers to used-car buyers, they would manage large fleets of vehicles and customer relationships on a continuing basis. Another candidate would be the current-day car rental agencies, which are already experienced in managing large fleets but only for short-term use and often to strangers.

Firms that don't make sense for this concept—but which would be certain to try—are the established car companies that always dream of moving closer to the customer, pushing the traditional dealers out of the way. A major problem for any manufacturer in becoming a solution provider for its own category of products is the unavoidable bias toward the products it makes when consumers want a complete range of choices from all manufacturers.

For example, during the recession of 1991, Don Runkle,

then the vice president for research and development at General Motors, proposed to senior management that GM dealers sell miles (that is, provide mobility) by providing the cars that customers wanted to take the hassle out of their consumption. The idea was to make the dealers GM's partners, rather than its adversaries, by offering them a new product that would attract customers to the dealerships and make GM money as well.

The general manager of the Buick Division signed up for an experiment. Then the question arose: Which brands of vehicles would be provided? Runkle argued that for the concept to be attractive to consumers it was important to provide any brand of vehicle, even Toyotas, on even terms. And that was the end of the proposal. Even though the math showed that GM and the dealer would be making more money by putting Toyotas in customer driveways than they would by trying to sell them Buicks, the idea of handling a competitor's product was too big a mental hurdle for GM's senior managers to overcome.[6]

Another problem car companies would face as mobility providers dealing directly with the customer would be the need to push the existing dealers out of the way. This is in a legal context where dealers are fully (and in our view unjustifiably) protected by franchise laws in every state and in every developed country, although they have begun to be relaxed in Europe. A better path is to find a new value-creating activity for existing dealers as fleet managers who help independent mobility providers—not car companies— offer consumers a full range of products as their needs and tastes change.

An Enormous Hidden Benefit of Solution Thinking

We pointed out at the outset of this book that the rich have always lived lives full of satisfying solutions. Steve Jobs and Paul Allen surely devote no mindshare to home repairs, personal logistics, or health insurance. Not surprisingly, the initial reaction we often encounter when describing the concept of a solution economy is that it sounds great, but that true solutions would cost too much for anyone but the wealthy. Indeed, many listeners cite an income constraint as the reason they spend so much of their own time on system integration to solve their problems.

In fact, a solution focus should *reduce* total costs for consumers and providers. It's easy to see why when we focus on the value stream for each solution, consisting of all of the consumer and provider actions required from start to finish to bring consumers the bundle of goods plus services that they need to solve a given problem.

Demand Smoothing

To begin this examination, take a piece of graph paper and a pencil (or a mouse pad and PowerPoint) and plot time in years on the horizontal axis and vehicle miles traveled per year in the U.S. (or practically any developed country) on the vertical axis. What you will see is a straight line. Plotting years against passenger miles traveled by air, weekly expenditures on food, square feet of residential space in use, bytes sent by e-mail, telephone calls placed, and items delivered by logistics services, produces similar straight lines with varying angles of upward slope. Together these graphs show that the actual use consumers make of the goods and services involved in solving their big problems is remarkably stable.

This should not be surprising because the number of us around is very stable from day to day and our needs for the basics of life are fairly constant.

Yet if you draw a second line on each graph showing the number of new motor vehicles, new commercial aircraft, new houses, new computers, and new telephones bought or installed every year what you see is chaos. Indeed, there are substantial ups and downs without a clear pattern. One consequence is massive inventories of finished products positioned to provide a high level of service in this sea of variable demand. A second consequence is absurd underutilization of production assets so that point capacity can accommodate spiky point demand. For example, in 2005 the value of finished vehicles on dealer lots in the U.S. was more than $80 billion, yet most of the automotive assembly system was running considerably below capacity.

Even worse, but largely unseen, are the large piles of inventory and excess capacity at every point up the value stream as each firm tries to cushion its operations from gyrating downstream demand. Worst of all, from the standpoint of managers in traditional businesses, this chaos has serious revenue implications. It leads to periodic sales and remaindering to move items produced just-in-case for inventory that is never wanted by customers.

We wonder what the world would look like if, instead of ordering these products in response to promotions from manufacturers designed to move products out of inventory, customers relied on a mobility provider or a shelter provider or a communications provider to obtain the items they need and to plan with that provider based on their projected future needs. We've already looked at this idea for car sales in Chapter 7. Let's see how it can be applied to practically any durable good or to any service provided on a continuing basis.

With a bit of planning—in cooperation with the mobility provider—to get the vehicles consumers want and need to solve their problems, providers could look ahead several months or even several years so that the desired vehicles could be ordered to exact customer specification. Then when the new vehicles arrive from the manufacturer (at an attractive price because they have been ordered in advance) they could be changed out for the old vehicles without the consumer needing to pay any attention. Or used vehicles meeting the consumer's changed circumstances could be obtained from other users no longer needing them, because many consumers don't care about the precise newness of the product. What they really want are the desired features and level of reliability.

As this begins to happen and mobility providers enter into long-term purchase agreements with car makers for stable volumes of vehicles (reflecting the stable pattern of actual vehicle use by their customers), inventories along the entire value stream could be steadily reduced. The total cost of the product would fall substantially and would help to offset solution-provider costs of managing demand and the vehicle fleet.

Of course, as we also saw in Chapter 7, some of us do want exactly the vehicle we want immediately. This is fine—if we are willing to pay a higher price for this convenience and manufacturers hold open some production slots for last-minute orders. As long as true impulse demand is a modest fraction of total demand and total demand is relatively stable, solution providers and their collaborating manufacturers can support "get it for me now" buyers while reducing solution costs for plan-ahead customers.

When we apply this same concept to communications, shelter, healthcare, financial management, and personal logistics, we see the same thing. If consumers and providers can have a frank and sustained conversation about their needs over an extended period it should be possible to eliminate the gyrations in order flow and to get consumers exactly what they need at lower total cost.

How Information Technology Can Support the Solution Economy

Another way to smooth demand and reduce costs lies in the full use of information technologies that are now in existence or rapidly emerging. Practically every item being manufactured today has built-in ability to report on its condition and to ask for help when needed. Cars, telecom devices and computers, home appliances, and even the human body (through strap-on or even implanted diagnostics) are rapidly gaining the ability to tell someone if they have a problem and suggest what to do about it. The cars, computers, and human bodies just don't have anyone to talk to.

Suppose, for example, that all of the electronic and electro-mechanical items in your home were connected to your shelter provider via the web. And suppose that your shelter provider had the full database on all this equipment on your home.[7] By listening continuously for trouble signs from equipment and by looking at available technician time, it should be possible to send the right technician with the right tools and parts to work on your home before anything fails.

What's more, a shelter provider with a large customer base would start to collect valuable data about what fails and why. Just as with the help desks we studied in Chapter 3, the shelter provider could start talking with manufacturers about why their equipment experiences significant failure rates and suggest better designs. Doing this would reduce the costs of a given repair but, more important, would reduce the number of items needing repair over time.

If smart products communicate with solution providers through the web, costly labor for customer support can be minimized. This is crucial because one of the most significant things happening in the shift to a solution economy is the conversion of large amounts of unpaid labor supplied by the customer—for example, to take their vehicles in for repairs, inspections, and maintenance or to track their own orders—into paid activities by the personnel of the solution provider. If these activities were performed as inefficiently as most of us conduct them now as consumers, solutions would indeed be only for the wealthy.

To return to our mobility example one last time, currently available technologies, including vehicle locating devices using GPS, make it possible for a mobility provider managing thousands of vehicles to do so with very little effort. The vehicles can report on their whereabouts and condition—mileage, time to periodic maintenance, and current operating problems. And they can call for help in the event of emergency. This information can be converted into billings, and customers can periodically report on their current and future needs via e-mail and the web. And in the future, vehicles will be increasingly able to report on not only their current condition but on the nature and timing of likely future failures through prognostic devices. Then by grouping service runs and providing technicians with the right parts, tools, and information via the web in order to fix any vehicle with one quick service call, it will be possible to maintain large fleets in the field without incurring large costs per vehicle. (The information needed to do this presents a civil liberties issue, of course, that we will address in a moment.)

As equipment of every sort, especially software, comes under the management of solution providers, the engineering philosophy of element providers is certain to change. Solution providers will want to move product designs away from the "bleeding edge" toward reliability, and will also want to move designs toward higher durability with little need for maintenance. When the solution provider is hurt by the need for repairs and service parts, rather than economically rewarded, then products will miraculously improve. Providers paid by usage will make more money when the total costs for a given amount of usage declines.

By contrast many current designs implicitly assume that the consumer will be willing to devote significant time to debugging and trips to service outlets. Imagine if Bill Gates had to come to the customer's home to debug software or if Bill Ford had to get the customer's car to change the oil or replace faulty parts. Would Microsoft code be so buggy? Would Fords need oil changes every 7,500 miles and a good bit of scheduled maintenance plus breakdown repairs during the first 100,000 miles of use? Solution providers are certain to demand much more capable products with much longer maintenance intervals and service lives.

Combining more durable designs with sensible uses of the web and smoothed demand can lower the real cost of consumer solutions below the current cost (the sum of isolated elements). We believe that over time cost-effective solutions and lower total-cost solutions can be available to everyone.

The Societal Benefits of Solution Thinking

A solution focus also can benefit society because internalizing the externalities of current industrial civilization becomes much easier and cheaper. We have already noted that product designs will tend toward durability and longevity, and solution providers will act to minimize total life-cycle costs—including energy costs—because they will control the assets from delivery to recycling. Doing this almost always reduces the amount of resources and energy needed to provide a given level of mobility, shelter, communications, or whatever. Much of the degradation and early scrapping of current-day manufactured goods is due to the inability of millions of individual users to understand or apply life-cycle costing and to introduce upgrades rather than buying entirely new products.

Management of many consumer assets by large, sophisticated organizations will also lead to better compliance with environmental and safety mandates. For example, will 120 million American vehicle owners, each pressed for time and looking only at short-term, out-of-pocket costs, maintain the emissions and safety performance of their vehicles as well as a few large mobility providers? The latter will have sophisticated technologies for emissions and safety management and large downside risks should they be found by governments to have failed to maintain standards.

The Challenges to Solution Thinking

We've now done the easy part. We've described the solution concept and portrayed some of its benefits. However, as we present these ideas to business audiences we typically hear of three problems that might obstruct the path.

First, they point out that whole new categories of businesses seem to be needed as solution providers, and it is not clear how the solution value stream should be divided vertically between different types of firms. These include solution providers, producers of solution elements (e.g., the car, the software, the hip-replacement operation), component providers selling to these producers, and raw material producers. Nor is it clear how solutions should be grouped horizontally. Should a mobility provider seek to solve all mobility problems or just those utilizing private cars? Should a shelter provider only handle the routine issues of home ownership or handle remodeling and upgrades as well? In addition, considerable amounts of assets in existing businesses are suddenly at risk. Just who is going to "architect" each solution's value stream, and who will take the hit on surplus and irrelevant assets?

Second, they point out that privacy looms as a major issue because the effectiveness of the solution provider is directly proportional to the amount of information continuously shared between the consumer and the provider. As one listener put it, "To continuously help me, my mobility provider must always know where I am and how I am treating the vehicles. This may be more than I want anyone to know." The generalized concern is that the solution provider will sell or barter or just plain give the information collected to everyone from curious spouses to spammers to governments.[8] And this concern is repeated as one moves up the value stream, because to truly solve the downstream customer's problem, every upstream provider must know a lot about the downstream business. And knowledge, as everyone agrees, is power.

Finally, they cite a companion concern to privacy, which is imprisonment. This is the fear that an investment of time and energy in selecting one provider for a given solution will lock the consumer into a gilded cage with that provider. Indeed, the original use of the term "solutions" in business foretold this risk. IBM in the 1950s advertised itself as every corporation's "data processing solution," promising to install its own hardware and software and to provide closed-source maintenance and code enhancement. It did this very well and, as the old joke went, no one ever got fired for buying IBM. However, the feeling of claustrophobia that this created for corporate managers over time was one of the prime forces behind the movement for software supplied by other firms and for decentralized computing with machines obtained from competing vendors.

In light of this experience and in keeping with the general feeling of our time that economic independence is priceless, our listeners tell us clearly that gilded cages are not a "solution."

The Challenges Resolved

Fortunately, there are some simple answers to these challenges.

Designing new value streams and putting other's assets at risk is what entrepreneurs do, as we explained in the previous chapter. Many of them took a bath at the end of the 1990s by trying to solve the wrong problems with brilliant technologies. But the entrepreneurial instinct is surely as strong as ever. Our simple objective is to raise the consciousness of entrepreneurs (indeed, to create lean solution thinkers) and point them in the right direction. No doubt experimentation will be needed with regard to the best horizontal segmentation of solutions and the best approach to vertical segmentation as well, but many experiments can be conducted with relatively low risk by redeploying existing assets rather than creating entirely new ones.

Once consciousness is raised and successes begin to emerge, entrepreneurs won't be the only ones that find solution thinking attractive. Many large businesses will discover that they can pioneer a new future in solutions going beyond their traditional activities. For example, credit-card companies, travel companies, postindustrial manufacturing companies, rental and leasing companies, and construction companies can all find opportunities to become solution providers.

The biggest challenges will face those firms that are

already in an industry as element providers, who wish to become solution providers as well. We understand their desire, having talked directly with a number of them. But in our experience this is unlikely to work. The solution provider needs a choice of element providers. Trying to yoke element provision to solution provision almost always produces an "asset backward" situation in which the real purpose of the new solution business is to push the elements made by the old business.

Our advice to element providers is simple: If you want to provide solutions instead, you have two choices. Either sell your element business and move next to the customer to solve complete problems, or keep your element businesses, while working with emerging solution providers, and tackle solutions to entirely different problems with different customers in a different industry.

As for privacy issues, because of the falling price of information capture and the growing ease of information sharing, these concerns are now emerging in every activity from supplying tiny parts to downstream manufacturers to providing complete solutions to end-consumers. It follows that ironclad privacy policies with legally enforceable penalties will be business standards within a few years as the implications of the web and e-everything settle into public consciousness. Thus the problem for the solution business is no different from any other information management business, including element businesses like credit checking, credit cards, or database management. Our belief is that the industry standard for solution providers will be that no one—without a court order—will be given access to any personal data for any reason, unless consumers agree to make their data available.

Finally, because solution provision works best when customer and provider are in a stable long-term relationship, the issue of choice and freedom to switch providers is, in our view, the most important challenge. In fact, customers don't want to switch if the provider is solving their problem, but will feel that they must if their provider is no longer cost-effective or responsive. In other words, if the provider is offering second-rate solutions and charging too much for them.

Fortunately, new information technologies—if properly deployed—can provide a way to introduce cost checks by means of web-based auction prices for solution elements. By reference to current auction prices the consumer could determine quickly and inexpensively whether the solutions being provided are cost-effective. Just stack up the solution elements and compare the total with the cost of the solution.

If this is not sufficient, end consumers can still do what most manufacturers and their first tier have been doing since the early 1990s. This is to reduce their supply base drastically but to retain relations with two providers for every problem. They then switch their business only as necessary based on comparisons of the performance of the two competing providers.

Moving further up the value stream, this will doubtless become the standard way of proceeding as each firm lines up two or three solution providers for every problem. However, even here web-based auctions may avoid the need for switching if the products being provided are sufficiently commoditized and performance terms can be determined easily. Customers then simply tell suppliers to meet the market price, at a minimum level of quality, delivery, and product performance or lose the business.

Price is, of course, only one dimension in evaluating a solution. Quality, a lack of hassles, and responsiveness to customer problems may actually be more important for many types of problems, such as healthcare. Here help also is on the way through the steady growth of publicly available customer performance evaluations by organizations like J.D. Power and Associates. When there are thousands of small providers, gathering valid data is hard to do cost-effectively. But when there are only a few big providers, it is much easier. And we think solution providers inevitably will grow large over time in order to solve consumer problems on a continuing basis in a highly mobile society.

We anticipate that the performance of each of these organizations in solving consumer problems in a timely manner at reasonable cost with a high level of quality will be widely available to consumers at practically no cost.

The Solution Opportunity

To reach a conclusion about the attractiveness of a few providers solving complete consumption problems permanently, just ask a simple question. Would consumers choose to continue down the current path of a large and growing number of economic relationships, most of them with strangers and each requiring a significant amount of their time and mindshare? Or would they rather slash their unpaid time by dealing with only a few high-quality providers solving their major problems at lower total cost? We are confident that there is demand. What's unknown is the precise form and timing of the supply.

Conclusion

Lean Solutions

We have now covered a lot of ground. By employing something so simple as maps of consumption and provision that anyone can draw on the back of an envelope, we have been able to see how the efforts of the consumer must fit together with the efforts of the provider if we are all going to solve our problems. To do this we need to move beyond the era of mass consumption facilitated by mass production, a world in which one format fits all at an ever-higher scale—the big-box retailer, the big-box hub airport, the big-box medical center—as ever-increasing product variety is substituted for true customer desire. The signature of the new age of consumption is to minimize the total cost—and in particular the time cost—of solving life's problems.

We have proposed some simple principles for a new way of proceeding that we call lean consumption. Let's restate them, now joining the view of the consumer with the view of the provider:

- Solve our problem completely.
- Don't waste our time.

- Provide exactly what we want.
- Provide value where we want.
- Provide value when we want.
- Provide the value we really desire,
  not just the existing options.
- Solve our complete problems permanently.

Can real providers working with real consumers do this? We have no doubt that they can—if the issues are only technical. The means to discover root causes of chronic problems, to remove time wastes from value streams, to get the right goods and services to the right place at the right time, and even to solve complete problems permanently with the aid of emerging information technologies and new institutional forms are easily at hand. We have described them in this book. The problem, therefore, is not technology or organization. The problem is us.

We are all deeply immersed in a view of consumption that is atomistic and adversarial, us against them, strangers dealing with strangers in one-time interactions. The arms-length markets most of us have lived with in the world of mass consumption do provide many splendid things, in particular an ever-growing range of brilliant objects. But, as we have seen, the steady progression of choice and variety often chokes our lives with parts not adding up to wholes because of the lack of a broader context.

What we need to move ahead is a grander vision of consumption and provision as a shared process that is clearly visible to everyone and in which problems are jointly defined and resolved. Indeed, we need to unify the two parts of our own heads—the way we think and act as consumers that conflicts sharply with the way that we think and act in our other role as providers.

Because consumers can't take the lead in fixing bad

processes, the real change agent for the age of lean consumption must be the provider. Within established businesses it must be the provision stream manager and, when new businesses are needed, it must be the lean entrepreneur.

We tend to think that our unavoidable role as managers is to work around broken processes, making excuses to the customer as necessary. However, life can be very different for the lean manager who clearly identifies the consumption and provision streams and makes their logic apparent both to customers and to provider organizations. The great leap then is to lead a joint walk of discovery to see how consumption and provision can be united in a lean value stream that makes customers and employees better off.

Similarly, we tend to think of entrepreneurs as self-optimizers, who strive for great wealth whatever the consequences for society. And often this has been true. It is not hard to think of entrepreneurs who have prospered mainly by off-loading costs onto other participants in value streams while grabbing the lion's share of value-stream profits.

The lean entrepreneur, however, can be a social optimizer who designs and puts in place new provision streams interlocked with enhanced consumption streams that make higher returns for the provider while making life better for the consumer. At the same time, the lean entrepreneur can provide the consumer the option that is really wanted. This is just what Adam Smith—who always viewed himself as a moral philosopher rather than an economist—intended as the outcome of market-based competition.

Pursuing a lean path has a green advantage as well. Supplying just what consumers need just where they need it in stable relationships with a life-cycle focus reduces the burden on the environment for any given level of material well being.

Transitioning to lean consumption also has a pronounced social advantage. Lean providers employ highly skilled people solving problems in deep collaboration with consumers rather than unskilled people repetitively fixing the same problems in the superficial relationships of the world of mass consumption. This gives work real meaning, and consumption a social aspect.

Traveling the full path from mass to lean consumption is not the work of a year or a decade. Indeed, we have only just begun. Mass consumption is deeply rooted and not just in consciousness. It resides in assets and organizations on a vast scale. All those big boxes and failure-industry bureaucracies won't go away quietly or easily. The objective of this book, therefore, has been to lay out the fundamental ideas of lean consumption for the first time in hopes of spurring a leap in consciousness by both consumers and providers. Coupled with bold action by managers and entrepreneurs to rethink consumption and provision streams in combination, the first instances of which we have described in these pages, we are now on our way toward lean solutions.

Acknowledgments

The Story of This Book

As we complete our fifth book, we realize once more that the story of how a book came to be could take as much time to tell as the story in the book. We won't write another book here, but we do need to tell just a bit of the story because it is the best way to thank those who have helped us along the way.

We have been thinking about consumption for almost as long as we have been thinking and writing about production. In the late 1980s, while visiting Japan to gather material on car distribution for *The Machine that Changed the World*, it dawned on us that Toyota thought quite differently about sales, distribution, and its fundamental relationship with its customers in Japan. This was how we first started to think backward from the perspective of the consumer.

Senior managers in Toyota recounted the painful lessons they learned while selling cars door-to-door as part of their early training—time they spent in addition to building cars on the production line, where they learned the importance of production. In Japan, it was commonplace for companies like Toyota to conduct door-to-door selling with sales staff tracking the needs of households over time. This led to a personal and continuing relationship with many Toyota customers that enabled sales staff to precisely understand and predict their needs. What was more, customer needs could be balanced with the need to smooth production orders, pulling forward or delaying production and delivery dates accordingly.

In dense urban areas in Japan, car dealers lacked the space to hold large stocks of finished vehicles. As a result, the ordering and planning system was geared to building and delivering customer's cars to precise time windows, in less than a month from placing the order. This meant that there were practically no unsold vehicles on dealer lots. By contrast, export orders created a stable base load for Toyota factories. These vehicles were scheduled with several months of lead time, in response to forecasts from import companies abroad, and offered with far fewer options.

At that time, door-to-door selling of any item was a distant memory in the West and no one was interested in learning about seemingly antiquated car-selling methods in Japan. This view was strengthened by the decision of firms like Toyota to employ traditional Western approaches to car retailing as it moved abroad.

However, in Europe there was an interest in looking for leaner ways of organizing car distribution from the factory to the dealer. The national distribution system supplying dealers in each country operated at cross-purposes with the factory and the dealers, often increasing costs and reducing responsiveness to changing demand. This led Dan to set up the International Car Distribution Programme (ICDP) in 1993, together with Malcolm Harbour, Jonathan Brown, and Philip Wade.

ICDP is an industry-funded research program that continues to this day, now led by John Whiteman and Andrew

Tongue. It has amassed an influential body of research on car distribution (a full list of reports can be found at www.icdp.net). ICDP research on customer fulfillment by John Kiff and on lean dealer operations by David Brunt forms the basis for material in several chapters in this book. David tested his ideas while subsequently working for Porsche GB and his work was picked up and implemented successfully by GFS in Portugal as related in Chapter 4.

A second opportunity to think about the challenge of provision arose when Dan was invited by CEO John Neill to head the new company university at the Unipart Group, a distributor and manufacturer of car parts in the UK. Here he learned the nuts and bolts of aftermarket parts distribution and warehousing and came to understand the significance of the Toyota Parts Distribution System, which was then being rolled out across the world. Bob Bennett and Bob Arndt, then at Toyota Motor Sales in the U.S., helped describe how this system worked in Chapter 4 of *Lean Thinking*.

It turned out that the Toyota parts system was also the right starting point when Dan was asked by Graham Booth, then supply chain director of Tesco, to explore the implications of lean grocery retailing. As other retailers began to realize the significance of what Tesco was doing, Graham and Dan took the lean message to the European Efficient Consumer Response (ECR) movement. ECR Europe is the largest organization in the world devoted to promoting collaboration between retailers and suppliers, attracting more than 3,000 delegates to its annual conferences. Dan joined the ECR Academic Advisory Panel and is one of the founding editors of the *ECR Journal* (www.ecr-journal.org), together with Daniel Corsten, Alan Mitchell, and Arnd Huchsermeier. This journal has published many seminal articles, several of which we have cited in this book, on retailing for fast-moving consumer goods and supply-chain cooperation.

As we deepened our interest in consumption and determined to make lean consumption the subject of our next book, we faced the problem that all authors encounter: How would we support a research team and pay the mortgage while researching and writing?

For previous books we had relied on university research grants and publisher advances. However, we knew that this project would take several years and would entail expenses larger than our traditional sources could support. This situation called for something new, and we tackled it in a new way. We contacted several large companies whose senior executives we had known in our past work and asked them to provide a loan to support the project with the understanding that the loan would be repaid from sales of the book. We explained that we were going to work backward from the needs of the consumer to create new types of provision processes that would be relevant to the work of their companies. Thus we offered to make them a test bed for our ideas while they supported the research.

Fortunately, leaders from two Fortune 100 companies, Delphi and United Technologies (UTC), came forward with offers of corporate support and we were able to launch the project in 2001. We made clear that we wanted to test our ideas in their organizations but that we did not want to write about their companies, no matter how brilliant they might be as lean providers. We have had a policy from the beginning of our collaboration never to write about companies in which we have any financial interest, and we have continued this practice.[1] So we extend our heartfelt thanks to Chairman and CEO J.T. Battenberg of Delphi and to President and COO Karl Krapek of UTC (both of whom have since retired) and hope that the lessons learned were worth the risk of their investment.

At the same time, we were also looking upstream from the

consumer all the way to raw materials and utilized the resources of the Lean Enterprise Institute to prepare *Seeing the Whole*, a workbook designed to help firms map their extended value streams.[2] While doing this, it became clear that most companies have no formal methodology for calculating and minimizing the total cost of production and design, by location across the world, for a given product for a given customer. So Jim collaborated on the Lean Location Logic (L3) Project with the International Motor Vehicle Program to develop a practical method of calculating total cost.[3]

As our research progressed, we carried out many research visits to retailers, distributors, healthcare organizations, maintenance providers, and service businesses in Europe and the U.S. These interactions convinced us that the same value-stream mapping method could be helpful in understanding both the consumption and the provision processes. This discovery, plus our growing frustration with our own consumption experiences, led us to shape this book in its final form.

As we entered the final stretch of research, Nick Rich from the Cardiff Business School put us in touch with Steve Parry, who was just leaving Fujitsu Services. Steve and his colleagues Mark Kell and Caroline Swain shared the impressive results they had achieved by applying lean thinking to customer support operations.

As we look back on four years of effort, we need to specially thank our editorial team: researchers Atisa Sioshansi and Andrea Crandall, editorial advisor Tom Ehrenfeld, designers Thomas and Jennifer Skehan at OffPiste Design, copy editor Patrick Hernan, and project manager George Taninecz. We also want to express special thanks to Tom Stewart, the Editor of the *Harvard Business Review*, for his early encouragement of our work leading to our *Lean*

Consumption article in the March 2005 issue. Gardiner Morse of HBR provided additional assistance during the editorial process for the article and in reviewing the book manuscript.

At Free Press, Dominick Anfuso has been our longtime editor, always ready for the next project, and Michele Jacob has handled publicity. Wylie O'Sullivan pulled everything together to get us from contract to launch. We arrived at Free Press with guidance from Rafe Sagalyn, our longtime agent who provided help when we most needed it to properly balance the book between the differing perspectives of providers and consumers. (Our personal frustration as consumers had made us overemphasize the consumption process and underemphasize the provision process in early drafts.)

We would also like to thank the management teams at our research and education institutes. At the Lean Enterprise Institute: Helen Zak, Jon Carpenter, Chet Marchwinski, Rachel Regan, Jeff Durham, and Phil Verbeek, with special assistance from board member Germaine Gibara and faculty member Guy Parsons. At the Lean Enterprise Academy: David Brunt, Ian Glenday, Lizzie Lewis, and Amber Thomas. They ran our organizations while we were away for extended periods researching and writing.

It wouldn't be right to conclude these acknowledgements without noting the immense debt of gratitude we owe to Toyota and its current and former employees. Ours has been an unusual relationship in that we have never worked for Toyota, we have never consulted to Toyota, and we have never received any financial support from Toyota. Indeed, we have never even owned any of its products. But we have received the gift of access and continuing conversation. And sometimes we have had the even more valuable gift of frank criticism of our efforts. We truly are lucky that Toyota happened to be pioneering a new way of thinking across the world—based on process-focused management—when we happened to be passing by its global construction site and could watch over the fence. We've simply explained to others what we saw.

Finally we would like to thank all the individuals who shared their knowledge and experiences with us during this book's development, many of whom also read drafts of the work:

Richard Anders, Matt Andersson, Michael Ballé, Don Berwick, Maureen Bisognano, Graham Booth, Dave Brunt, Philip Clarke, Curtis Cook, Daniel Corsten, Anne Esain, José Ferro, Dave Fitzpatrick, Jay Gershuny, Germaine Gibara, Ian Glenday, Chris Harris, Rick Harris, Bruce Henderson, Matthias Holweg, Steve Hughes, Peter Ickes, Kurt Kammerer, Mark Kell, John Kiff, Chuck Kilo, Barry Knichel, Pat Lancaster, Sir Terry Leahy, Dave Logozzo, John Long, Ricardo Lopes, John Paul MacDuffie, Robert Mann, Roger Mansfield, Robert Mason, Alan Mitchell, Gordon Moore, Bob Morgan, Brennan Mulligan, Mark Murray, Steve Parry, Guy Parsons, Mark Powell, Pat Quintal, Nick Rich, Curt Roberts, Don Runkle, Pat Rutherford, John Shook, Pedro Simao, David Simons, Art Smalley, Steve Spear, Gail Strand, Caroline Swain, Cynthia Swank, Mike Tansey, Dave Taylor, Andrew Tongue, John Whiteman, Scott Whitaker, Bodo Wiegand, Solveig Wikstrom, and John Womack.

These individuals did the best they could to set us straight. If any problems remain, and surely they do, we are the root cause.

Lean Global Network

We could not have written this book without an institutional base for our efforts and we wish to thank our many global collaborators in the Lean Global Network.

In 1997, upon the completion of our previous book, Jim founded the nonprofit Lean Enterprise Institute in Boston (www.lean.org). LEI's mission is to write down the building blocks of lean knowledge in action-learning workbooks and to teach this knowledge to lean leaders and managers in public and in-house workshops. LEI also tries to raise consciousness of lean thinking and to spread it to new activities in new industries through a continuing series of public conferences. LEI's teaching faculty and authors include an extensive network of lean experts. Many of these individuals, like John Shook and Art Smalley, were members of the original generation of Westerners who went to Japan in the 1980s to learn Toyota's methods directly and to lead the initial efforts by Toyota to transfer its methods across the world in Toyota's own operations and among its suppliers.

The Lean Global Network has grown steadily since 1997. The method in every country has been to hold initial awareness-raising events for the public under the banner of Lean Summits and then to progress as quickly as possible to the creation of independent, nonprofit lean institutes under the guidance of local leaders. The first Lean Summit outside the U.S. was held in the UK in 1997 and repeated annually before leading to the founding of the Lean Enterprise Academy under Dan's leadership in 2003 (www.leanuk.org).

Events moved more quickly in Brazil, where the initial Lean Summit in 1997 led to the formation of Lean Institute Brasil under the leadership of Professor José Ferro in 1998 (www.lean.org.br).

The pattern in Turkey was similar to that in the UK, with an initial lean summit in 1998 leading to the formation of Lean Institute Turkey in Istanbul in 2003 under the leadership of Yalcin Ipbuken (www.yalienstitu.org.tr).

Affiliate arrangements have now been established in Poland at the Wroclaw Technical University under the direction of Professor Tomasz Koch (www.lean.org.pl), at the Lean Enterprise Institute Australia (in Melbourne) under the leadership of Peter Walsh (www.lean.org.au), in Germany (at Aachen) at the Lean Management Institut founded by Dr. Bodo Wiegand (www.lean-management-institut.de), in the Netherlands at Lean Management Institut founded by Rene Arnoudts (www.leaninstituut.nl), and in France at the Projet Lean Entreprise founded by Michael Ballé and Freddy Ballé (www.lean.enst.fr).

Each of these organizations seeks to translate lean teaching materials, conduct courses to teach these materials, and conduct lean summits to raise awareness.

Lean Summits have also been organized recently in China, Denmark, India, Mexico, and South Africa, and we hope that leaders will emerge soon in every country with an interest in dramatically improving its core value-creating processes.

The current focus of the lean institutes in the U.S. and UK is to expand the boundaries of lean thinking through public events devoted to services, business processes, healthcare, and the public sector.

Anyone interested in these activities or in initiating new activities should contact Professor José Ferro, our Global Lean Ambassador, based in Sao Paulo, Brazil, at ferro@lean.org.br.

Our objective is to continually increase global awareness and to build the capability to teach lean knowledge to any organization in any industry in any country.

Notes

Preface

1. James P. Womack, Daniel T. Jones, and Daniel Roos, *The Machine That Changed the World: The Story of Lean Production*. New York: Rawson McMillan, 1990.

2. James P. Womack and Daniel T. Jones, *Lean Thinking: Banish Waste and Create Wealth in Your Corporation*. New York: Simon & Schuster, 1996, Second Edition, 2003.

3. For example, the J.D. Power and Associates Initial Quality Study shows a 33 percent drop in the average number of defects in new vehicles of all brands between 1998 and 2005. The U.S. Bureau of Labor Statistics reports in its Consumer Price Index that the real, inflation-adjusted price for a new car of a constant specification has fallen steadily since the mid-1990s.

4. See B. Joseph Pine II, *Mass Customization: The New Frontier in Business Competition*. Boston: Harvard Business School Press, 1992, for the classic statement of this strategy for producers.

5. At least up to a point. See Barry Schwartz, *The Paradox of Choice: Why More Is Less*. New York: Ecco, 2004, for a psychologist's explanation of why consumer choice past a certain point can become oppressive.

Introduction

1. Looking at the bright side, the rotation of the earth is slowing. In only 157 million years consumers will have the luxury of a 25-hour day.

2. See B. Joseph Pine II and James H. Gilmore, *The Experience Economy: Work is Theatre and Every Business a Stage*. Boston: Harvard Business School Press, 1999, for an interesting demonstration that many consumers value the experience involved in some types of consumption—going out to dinner, high-end shopping—more than the physical objects involved. This is absolutely true. However, it's our belief that most of us seek a very different experience in the great majority of our acts of consumption. This is obliviousness with zero mindshare and, as nearly as possible, zero time expenditure. This leaves time to focus on those few aspects of consumption where we seek a vivid experience.

Chapter 1

1. Andrew Tongue, John Whiteman, and Daniel T. Jones, *Progress on the Road to Customer Fulfillment: ICDP Research 2000–2003*. Solihull, UK: International Car Distribution Programme, 2003. The ICDP is a global research effort supported by car companies, large dealer groups, parts makers, financial organizations lending to the car industry, and governments. See *www.icdp.net* for details on the current program. Dan Jones was a founder and codirector from 1993 to 2005.

2. These "consumption maps" are an adaptation of a method long used by lean thinkers to draw value-stream maps of production processes. See Mike Rother and John Shook, *Learning to See: Value-Stream Mapping to Add Value and Eliminate Waste*. Brookline, MA: Lean Enterprise Institute, 1998, for a complete explanation of value-stream mapping in production environments. See Daniel T. Jones and James P. Womack, *Seeing the Whole: Mapping the Extended Value Stream*. Brookline, MA: Lean Enterprise Institute, 2002, for an extension of this method to entire production processes, from raw materials to finished product.

3. The best summary of this body of work is Jonathan Gershuny, *Changing Times: Work and Leisure in Postindustrial Society*. London: Oxford University Press, 2000.

Chapter 3

1. Philip B. Crosby, *Quality Is Free: The Art of Making Quality Certain*. New York: McGraw-Hill, 1979

2. We are indebted for much of the material in this section to Steve Parry, formerly Head of Strategy and Change at Fujitsu Services in the UK. For a summary of his thought process, see Susan Barlow, Stephen Parry, and Mike Faulkner, *Sense and Respond: The Journey to Customer Purpose*. London: Palgrave Macmillan, 2005.

3. Note that in this example, the customers being helped were BMI employees, such as the check-in staff who were using hardware and software supplied by a variety of vendor firms. Help desks work exactly the same way when they serve end consumers.

Chapter 4

1. Toyota dealers in Japan, where the Toyota Motor Corporation has an equity stake in the dealing system, are an entirely different matter, as we reported in Chapter 7 of *The Machine That Changed the World*. Elsewhere in the world, Toyota has conformed to standard practice by selling its vehicles to independent dealers for resale to the public.

2. Then a Senior Research Associate at the Lean Enterprise Research Centre, Cardiff Business School, and now a director of the ICDP.

3. Then a Senior Research Associate at the Lean Enterprise Research Centre, Cardiff Business School, and now a faculty member at the Lean Enterprise Academy.

4. This paper was subsequently published as John S. Kiff, "The Lean Dealership—A Vision for the Future: From Hunting to Farming," *Marketing and Intelligence Planning*, Volume 18, Number 3, 2000, pp. 112–126.

5. *5S* refers to a group of exercises derived from Toyota practice, in which five related terms that start with the letter S describe practices that are conducive to visual control and lean production.

6. For a summary of Dr. Murray's experiment see Julie A. Jacob, "Same Day Appointments Catching on with Doctors," *Amednews.com: The Newspaper for America's Physicians*, Jan. 29, 2001, www.ama-assn.org/amednews/2001/01/29/bisa0129.htm

7. In our experience, it's nurses—not doctors or medical managers—who first grasp process thinking. And among

doctors, we've often been impressed with anesthesiologists because they want to minimize the time patients are unconscious and therefore urge the introduction of flow methods in operating rooms.

8. For a recent summary of experience with open access see Greg Randolph, Mark Murray, Jill Swanson, and Peter Margolis, "Behind Schedule: Improving Access to Care for Children One Practice at a Time," *Pediatrics*, Vol. 113, No. 3, March 2004, pp. 230–237.

Chapter 5

1. At least some readers will wonder how price markdowns can be "bad" for consumers. And if the item wanted is the item being marked down, the consumer is certainly better off. But what about the average price of all shoes sold? The extra costs inherent in overproduction, inventories, and the management of complex safety valves must be paid for by someone. That someone is the average consumer because the average cost and price of all the shoes sold is higher than it needs to be. Stated another way, savings on sale-priced items are more than offset by extra spending on the regular-priced items bought, because the "regular" price is higher than it needs to be. But most consumers only notice the sale prices, not the average prices.

2. For a full explanation of value-stream maps for extended value streams such as the one shown, see Daniel T. Jones and James P. Womack, *Seeing the Whole: Mapping the Extended Value Stream*. Brookline, MA: Lean Enterprise Institute, 2002.

3. See Thomas Gruen and Daniel Corsten, "Rising to the Challenge of Out of Stocks,"*ECR Journal*, Vol. 2, No. 2, Winter 2002, for a summary of 52 studies of level of service

conducted across the world. The authors report that 50 percent of OSS are due to errors in retail-store orders and forecasts, 25 percent are due to poor shelf replenishment practices inside the store, and 25 percent are due to delivery failures, information errors, and production problems in upstream replenishment activities.

4. In recent years, many retailers have also tried to improve level of service by taking order discretion away from managers at individual stores and by introducing regional distribution warehouses that serve each store rather than having each store receive direct deliveries from each supplier. (Wal-Mart is perhaps the most visible example.) These are positive steps, but when combined with traditional information management systems and infrequent deliveries their potential for improving the level of service is modest.

5. Some readers may find this description familiar from experience with The Beer Game, an inventory management exercise for teams that was popularized in Peter Senge's *The Fifth Discipline: The Art and Practice of the Learning Organization.* New York: Doubleday/Currency, 1990. Where we differ from Senge is in our solution to the problem.

6. Ideally, the flow of information will be tightly interlocked with the flow of materials. Toyota, for example, uses kanban signals sent upstream by the same replenishment loop that brings the requested materials via the same replenishment loop. Outside Toyota's factory walls and at the factories of suppliers within a very short travel time, electronic kanban are substituted for the traditional kanban cards. A full description of Toyota's reflexive pull system is contained in Art Smalley, *Creating Level Pull: A Lean Production-System Improvement Guide for Production-Control, Operations, and*

Engineering Professionals. Brookline, MA: Lean Enterprise Institute, 2004.

7. Toyota's parts distribution system, described in Chapter 4 of *Lean Thinking*, is still the most complete example. Some 60 percent of its spare-parts suppliers are making and shipping parts every day to Toyota's Regional Distribution Centers in North America in response to deliveries by the RDCs to car dealers the previous day, *Lean Thinking*, 2nd Edition, page 302.

8. *Lean Thinking*, Chapter 2, pp. 38–48. As we prepared this example in 1996, Tesco had just become one of the sponsors of the Lean Enterprise Research Centre at the Cardiff University Business School in order to carry out proof-of-concept trials on applying lean thinking to the grocery industry. Now, after nine years and dozens of pilots and rollout projects, Tesco is very close to achieving continuous flow in canned beverages and has applied these ideas to many of the fast-moving products in its provision streams. The example presented here is based on numerous value-stream exercises carried out with Tesco by Dan Jones along with Cardiff researchers Nick Rich and David Simons. These experiments are summarized in Daniel Jones and Philip Clarke, "Creating the Customer Driven Supply Chain," *ECR Journal*, Vol. 2, No 2, Winter 2002.

9. Regular surveys in the UK reveal that delivery trucks are only utilized during 28 percent of the available time, are running empty 20 percent of the time, and on average are only half full. See Alan McKinnon et.al, "Running on Empty?" *ECR Journal*, Vol, 3, No. 1, Spring 2003. This contrasts with the use of mixed-product milk runs by Toyota suppliers and Seven-Eleven stores in Japan, where pickup and delivery times are tightly synchronized. See Hirofumi Matsuo and

Yasuaki Takeda, "ECR: A 'Fresh' Look from Japan," *ECR Journal*, Vol. 2, No. 2, Winter 2002. When trucks make frequent runs with many stops and almost always carry substantial loads, the total number of miles of travel needed to deliver a given quantity of material can be substantially reduced.

10. It is best to manage these spikes separately. It is our belief that as companies learn more about lean provision and learn better to calculate the total costs and benefits of promotions (which are much higher than managers looking only at "point costs" suspect), this approach to retailing will gradually disappear. We'll talk further about this in our discussion of "big box" retailing in Chapter 6.

11. The provision streams for perishable goods are being leaned as well, as Tesco takes part in a UK-government sponsored project to map provisions streams for red meat and dairy and grain products all the way back to the farm. See David Simons, Mark Francis, and Daniel T. Jones, "Food Value Chain Analysis," in *Consumer Driven Electronic Transformation: Applying New Technologies to Enthuse Consumers and Transform the Supply Chain*, ed. by Georgis Doukidis et al, Amsterdam: Elsevier, 2005.

12. The classic statement of this position is Frances Cairncross, *The Death of Distance: How the Communications Revolution Will Change Our Lives*. Boston: Harvard Business School Press, 1997.

13. Many managers with a casual interest in lean thinking seem to have concluded that a truly lean production system, like Toyota's, will have zero inventories anywhere. But this can only work if customer demand is completely smooth and

predictable and if upstream supply is completely reliable. Instead of zero inventories, lean thinkers look to create small inventories at one or a few points in any provision stream making standardized products. In the shoe case, the store would have substantially no inventory while the distribution warehouse would have a small inventory to cushion against sudden surges in customer demand, and the factory would have an additional small inventory to cushion against disruptions in upstream supply. (These are what Toyota would call "standard inventories," whose size can be precisely calculated for each point based on the volatility of downstream orders and the reliability of upstream supplies.)

However, these small inventories—which facilitate a very high level of service—are a tiny fraction of the traditional inventories at every point in the provision stream, inventories that still provide a low level of service for the end customer. Equally important, small standard inventories permit the distribution centers and the factories to conduct their work very smoothly, without constant and costly interruptions in production and shipping schedules to deal with sudden shortages in demand or shortfalls in supply. See Art Smalley, *Creating Level Pull*. Brookline, MA: Lean Enterprise Institute, 2004, for a thorough explanation of how to calculate standard inventories.

14. We are always amazed that companies seem to search for a single best global location for production. In our approach of simply counting total costs, it is almost always the case that different locations provide the lowest cost for serving customers in different markets. In other words, the best location for making shoes for American consumers is not likely to be the best location for making shoes for European or Chinese consumers.

15. Note that "total cost" is all of the costs incurred by the contract manufacturer, the shoe company, the retailer, and the shipping companies combined.

16. However, it's important to note that NuSewCo is an advanced practitioner of what is sometimes called the "Toyota Sewing System." This is a set of techniques for lean factory operations for garment manufacture that has been pioneered by companies in the Toyota Group in Japan. Without deploying these methods, which have doubled NuSewCo's labor productivity over the past few years compared with its previous practices common to this industry, NuSewCo would probably not be cost-competitive at its California location.

17. We have taken a direct hand in creating nonprofit lean institutes in Brazil, Turkey, Poland, and Mexico to teach lean methods, and we expect to help create many more teaching organizations in the years ahead. See the material on "Lean Global Network" at the conclusion of this volume for further details.

18. For a summary of thinking on the issue of location see the working paper by James P. Womack, "Lean Location Logic," Brookline, MA: Lean Enterprise Institute, 2005.

19. A Mongolian tent (also called a *ger*) made in Mongolia for Mongolian users but also made in North America, in derivative versions, for North American customers.

20. An additional issue, in some cases, is the minimum scale of production required to exhaust volume economies. Traditional mass production thinkers typically consult the machinery industry or components vendors about existing

technologies. They are told that scale economies demand the production of the world demand for some items—tiny electronics components are probably the leading current-day example—on one machine in one room.

Whenever we hear this we ask a simple question: Why does it cost less to produce a billion items in one room than 100 million items in each of 10 rooms located much closer to customers? Where are the data? And it often turns out that there are no data. The process designers—often working within the electronics supplier—are simply following a technological trajectory to its logical conclusion, thinking that bigger machines running faster to make higher volumes of parts must always lead to lower costs per part. As a result, no one has ever investigated "right sizing" process technologies to meet needs in widely dispersed markets with rapid response at lowest total cost. It was experiences of this type that many years ago convinced Toyota to build its own right-sized process technologies rather than to listen to vendors, and we hope you will adopt the same stance.

Chapter 6

1. A separate stock-keeping unit is created for every product that is in any way different in specification. For example, in the case of the cola discussed in the last chapter, each type—Coke, Diet Coke, Classic Coke, Cherry Coke—has a different SKU. But the same type of cola in a different container—12-oz. can, 32-oz. plastic bottle, and 64-oz. plastic bottle—also has a different SKU. And the same type of product in the same type of container packed in different amounts—standalone cans of Coke, Coke in six-packs, Coke in cases of 24—also has a different SKU. And then there is the issue of promotions, to be discussed later, in which the same product in the same size container in the same pack size may still carry a different SKU because of a promotion involving discount coupons, "two for

the price of one," etc. All of this information is captured in the product bar codes and is therefore easy for the retailer to gather by scanning at checkout.

2. When shopping these formats, we always enjoy examining the packaging to see how many extra steps are actually required in order to "save" costs. For example, the large jars of mustard in the twin pack require two extra steps: Pasting a sticker over the barcode on each jar so that the checkout scanner will not think it is seeing a single jar, and shrink-wrapping the two jars together while applying a new, twin-pack barcode. With the recent growth of big-box grocery formats, this challenge has become widespread, as we learned while examining one of the largest manufacturers of packaged groceries. This firm is repacking 30 percent of its total output, with several extra steps required for each repack, in order to go from traditional singles presentations for grocery stores to multipacks for big boxes. There are reasons why prices are lower at big-box food outlets, but packaging economies is not one of them.

3. There is also the matter of community opposition to large traffic generators, with the result that big boxes are increasingly difficult to construct in densely populated areas in North America and Europe.

4. Obviously, all 80,000 SKUs are relevant to some household or they wouldn't be in the store. The problem here is the simple one that each household is sharing a vast store with thousands of other households, each wanting something at least slightly different.

5. For the classic statement of this view see Naomi Klein, *No Logo: Taking Aim at Brand Bullies*. New York: Picador, 2000.

6. For an excellent review of this tradition and its weaknesses, see Clayton Christensen and Michael Raynor, *The Innovator's Solution: Creating and Sustaining Successful Growth*. Boston: Harvard Business School Press, 2003.

7. Christensen and Raynor have a nice aphorism for this: "Customers hire a product to do a job." They note that the job may change for the same product as customer circumstances change. In their famous milkshake example, a product is bought on the way to work in the morning as a quick breakfast for the commuter and bought in the evening at the same outlet by the same customer with the same attributes as a pacifier for the kids. We've given this formulation a geographic dimension by pointing out that customers often buy the same product in different formats as their circumstances change. And we'll broaden the formulation further in Chapter 10 by showing that customers often don't really seek a product at all. Instead, they want to obtain a hassle-free solution to a problem.

8. Indeed, with 29 percent of the UK full-sized grocery market, Tesco's more recent problem has been government antimonopoly laws. A bid to buy Safeway was recently turned down by the Monopolies Commission, and Tesco is now working even harder to develop a range of formats so it can continue to grow its total market without being perceived as a monopolist in any individual format.

9. The full story of how Tesco and Dun Humby, its market research and software subsidiary, managed to analyze the mountains of data from Clubcard is told in Clive Humby, Terry Hunt, and Tim Phillips, *Scoring Points: How Tesco Is Winning Customer Loyalty*. London: Kogan Page, 2003.

10. See Isao Shinohara, *NPS—New Production System: JIT Crossing Industry Boundaries*. Norwalk, CT: Productivity Press, 1988.

11. The Seven-Eleven story is summarized in Hau Lee, "The Triple A Supply Chain," *Harvard Business Review*, October 2004; Hau Lee, "Intelligent Demand Based Management," *ECR Journal*, Spring 2002; and Hirofumi Matsuo and Yasuaki Takeda, "ECR: A Fresh Look from Japan," *ECR Journal*, Winter 2002.

12. This would be the food equivalent of what Amazon does with books. As you become a regular user, Amazon's software looks at your purchase pattern and automatically suggests new titles that seem to fit your preferences. This concept should be equally attractive in any shopping venue. It would inform you about new offerings you are likely to value, but without wasting your time on the thousands of irrelevant new offerings pushed annually into every retail channel. The current method of determining consumer acceptance by putting thousands of new products on the shelf every year results in 95 percent of the products failing even as consumers are required to sort their way through the clutter.

13. This is a typical Japanese metaphor based on observation of nature, where water spiders flit across the surface of a pond, going from one feeding spot to the next. The rapid and frequent movements of these tiny creatures is today replicated in Toyota facilities all over the world by the materials handlers. See Rick Harris, Chris Harris, and Earl Wilson, *Making Materials Flow: A Lean Material-Handling Guide for Operations, Production-Control, and Engineering Professionals*. Brookline, MA: Lean Enterprise Institute,

2003, for details on how this system works in a factory environment.

14. See Art Smalley, *Creating Level Pull*. Brookline, MA: Lean Enterprise Institute, 2004, for a complete explanation of material delivery systems in combination with information delivery systems.

Chapter 7

1. See Michael Dell, *Direct From Dell: Strategies That Revolutionized an Industry*. New York: Harper Business, 1999, for a clear statement of the value proposition and a partial explanation of how the production system actually works. The key points are that Dell exclusively builds to order with very short lead times (p. 189) and asks its suppliers to set up plants next to each of Dell's six global assembly complexes (p. 178). These supply parts in small amounts frequently so that Dell needs only four to six days of supplier parts in its assembly complexes. This is all true but leaves out the more interesting fact that many supplier "plants" are simply the large warehouses storing parts shipped from production sites across the world.

2. These facilities are what Dell means when it says that suppliers are requested to locate adjacent to Dell assembly sites.

3. Of course, the suppliers may face a production capacity problem of their own, making it impossible for them to respond quickly even with air expediting.

4. Dell faces the same situation in the electronics industry that firms like Adidas, Reebok, and Nike face in the shoe business. The manufacturing base for the items they most

need is concentrated among a few firms in Southeast Asia, and these firms have so far had no incentive to globalize their operations to get near their customers. We believe that this situation will change substantially in the next decade, as we explained in Chapter 6, but it will be some time before the typical electronics manufacturer (or shoe producer) is able to locate most of its supply base close to the point of final assembly and testing, within the region of sale.

5.   For an exhaustive examination of modularity as a design principle see Carliss Y. Baldwin and Kim B. Clark, *Design Rules: The Power of Modularity*, Cambridge, MA: MIT Press, 2000.

6.   For details on the history of inventories in the auto industry and a thorough discussion of the options facing automakers in moving to make-to-order systems, see Matthias Holweg and Fritz Pils, *The Second Century*, Cambridge, MA: MIT Press, 2004. Holweg and Pils are among the current generation of researchers in the International Motor Vehicle Program, the MIT-originated study of the global motor vehicle industry that was the organizational base for our 1990 book (co-authored with Dan Roos), *The Machine That Changed the World*.

7.   The car maker must worry about "line balance," meaning that the differing amount of work required to assemble complicated models in contrast with simple models prevents running certain combinations of cars in a sequence. The company must also think about parts availability, particularly for low-volume, infrequently ordered options that require special arrangements with suppliers and special materials handling.

8. International Car Distribution Programme, *Fulfilling the Promise: What Future for Car Distribution?* Solihull, UK: International Car Distribution Programme, 2001, p. 7.

9. This is partly due to the curious but common airline practice of offering refunds or travel at a future date if the passenger misses the flight. By contrast, if you bought a car that evaporated if you failed to pick it up from a dealer on a given date, car companies would surely not give you another car for free!

10. In addition, they introduced length-of-stay requirements, including the notorious "Saturday night stay," to separate the more price-sensitive holiday travelers from the more time-sensitive business travelers.

11. But to repeat, we are in different circumstances as consumers at different times. So the value to us of the same seat going to the same place changes with time. And all provision systems must respond to the consumer's changing definition of value. Otherwise, there is no way to determine what a provider should be providing.

12. Note that the precise specification of each product is not planned. By definition, it can't be. What's planned is holding the specification of perhaps 10 percent of slots—let's say every 10th car in the case of a car assembly line—open long past the 10 days needed for the other 90 percent of production, so the precise specification can be set even at the instant it starts down the line.

13. Perhaps we are straining the reader's credulity, but we see car salespeople as one of the worst cases of good people in a

bad process, who over time become as "bad" as the process they are stuck in.

14. Readers outside the U.S. and the UK may be unfamiliar with this term but doubtless have experienced applications of the concept. For decades dealers have announced, immediately after the formal agreement to purchase was reached, that there is an urgent need for special treatments to the vehicle—the most common being a spray coating under the vehicle to prevent alleged risks of corrosion. These are depicted as essential to protect the buyer's new investment. Most experts in the field have viewed these add-ons as adding significant cost with little value, but as one has been debunked another has soon emerged to take its place.

Chapter 8

1. Alfred D. Chandler, *Strategy and Structure: Chapters in the History of the American Industrial Enterprise*. Cambridge, MA: MIT Press, 1962.

2. In this section we are indebted to Kent Sears, Vice President for Quality, General Motors, for sharing his experience in rethinking GM's core business processes, using methods very similar to those described.

3. Michael Hammer and James Champy, *Reengineering the Corporation: A Manifesto for Business Revolution*, New York: Harper Business, 1993.

4. See Cindy Swank, "The Lean Service Machine," *Harvard Business Review*, Vol. 81, No. 10, October 2003, pp. 123–129 for details. We have done additional investigations of their progress.

5. The principles of lean production are fully explained in Chapters 1–5 of James P. Womack and Daniel T. Jones, *Lean Thinking: (Second Edition)*. New York: Free Press, 2003.

6. See Rick Harris, Chris Harris, and Earl Wilson, *Making Materials Flow*. Brookline, MA: Lean Enterprise Institute, 2003, Part II, pp. 15–22, for details on the creation of a plan for every part.

7. The PDCA cycle is a sequence of actions devised by Deming, based on the scientific method of proposing a change in a process, implementing the change, measuring the results, and taking appropriate action. The sequence has four stages. Plan: determine goals for a process and needed changes to achieve them. Do: implement the changes. Check: evaluate the results in terms of performance. Act: standardize and stabilize the cycle again, depending on the results.

Chapter 9

1. In *Lean Thinking* we gave two personal examples, a business trip from Jamestown, NY, to Holland, MI, and a pleasure trip from Hereford in the UK to Crete, and we've been amazed how many readers tell us that the examples were deeply telling about their personal travel experiences. For many travelers, getting from A to B has been a truly awful experience, and this was the case far before Sept. 11, 2001. Here we've chosen a mythical origin and destination to generalize our key points.

2. Compared with the fast-moving consumer goods being cross-docked in Chapter 6, think of passengers as packages with feet that follow their own routing instructions.

3. Because costs per trip were truly difficult to calculate in this environment, a hub operator could easily use the yield

management computers to instantly adjust fares on any route flown by a new entrant to a level that could force out the new entrant. More importantly, the hub operator could do this without much risk of anticompetitive scrutiny by governments.

4. As we have seen in Chapter 7, slot systems of this sort have an important role in a manufacturing environment where every product is different and the manufacturer faces a real cost in trying to get every customer the precise product desired with no lead time. Separating those who can plan from those who can't and offering the former group of customers a lower price makes eminent sense for cars and computers. However, in the airline world, where slot pricing originated, products are practically identical—excepting a larger seat and a free drink for the "first class" customer—yet every seat is priced differently.

5. It is possible to book a ticket calling for a change of planes at an airport where a point-to-point airline has many flights (e.g., Love Field in Dallas for Southwest). But the arrivals and departures of connecting flights are not coordinated to save the traveler's time and these carriers do not "interline" by writing tickets with or transferring bags to other carriers. In addition, they don't cooperate with travel agents to simplify ticket writing for complex itineraries, but rely instead on web bookings. It's not surprising that a very high fraction of their passengers are only traveling from the city where the flight originates to the city where it lands.

6. Our favorite metric for the cabin environment is whether we can get our notebook computer open without fear it will be crushed as the traveler in the seat ahead of us tries to recline.

7. We've been contacted by several hub-and-spoke airlines in recent years, asking how lean thinking could be applied to their operations. In particular, they've asked if stretching out the pulses when all aircraft arrive and depart at very nearly the same time would be a good way to level the operation. The problem is that while this saves the airline money (by increasing aircraft and staff utilization), it leaves the passenger worse off because the connecting time between most flights increases substantially. A better idea, but not attractive so far to the airlines, is to decrease batch size by flying planes half the size twice as often from each originating point into the hubs, with a smooth pattern of aircraft arrivals and departures through the day. Even though inbound and outbound schedules would not be synchronized, connect times for the average passenger would be no greater and asset utilization would be much better.

An additional innovation might be to load planes from both front and rear doors and give passengers baggage cubicles with their seat number as they enter the plane to cut down in the time needed to lift heavy bags into overhead racks. These innovations are similar in concept to the setup reduction exercises routinely undertaken by lean thinkers for manufacturing machinery in order to reduce changeover times from one product to the next and to shrink production batches.

8. Oddly, some hub-and-spoke carriers have pursued this option for international flights. Continental, Lufthansa, and others are experimenting with the use of smaller planes for trans-Atlantic trips (Boeing 757s vs. 767s) and fitting the planes with only business-class seats. The idea is to segregate passengers so everyone on a given flight is expecting the same product and paying the same fare as the plane flies nonstop between smaller cities in Europe and America to eliminate

the need to go through hubs. Still smaller planes—737s and A320s—have comparable range in their special business-jet configurations and could serve even smaller cities.

9. We've even asked Robert B. Brown, the retired chief engineer of the Boeing Commercial Airplane Company, to create some small, "lean" airplanes for us that can be turned in only a few minutes, operated for days with very little line maintenance, and flown so as to avoid off-airport noise at small airports. While these are purely conceptual, it's amazing how many new ideas designers can come up with when freed from traditional restraints.

10. When we propose this concept to audiences, the frequent response is that this increases the customer's unpaid work. But think about this carefully. Would you rather wait 30 minutes in the terminal and 20 minutes on the plane as it loads while others do the work? Or would you rather perform some simple tasks yourself in cooperation with staff and other passengers so that everyone saves time. One of the features we do admire about the point-to-point carriers like Southwest is that they have been good at explaining the boarding and deboarding process to passengers so they cooperate actively with the cabin crew to get everyone on and off faster. We find that consumers cooperate cheerfully with a lean process that is carefully explained and which saves everyone's time.

11. The Eclipse 500, the initial aircraft in this category, carries five passengers plus a pilot at jet speeds and altitudes for a purchase price of about $1.3 million. The other announced projects are the Adam Aircraft A700, the Cessna Citation Mustang, and the Embraer VLJ. The latter may be particularly significant because it is the first plane offered by a traditional

commercial aircraft manufacturer accustomed to building rugged airframes for high daily utilization.

12. An additional and important issue is community relations with airport neighbors. To land near the homes of business travelers means much higher standards for off-airport noise as well as road improvements to avoid traffic in residential neighborhoods.

13. Part of the issue is the severe consequences for doctor and patient of being wrong about the diagnosis. The natural instinct of the doctor is to recommend more tests from a higher level of specialist whenever there is any doubt. The lean thinker, of course, wants to find ways to move knowledge closer to the patient so that steps and waits are eliminated without reducing the quality of care.

14. We are often struck by the fact that medical centers are the most complex and disorientating buildings we ever encounter. There is a good reason for this given their current multifunction mission, as we will see in a moment, but their complexity raises some profound questions about the physical configuration of healthcare.

15. It's provocative to think just how far this process might go. Dr. Gordon Moore, a family practice physician in Rochester, NY, decided several years ago that even this degree of simplification was not enough. He resigned from a large HMO and set up a one-person practice. By using the latest technology for medical records, microtesting equipment, patient e-mail, patient voice mail, and electronic billing, and by scheduling appointments at longer intervals than standard practice, he has found that he can run a complete medical practice in one room (sharing a waiting room with another

physician) with no receptionist, no nurse, and no record-keeping staff. He has become a truly solo physician with practically no assets or overhead. Moore has reported that 99 percent of his patients can obtain an appointment the same day, that many of his regular patients can be treated over the phone or e-mail without coming in, and that patient-outcome measures—blood pressure, blood sugar, cholesterol, etc.—are better than those achieved by his patients when in the large practice he left. This is because the patients are always dealing with their personal physician who knows the details of their medical problems. (See *Family Practice Management*, published by the American Academy of Family Physicians, Gordon Moore, "Going Solo: One Doc, One Room, One Year Later," March 2002, at www.aafp.org).

Chapter 10

1. Oddly, their consumption solution creates a new problem: Managing those who manage their problems. The media periodically cover cases of the truly wealthy who are defrauded or abused by their problem-solving staff, and there are doubtless many additional instances never receiving public attention. The "who watches the watchmen" problem is as old as human history and can never be solved by simply adding additional layers of management. The better approach is to eliminate the need for management.

2. This is Herbert Simon's term, invented more than 40 years ago when communications options were vastly simpler than today, to describe a situation in which gathering all of the information necessary to truly optimize one's consumption was more trouble than it was worth. He gave everyone failing the optimization challenge a new lease on self-esteem by arguing that gathering just enough information to make a good decision was often more

"rational" than gathering all the information needed to make a perfect decision. The Nobel Prize in Economics committee, a group of busy people probably flunking the optimization challenge themselves, responded with enthusiasm to this concept and awarded Simon the Nobel Prize in economics for his insight in 1978.

3. See Michael Porter and Elizabeth Olmsted Teisberg, "Redefining Competition in Health Care," *Harvard Business Review*, June 2004, for the most recent in an escalating series of economic analysis arguing that breaking healthcare up into independent value streams focused on specific problems is the best approach to cost containment. We applaud much of this analysis, and have advocated similar steps in Chapter 9, but we note that the certain consequence is that consumers will have many more providers to manage in creating their own healthcare solution.

4. The other aspect is whether the medical system actually knows what to do about the patient's problem and consistently provides the best treatment at the best time. This is another process problem but one beyond our scope here. Readers with an interest in this topic should become acquainted with the groundbreaking work of the Institute for Healthcare Improvement at www.ihi.org.

5. This also would make the most significant contribution to reducing the impact of shopping on the environment, and greenhouse emissions in particular. Mapping the value stream for food from the farm to the plate reveals that consumers driving to the store and then storing products in their refrigerators account for more CO_2 emissions than the combined effects of production, storage, distribution, and retail activities for any food product, see Simons, David, and

Robert Mason, "Lean and Green: Doing More with Less," *ECR Journal*, Vol. 3, No. 1, Spring 2003, pp.84–91.

6. We are grateful to Don, who subsequently was Vice Chairman of Delphi Corp., for sharing with us his extensive files on the brief life of this concept at GM. Surely these ideas have a bright future in the right type of organization.

7. The first step toward providing this capability has just been taken by large homebuilders and major suppliers of equipment going into new homes. Their joint venture, The Homebuilder Site (www.homebuildersite.com) has just launched its Envision Life Style service that creates a complete database for new homes as completed, showing all details of construction and all appliances and equipment including serial numbers. By linking the data file for each home to the builder and to the equipment providers, it is easily possible to create maintenance task lists and to determine what to do in the case of problems. What is still lacking is a single provider who can offer all the maintenance and service needed by the homeowner without any need for the homeowner to think about it.

8. For the nightmare vision of where this could lead, see Jeremy Rifkin, *The Age of Access: The New Culture Hypercapitalism, Where All of Life is a Paid-For Experience.* New York: Jeremy P. Tarcher/Putnam, 2000.

Acknowledgments

1. We pioneered this method at MIT in the 1980s when we worked to obtain foundation and government support for the Future of the Automobile Project during 1979–84 and industry support through a special mechanism during

1985–90 for the International Motor Vehicle Program. For the latter program, we approached all of the world's car companies and the largest automotive suppliers and asked them to contribute to a special fund through their industry associations in each country. All of the funds went into a central account used by the research teams that accepted no restrictions on its work from any of the companies.

2. Daniel T. Jones and James P. Womack, *Seeing the Whole: Mapping the Extended Value Stream*. Brookline, MA: Lean Enterprise Institute, 2002.

3. The results are available in the working paper by James P. Womack, "Lean Location Logic," Brookline, MA: Lean Enterprise Institute, 2005.

Bibliography

Baldwin, Carliss Y., and Kim B. Clark, *Design Rules: The Power of Modularity*, Cambridge, MA: MIT Press, 2000.

Barlow, Sue, Steve Parry, and Mike Faulkner, *Sense and Respond: The Journey to Customer Purpose*. London: Palgrave Macmillan, 2005.

Browett, John, "Tesco.com: Delivering Home Shopping," *ECR Journal*, Vol. 1, No. 1, Summer 2001, pp. 36–43.

Cairncross, Frances, *The Death of Distance*, Boston: Harvard Business School Press, 1997.

Chandler, Alfred D., *Strategy and Structure: Chapters in the History of the American Industrial Enterprise*, Cambridge, MA: MIT Press, 1962.

Christensen, Clayton M., and Michael E. Raynor, *The Innovator's Solution: Creating and Sustaining Successful Growth*. Boston: Harvard Business School Press, 2003.

Christensen, Clayton M., Scott D. Anthony, and Erik A. Roth, *Seeing What's Next: Using Theories of Innovation to Predict Industry Change*. Boston: Harvard Business School Press, 2004.

Crosby, Philip B., *Quality Is Free: The Art of Making Quality Certain*. New York: McGraw-Hill, 1979.

Dell, *Michael, Direct from Dell: Strategies that Revolutionized an Industry*. New York: Harper Business, 1999.

W. Edwards Deming, *Out of the Crisis*. Cambridge, MA: MIT Press, 1982.

Evans, Philip, and Thomas S. Wurster, *Blown to Bits: How the New Economics of Information Transforms Strategy*. Boston: Harvard Business School Press, 2000.

Gershuny, Jonathan, *Changing Times: Work and Leisure in Postindustrial Society*. London: Oxford University Press, 2000.

Gruen, Thomas, and Daniel Corsten, "Rising to the Challenge of Out-of-Stocks," *ECR Journal*, Vol. 2, No. 2, Winter 2002, pp.44–58.

Hammer, Michael, and James Champy, *Reengineering the Corporation: A Manifesto for Business Revolution*. New York: Harper Business, 1993.

Harris, Rick, Chris Harris, and Earl Wilson, *Making Materials Flow: A Lean Material-Handling Guide for Operations, Production-Control, and Engineering Professionals*. Brookline, MA: Lean Enterprise Institute, 2003.

Hawken, Paul, Amory B. Lovins, and L. Hunter Lovins, *Natural Capitalism: The Next Industrial Revolution*. London: Earthscan, 1999.

Holweg, Matthias, and Fritz Pil, *The Second Century: Reconnecting Customer and Value Chain through Build-to-Order*. Cambridge, MA: MIT Press, 2004.

Humby, Clive, Terry Hunt, and Tim Phillips, *Scoring Points: How*

Tesco is Winning Customer Loyalty. London: Kogan Page, 2003.

International Car Distribution Programme, *Fulfilling the Promise: What Future for Car Distribution?* Solihull, UK: International Car Distribution Programme, 2001.

Jacob, Julie, "Same Day Appointments Catching on with Doctors," Amednews.com, January 29, 2001, www.ama-assn.org/amednews/2001/01/29/bisa0129.htm.

Johnson, Maureen, "The Store of Tomorrow," *ECR Journal*, Vol. 2, No. 1, Spring 2002, pp. 82–93.

Jones, Daniel T., "Thinking Outside the Box," *ECR Journal*, Vol. 1, No. 1, Summer 2001, pp. 80–89.

Jones, Daniel T., and Philip Clarke, "Creating a Customer Driven Supply Chain," *ECR Journal*, Vol. 2, No. 2, Winter 2002, pp. 28–37.

Jones, Daniel T., and James P. Womack, *Seeing the Whole: Mapping the Extended Value Stream.* Brookline, MA: Lean Enterprise Institute, 2002.

Kiff, John, "The Lean Dealership—A Vision for the Future: 'From Farming to Hunting,'" *Marketing and Intelligence Planning*, Volume 18, Number 3, 2000, pp. 112–126.

Klein, Naomi, *No Logo: Taking Aim at Brand Bullies*, New York: Picador, 2000.

Lean Enterprise Institute, *Lean Lexicon: A Graphical Glossary for Lean Thinkers.* Brookline, MA: Lean Enterprise Institute, 2004.

Lee, Hau L., "Intelligent Demand Based Management," *ECR Journal*, Spring 2002.

Lee, Hau L., "The Triple A Supply Chain," *Harvard Business Review*, October 2004.

Lee, Hau L., "Unleashing the Power of Intelligence," *ECR Journal*, Vol. 2, No. 1, Spring 2002, pp. 60–73.

Liker, Jeffrey K., *The Toyota Way*, New York: McGraw Hill, 2004.

Matsuo, Hirofumi, and Yasuaki Takeda, "ECR: A "Fresh" Look from Japan," *ECR Journal*, Vol. 2, No. 2, Winter 2002, pp. 16–27.

McKinnon, Alan, et.al., "Running on Empty?", *ECR Journal*, Vol. 3, No. 1, Spring 2003, pp. 73–82.

Mitchell, Alan, *Right Side Up: Building Brands in the Age of the Organized Consumer*. London: Harper Collins, 2001.

Moore, Gordon, "Going Solo: One Doc, One Room, One Year Later," *Family Practice Management*, March 2002, www.aafp.org/fpm/20020300/25goin.html.

Pine, Joseph B., *Mass Customization: The New Frontier to Business Competition*. Boston: Harvard University Press, 1993.

Pine, Joseph B., and James H. Gilmore, *The Experience Economy: Work is Theatre and Every Business a Stage*. Boston: Harvard Business School Press, 1999.

Porter, Michael, and Elizabeth Olmsted Teisberg, "Redefining Competition in Health Care," *Harvard Business Review*, June 2004.

Randolph, Greg, Mark Murray, Jill Swanson, and Peter Margolis, "Behind Schedule: Improving Access to Care for Children One Practice at a Time," *Pediatrics*, Vol. 113, No. 3, March 2004, pp. 230–237.

Rifkin, Jeremy, *The Age of Access: The New Culture of Hypercapitalism Where All of Life is a Paid-for Experience*. New York: Penguin Putnam, 2000.

Romm, Joseph J., *Lean and Clean Management: How to Boost Profits and Productivity by Reducing Pollution*. New York: Kodansha International, 1994.

Rother, Mike, and John Shook, *Learning to See: Value Stream Mapping to Add Value and Eliminate Muda*. Brookline, MA: Lean Enterprise Institute, 1998.

Schwartz, Barry, *The Paradox of Choice: How More Is Less*. New York: Ecco, 2004.

Senge, Peter M., *The Fifth Discipline: The Art and Practice of the Learning Organization*. New York: Doubleday, 1990.

Sewell, Carl, *Customers for Life: How to Turn a One-Time Buyer into a Lifetime Customer*. New York: Doubleday, 1990.

Shinohara, Isao, *NPS—New Production System: JIT Crossing Industry Boundaries*. Norwalk, CT: Productivity Press, 1988.

Simons, David, Mark Francis, and Daniel T. Jones, "Food Value Chain Analysis," in *Consumer Driven Electronic Transformation: Applying New Technologies to Enthuse Consumers and Transform the Supply Chain*, ed. by Georgis Doukidis et al, Amsterdam: Elsevier, 2005.

Simons, David, and Robert Mason, "Lean and Green: Doing More With Less," *ECR Journal*, Vol. 3, No. 1, Spring 2003, pp. 84–91.

Smalley, Art, *Creating Level Pull*. Brookline, MA: Lean Enterprise Institute, 2004.

Swank, Cynthia K., "The Lean Service Machine," *Harvard Business Review*, Vol. 81, No. 10, October 2003, pp. 123–129.

Toffler, Alvin, *The Third Wave*. New York: William Morrow, 1980.

Tongue, Andrew, John Whiteman, and Daniel T. Jones, *Progress on the Road to Customer Fulfilment: ICDP Research*

2000–2003. Solihull, UK: International Car Distribution Programme, 2003.

Underhill, Paco, *Call of the Mall*. New York: Simon & Schuster, 2004.

Underhill, Paco, *Why We Buy: The Science of Shopping*. New York: Touchstone, 1999.

Wikstrom, Solveig, and Richard Norman, *Knowledge and Value: A New Perspective on Corporate Transformation*. London: Routledge, 1994.

Womack, James P., Daniel T. Jones, and Daniel Roos, *The Machine that Changed the World*. New York: Rawson Macmillan, 1990.

Womack, James P., and Daniel T. Jones, *Lean Thinking: Banish Waste and Create Wealth in your Corporation*, 2nd Edition. New York: Free Press, 2003.

Womack, James P., and Daniel T. Jones, "From Lean Production to the Lean Enterprise," *Harvard Business Review*, Vol. 72, No. 2, March–April 1994, pp. 93–103.

Womack, James P., and Daniel T. Jones, "Beyond Toyota: How to Root out Waste and Pursue Perfection," *Harvard Business Review*, Vol. 74, No. 5, September–October 1996, pp. 140–158.

Womack, James P., and Daniel T. Jones, "Lean Consumption," *Harvard Business Review*, Vol. 83, No. 3, March 2005, pp. 58–68.

Wright, Robert, *Nonzero: The Logic of Human Destiny*. New York: Little Brown, 2000.

Zuboff, Shoshana and Jim Maxmin, *The Support Economy: Why Corporations Are Failing Individuals and the Next Episode of Capitalism*, New York: Viking, 2002.

Index

About the Authors

James P. Womack is the president and founder of the Lean Enterprise Institute (www.lean.org), a nonprofit education and research organization based in Brookline, MA. LEI is devoted to promoting lean thinking by presenting lean knowledge in workbook formats and teaching this knowledge in a variety of venues.

Daniel T. Jones is chairman and founder of the Lean Enterprise Academy (www.leanuk.org), a nonprofit education and research organization based in the UK. The Academy shares the mission of the Lean Enterprise Institute in the U.S. of raising lean consciousness and making lean knowledge available in a range of formats.